THE DECLINE OF THE DEATH PENALTY AND THE DISCOVERY OF INNOCENCE

Since 1996, death sentences in America have declined more than 60 percent, reversing a generation-long trend toward greater acceptance of capital punishment. In theory, most Americans continue to support the death penalty. But it is no longer seen as a theoretical matter. Prosecutors, judges, and juries across the country have moved in large numbers to give much greater credence to the possibility of mistakes – mistakes that in this arena are potentially fatal. The discovery of innocence, documented through painstaking analyses of media coverage and with newly developed methods, has led to historic shifts in public opinion and to a sharp decline in the use of the death penalty by juries across the country. A social cascade, starting with legal clinics and innocence projects, has snowballed into a national phenomenon that may spell the end of the death penalty in America.

Frank R. Baumgartner is Miller-LaVigne Professor of Political Science at The Pennsylvania State University. His previous publications include *Comparative Studies of Policy Agendas* (2007), *The Politics of Attention: How Government Prioritizes Problems* (with Bryan D. Jones, 2005), *Policy Dynamics* (with Bryan D. Jones, 2002), and *Agendas and Instability in American Politics* (with Bryan D. Jones, 1993), winner of the 2001 Aaron Wildavsky Award, APSA Organized Section on Public Policy. He has been published widely in journals and serves on the editorial boards of *American Journal of Political Science*, *Political Research Quarterly*, *Journal of European Public Policy*, *Policy Studies Journal*, and *Journal of Information Technology and Politics*.

Suzanna L. De Boef is Associate Professor of Political Science at The Pennsylvania State University. Her research examines the dynamics of public opinion, elections, and public policy and the statistical methods used to analyze them. Her work has appeared in journals such as *American Political Science Review*, *American Journal of Politics*, *Political Analysis*, and *Statistics in Medicine*.

Amber E. Boydstun is a graduate student in political science at The Pennsylvania State University. Her research explores the influence of issue-definition on media agenda control. She has been published in *Mass Communication and Society* and expects to receive her PhD in 2008.

THE DECLINE OF THE DEATH PENALTY AND THE DISCOVERY OF INNOCENCE

Frank R. Baumgartner
The Pennsylvania State University

Suzanna L. De Boef
The Pennsylvania State University

Amber E. Boydstun
The Pennsylvania State University

CAMBRIDGE
UNIVERSITY PRESS

CAMBRIDGE UNIVERSITY PRESS
Cambridge, New York, Melbourne, Madrid, Cape Town,
Singapore, São Paulo, Delhi, Tokyo, Mexico City

Cambridge University Press
32 Avenue of the Americas, New York, NY 10013-2473, USA

www.cambridge.org
Information on this title: www.cambridge.org/9780521715249

First published 2008
Reprinted 2011

A catalog record for this publication is available from the British Library.

Library of Congress Cataloging in Publication Data

Baumgartner, Frank R., 1958–
The decline of the death penalty and the discovery of innocence / Frank R. Baumgartner,
Suzanna L. De Boef, Amber E. Boydstun.
   p.   cm.
Includes bibliographical references and index.
ISBN 978-0-521-88734-2 (hardback) – ISBN 978-0-521-71524-9 (pbk.)
   1. Capital punishment – United States – History.   2. Guilt (Law) – United States –
History.   3. Judicial error – United States – History.   4. Capital punishment – United
States – History.   I. De Boef, Suzanna, 1966–   II. Boydstun, Amber E., 1977–   III. Title.
KF9227.C2B38   2008
345.73´0773–dc22   2007025858

ISBN 978-0-521-88734-2 Hardback
ISBN 978-0-521-71524-9 Paperback

CONTENTS

LIST OF TABLES

LIST OF FIGURES

ACKNOWLEDGMENTS

This project began with a phone call. Peter Loge, a Washington-based advocate then working with The Justice Project, called Baumgartner in 2002, saying he had read some previous work about the importance of issue-definition and framing and that he was working on framing an issue, and he asked if we could discuss it. "What's the issue, and what's the frame?" Baumgartner asked. "Well, the issue is the death penalty, and the frame is that it's a government program run by bureaucrats, and it is prone to waste, inefficiency, and errors," Loge responded. With that intriguing beginning, Baumgartner agreed to come down to Washington to meet and find out more. Soon Cheryl Feeley, an undergraduate student at Penn State searching for a topic on which to write her senior honors thesis, had a new topic: investigate the history of how the death penalty has been discussed in America over several decades to see if it had, indeed, been reframed. Boydstun, then a first-year PhD student, got involved. After some time, as our analysis got more and more complicated, De Boef got interested in both the substance of our study and the methodological challenges we faced. Feeley graduated in 2003, having completed her thesis, and took a job in Washington with The Justice Project; she is now in law school, and we thank her first and foremost for her initial work. In the years since then, we three authors have learned a great deal about a topic on which none of us was originally expert; it has been shocking.

During the years we have been working on this project, we have benefited from the opportunity to present our results in many venues and learned greatly from the feedback we have gotten from colleagues. Thanks to colleagues at Aberdeen, Indiana, Manchester, Mount St. Mary's, Oxford, and Wisconsin universities, as well as at the European University Institute and the Public Policy Institute of California, for invitations to Baumgartner to present in departmental seminars. With regard to more applied settings, where we learned tremendously from those actually working in the area, thanks to the NAACP Legal Defense Fund Annual Capital Punishment Training Conference, The Justice Project, the

National Coalition to Abolish the Death Penalty, the UCLA Conference on Wrongful Convictions, and the Third World Congress to Abolish the Death Penalty for invitations to present our research. These events allowed us to meet activists in the area – and to get to know many of them – and to meet personally or hear the stories of many individuals who were exonerated from death rows across the United States. Their personal stories make our statistics look trivial. Yet, as Aaron Owens, a California exoneree who served ten years in prison, remarked to Baumgartner when they shared a panel for their very different presentations about the question of innocence, they are part of the same story.

Several institutions provided support for the research reported here. Most importantly, the Department of Political Science and the College of the Liberal Arts at Penn State University have housed and supported the project since its beginning. Boydstun has spent her entire graduate career working on this project while simultaneously developing her own dissertation ideas on issues related to framing but not associated with the death penalty (with Baumgartner and De Boef serving as co-chairs of her dissertation committee). Thanks to the department, the college, and Bruce Miller and Dean LaVigne for graduate fellowships that have supported her work. While on sabbaticals during which parts of this book were written, Baumgartner was lucky enough to be hosted by the European University Institute in Florence, Sciences Po (CEVIPOF) in Paris, and the Camargo Foundation in Cassis. Each of these institutions provided tremendous support for scholarly productivity, good colleagues, and a chance to be away from administrative responsibilities; thanks to each of them.

Baumgartner has benefited from two National Science Foundation (NSF) grants (0111611 and 0111224) for projects related to the theoretical ideas developed here, if not the substance of the death penalty. Neither the NSF nor the original collectors of the data bear any responsibility for the analysis reported here. Thanks to Bryan Jones, John McCarthy, Jeff Berry, Marie Hojnacki, Beth Leech, and David Kimball for participation in these related projects, from which many ideas have found their way into this book. We also owe thanks to Fuyuan Shen and Frank Dardis, with whom we conducted a separate but related experimental study investigating the cognitive effects of framing in the case of the death penalty, and whose intellectual contributions have benefited this book in many ways. Michelle Massie and Mary Beth Oliver also contributed their energies to the cognitive effects study, and their good ideas have aided us in our current endeavor.

Throughout the course of the project, we have benefited from the skills and dedication of a number of exceptional undergraduate research assistants at Penn State, including Amanda Blunt, Steve Dzubak, Scott Huffard, Christine MacAulay, Kimberly Roth, Trey Thomas, Denise Ziobro, and especially Mary Gardner. We also thank Jim Stimson for providing the initial set of survey data we used to develop our measure of public support for the death penalty and for writing the algorithm that made this measure possible in the first place; James Alan Fox for providing us with access to victim-level data from the Supplementary Homicide Reports File, 1976 to 2003, and for walking us through the weighting procedure; the staff at the U.S. Department of Justice, Bureau of Justice Statistics for providing supplementary homicide data; and Christine Mahoney and Daniel Jones-White for training Boydstun in the nuances of data management.

Finally, we are pleased to thank many individuals who have read and commented on parts or all of the manuscript. This list includes Bryan Jones, Jeff Berry, Beth Leech, Lisa Miller, Errol Henderson, Cal Golumbic, John McCarthy, Jim Eisenstein, Christoffer Green-Pedersen, Barbara Bowzer, Linda Walker, and two anonymous reviewers. Also, within the community of activists and death penalty scholars, we would like to thank Richard Dieter, Sam Gross, Sam Millsap, Steve Hall, and Peter Loge for their comments and suggestions about the manuscript. Baumgartner thanks his older brother, John, for pointing out a terrible error in our original manuscript that could have had devastating consequences for us if it had appeared in print; that's what brothers are for. De Boef thanks her sons, Jack, Adam, and Collin, for their indulgence of the inevitable blurring of family time and work time (and Microsoft for the Xbox); she loves those boys dearly. Boydstun thanks her parents for providing unconditional love, fortitude, and feedback and is especially grateful to Kyle Joyce for his gift of indelible partnership as both colleague and spouse. Last but not least: Mothers are required to do many things for their children, but reading their work is not one of them; only exceptional moms do that. In fact, all three of our mothers read parts or all of the manuscript and provided suggestions and encouragement throughout the project; thanks, moms.

We appreciate the cooperation of photographer Loren Santow, whose series of portraits of exonerated death row prisoners that we use on the cover and in our epilogue puts into greater clarity than our words can do the human cost of the issues that are at the core of our discussion throughout this book.

It is impossible to write a book on the topic of innocence in the death penalty debate without thinking of the individuals who are at the core of the analysis as either victims of violent crime in America or victims of a broken system. There is truly no greater disservice to society than to condemn the wrong individual for a vicious crime while the guilty party goes free. We dedicate the book to those who have been the victims of crime, to those who have been falsely convicted and punished for crimes they did not commit, and to those who have worked to bring this problem to the public consciousness.

I INNOCENCE AND THE DEATH PENALTY DEBATE

O N JULY 25, 1984, nine-year-old Dawn Hamilton went to play in the woods near her aunt's home in the Baltimore suburb of Rosedale, Maryland. When Dawn did not return, her aunt called the police. Several hours later, searchers found Dawn's body in the woods beaten, raped, and strangled. Her underwear was found hanging in a tree, and a bloody rock was found near the little girl's crushed head – a gruesome and horrifying scene.

At the time, former marine Kirk Noble Bloodsworth, twenty-three, was living in Baltimore County. He had no criminal background, but fit the description of the man who two boys, ages seven and ten, said they had seen entering the woods with Dawn that day. Police arrested Bloodsworth. The principal evidence linking him to the crime was testimony by five government witnesses (including the two boys) who identified Bloodsworth as the man they had seen with Dawn soon before she disappeared. This eyewitness testimony contradicted testimony by Bloodsworth's friends that he had been at home at the time of the incident. There was no physical evidence linking Bloodsworth to the crime, but prosecutors suggested that a shoe print left near the girl's body was the same size as a pair of Bloodsworth's shoes. Prosecutors also aggressively questioned the credibility of the defense witnesses. After serving in the marines, Bloodsworth had been unemployed and spent time partying, drinking, and associating with a shifting group of friends who did not make strong character or alibi witnesses. Though they said he could not have been at the scene, many admitted to alcohol or drug use. The jury found Bloodsworth guilty of sexual assault, rape, and first-degree premeditated murder. He was sentenced to death.

Before Bloodsworth's 1986 trial, police had begun to investigate another suspect in the slaying – a local newspaper delivery man who had helped search for the little girl and had been the one to find her underwear. An appeals court ruled that authorities had illegally withheld this exculpatory evidence from the defense and ordered a retrial. In April 1987, Bloodsworth was tried again, and again found guilty based on eye-witness testimony. This time he was sentenced to two consecutive life terms in prison. Sentences in both trials were imposed by the judge.

After his second trial, Bloodsworth received a new court-appointed attorney, Robert E. Morin. With the help of Centurion Ministries, a non-profit organization in Princeton, New Jersey, that works to help over-turn wrongful convictions of innocent individuals, Morin arranged to have evidence from Bloodsworth's case sent to California for DNA test-ing – a technology that had not been available in 1984. Even though in 1984 authorities had determined that the evidence from the case – the girl's shorts and underwear and a bloody stick found near the body – contained nothing of criminal value, fortunately for Bloodsworth the items had never been destroyed. Bloodsworth's family had exhausted its life savings in the course of mounting appeals against the two convic-tions, so Morin paid the $10,000 fee for the DNA testing out of his own pocket. After a long delay, the test results came back showing that semen on the underwear did not belong to Bloodsworth. The prosecu-tor, still believing Bloodsworth was guilty in spite of this evidence to the contrary, insisted on a second test. Subsequent testing by the Federal Bureau of Investigation (FBI) confirmed the results. Kirk Bloodsworth was innocent.

It would take three months for the paperwork to be processed, but on June 28, 1993, after spending eight years, eleven months, and nine-teen days in prison, including two years on death row, Bloodsworth was exonerated. Three months later, in December 1993, Maryland governor William Donald Schaefer issued Bloodsworth a full pardon. The fol-lowing year in June 1994, the state of Maryland awarded Bloodsworth $300,000 for lost income, based on the calculation that Bloodsworth would have earned approximately $30,000 each year he was imprisoned. There was no payment for injuries, though while in prison as a con-victed child rapist and murderer he had been treated harshly by the other inmates.

Bloodsworth and others continued to press prosecutors to find the real criminal by comparing the DNA results to those of possible suspects in the crime, suspects who had gotten away, suspects about whom police had not followed up on leads. On September 5, 2003, nearly two decades after Dawn Hamilton was raped and murdered, a match was found. The murderer was Kimberly Shay Ruffner, a convicted sex offender. In a twist of fate, Bloodsworth and Ruffner had been imprisoned together – Ruffner was there on a different child sexual assault conviction – and the two men had interacted frequently. It was only after conclusive proof that another person had committed the crime that the state prosecutor apologized to Bloodsworth.[1]

Kirk Bloodsworth was the first death row inmate in the history of the United States to be released on the basis of DNA evidence and the forty-ninth individual to be exonerated after serving time on death row since 1973. Ten years later, Ray Krone became the 100th death row inmate to be exonerated. As of 2007, 123 men and women have been exonerated from death row, 14 of them directly as a result of DNA testing (Death Penalty Information Center [DPIC] 2006e).

In fact, exonerations are nothing new in this country. In spite of many safeguards, mistakes have always occurred. For example, in 1819 two Vermont brothers were scheduled to be executed for the murder of Russell Colvin when Colvin himself showed up to witness the hanging (Banner 2002, 122). In 1835 Charles Boyington was executed in Alabama for a murder in a tavern; several years later the owner of the tavern, on his deathbed, confessed to the murder himself (ibid.). Examples from throughout history can be found of people either convicted or executed for the murders of people who later turned up alive or whose real murderer was subsequently identified (see Radelet et al. 1992). Mistakes happen.

One response to these examples is utilitarian – perhaps the value of the death penalty outweighs the cost of a few errors. In a 1985 congressional hearing, Senator Jeremiah Denton of Alabama expressed this view: "I do not want to be overly simplistic, but saying that we should not have the death penalty because we may accidentally execute an innocent man is like saying we should not have automobiles because some innocent people might accidentally be killed in them" (quoted in Banner 2002, 304). This argument does indeed have a parallel with the death penalty. The logic is to compare the benefit with the cost.

Although people recognize that cars do indeed crash (and more than 40,000 people regularly die on the highways each year), the difference in purpose between automobiles and the death penalty makes the analogy hollow. The purpose of cars is not to kill people with the hope that they are all deserving. The purpose of the death penalty, however, *is* to kill individuals – those individuals judged to be guilty. Most Americans find abhorrent the idea that executions would be performed without complete confidence that the people being executed actually deserve the punishment. This idea of executing someone who may be innocent is objectionable even to people who support the death penalty in theory and in those cases in which there is no doubt about guilt.

THE DISCOVERY OF INNOCENCE

This book is about Americans' discovery of the concept of innocence. Although it is obvious on one level that any human-designed institution is imperfect, until recently most Americans did not think much about the possibility that some percentage of people sentenced to death might actually be innocent. The occasional exoneration of someone from death row was often seen more as proof that the system works (because they were not executed) rather than as a sign of imperfections perhaps pervading the system. All this has begun to change, and in fact has changed dramatically, over the past twenty years or so. Today, the concept of innocence pervades public and official discussion of the death penalty in a way unlike that of any period in previous history. State legislatures are establishing "innocence commissions," putting the death penalty on hold as they review the vulnerability of their state justice systems to potentially fatal errors, and reviewing the possible mechanisms to establish a "foolproof" death penalty. In December 2006, the number one best-seller on the *New York Times* hardcover nonfiction list was John Grisham's *The Innocent Man*, the story of Ron Williamson, a former major league baseball prospect who was wrongly convicted of murder and spent eleven years on Oklahoma's death row for a 1982 crime he did not commit (Grisham 2006). These developments come after hundreds of years of experience with the death penalty and more than 1,000 executions in the modern era (since 1976) alone. Why now? And what effect is this new debate having on the death penalty in the public eye and in practice? Can there be such a thing as a foolproof bureaucratic institution of the scope of the U.S. criminal justice system?

The answers to these questions lie in the process of "framing," defining an issue along a particular dimension (e.g., fairness and innocence) at the exclusion of alternate dimensions (e.g., morality, constitutionality, or cost).[2] Framing is a natural part of the political process, but rarely does framing result in a near-complete overhaul of an issue debate, as in the case of the death penalty over the last decade.

The strength and even the occurrence of the "innocence frame" is somewhat surprising because, once one pauses a moment to think about it, it seems obvious that mistakes will occur, and probably have occurred, throughout the history of the death penalty, as in other criminal proceedings. How could *every single* judicial proceeding in all of American history have been perfect? What if a clinically depressed, suicidal, drug-addicted, or mentally handicapped defendant actually wanted to be executed and confessed to a crime, refused to cooperate in his own defense, and was connected to the crime through eyewitness testimony, association with known criminals, or some other evidence, or simply bore a resemblance to the real murderer? Could the system make such errors? Logically, it seems quite possible. And yet, except for one notable instance of Supreme Court intervention, a majority of American states have kept the death penalty on the books throughout our nation's history. So why all the fuss about wrongful convictions, and why now?

There are, of course, many reasons for the recent consideration of innocence. Some have to do with new scientific technologies such as DNA testing, which provides overwhelming evidence of innocence in particular criminal cases. But what more convincing evidence is there than seeing the supposed victim of a murder amble up to the execution site, as occurred back in 1819? Convincing demonstrations of the innocence of some proportion of those convicted of capital crimes have always been around us, and the numbers in recent years have not been startling by any historical standards. In this book, we argue that the rise of what we call "the innocence movement" has stemmed from a process of collective attention-shifting. As legal scholars, judges, journalists, and others have focused new attention on this old problem of innocence, the debate has been transformed. Once the process started, it was reinforced by further findings of innocence. Particular facts, which once might have been treated as one-of-a-kind historical flukes or lucky breaks for the wrongly condemned, were transformed into evidence of the entire system being flawed, framing the debate along a new dimension. More attention led to more efforts to find more cases. "Innocence projects" were established in journalism and law schools throughout the country, offering pro bono research and legal assistance to the wrongfully convicted. Scientific and cultural trends also reinforced these developments. DNA evidence and TV dramas (some factual, some fictionalized) that focused on problems in police crime labs added further credibility to the idea that concerns about mistakes are not just the product of self-interested statements by convicts attempting to save their skin but perhaps are indicative of serious and systematic problems that public officials should take seriously. The result of these self-reinforcing developments has been the redefinition of American public discourse about the death penalty. Although Americans remain supportive of capital punishment *in theory*, they are increasingly concerned that the system might not work as intended *in practice*. According to the Gallup Organization, public support for the death penalty has declined by ten percentage points in the last decade – a significant drop in aggregate public opinion.[3] And as public concern about the death penalty has grown, the system itself has changed; the average number of death sentences per year since 2000 (150) is just more than half the yearly average during the previous decade (288) (calculated from Snell 2005). The results have been dramatic.

A NEW ARGUMENT IN AN OLD DEBATE

The death penalty is an American tradition, but in recent decades a highly contested one. Whereas capital punishment for serious crimes was once common across the bulk of Western countries, since 1945 it has been increasingly rare in democratic nations and more geographically concentrated within the United States. Because the death penalty has such a long history in America and elsewhere, the arguments for and against it are quite familiar. Most familiar of course are moral and religious arguments – on both sides. Pro–death penalty moral arguments center around the biblical "an eye for an eye" code, emphasizing the need for harsh punishment for terrible crimes. Anti–death penalty moral arguments, often also couched in religious terms, stress forgiveness and redemption, question whether justice is served by what opponents call "state violence" or "state killing," or rely on the more homespun logic that "two wrongs do not make a right." In any case, morality is the main argument on both sides: Some oppose and some support the death penalty based on their own sense of what is right and wrong. This national ambivalence, of course, augurs extremely poorly for anyone who would hope to change attitudes or behaviors on the topic. People do not change their moral views on a whim.

Morality is not the only argument familiar to those who have followed the death penalty debate. Among experts, the bulk of the discussion in fact is on constitutionality and legal procedures. After all, death cases are always criminal trials, so they involve all the complicated questions of federal review over state procedures, due process, jury selection, use of evidence, right to effective counsel, and other issues that are the stuff of detailed analyses of constitutional law and criminal procedure as these relate to particular cases. This legal complexity is clearly not the set of terms on which ordinary Americans draw when thinking about or discussing the issue, but because of its nature the death penalty cannot be dissociated from issues of criminal procedure. Deterrence has been extensively debated, on both sides, with statistics, anecdotes, examples, and forceful arguments aplenty. Race, class, geography, and fairness issues have long been a part of the discussion. International comparisons have entered the debate. As most Western countries have abandoned the practice, the United States has become increasingly isolated. Internal geographic disparities have become important. States in the South have always been more prone to use the death penalty (though as Stuart Banner [2002] shows, in colonial times states of the North were also quite frequent users of capital punishment, though they imposed it more for moral crimes than the economic ones – including slavery – at focus in the South). But the modern death penalty has become even more geographically distinct. More than 80 percent of all the executions since 1976 have taken place in the South, and the bulk in only a handful of states. Even the method of execution, the functioning of the physical machinery of death, has become a periodic item of discussion. Malfunctioning electric chairs produced horrific scenes in a few instances in the 1980s, and faulty administrations of lethal injections, with gruesome consequences, recently became the source of controversy in the early 2000s, finally leading to the suspension of executions in many states, including Florida, in 2006 and 2007. The financial cost of the death penalty has become the focus of some discussion, with a shift over time from a sense that it was cheaper than the alternative of life in prison to the realization that court costs associated with capital trials – with substantial safeguards for the defense, including DNA testing – are tremendously high. Considering the low percentage of convicted murderers who are actually executed, the total cost per execution of most state capital punishment systems is staggering (more than $10 million per case in many states); many have begun to argue that the money could better be spent on alternative crime-related spending priorities while promoting life without parole as an alternative punishment.

In sum, the death penalty is certainly a complex issue. In fact, the paragraph above refers to nineteen distinct arguments, though our list is by no means comprehensive. For most of recent history, however, the death penalty in America has been characterized by entrenched feelings, stable policies, and little movement. Most states rarely use the death penalty, a few use it quite extensively, and most Americans support its use. Considering the multiple dimensions of evaluation that relate to the death penalty, and the multiplicity of concerns that Americans have, the death penalty is a good area in which to explore the process by which attention shifts from one dimension of evaluation to another, and with what consequence. Although the debate is complex, this complexity is not unusual; in fact this complexity – the multiple dimensions of evaluation – is typical of many debates in public policy. Consider global warming, homelessness, poverty, and educational opportunity; which of these issues is simple?

A POLICY REVERSAL

What *is* rare about the death penalty among other major U.S. policy areas is that it is in historic decline. From the beginning of the modern era of capital punishment in 1976 through the mid-1990s, the death penalty grew more common and was increasingly accepted as a "normal" part of American political life. In 1994, 314 death sentences were imposed and nearly 3,000 inmates were on the various death rows across the United States. Public opinion hovered around 80 percent in favor of capital punishment for persons convicted of murder, with less than 20 percent of Americans opposed, reflecting a steady increase in public support over a thirty-five-year period. Media coverage of the death penalty was increasingly positive as well, reflecting its wide use, constitutional acceptability, and public support. These trends reversed, however, in the mid-1990s, and by 2004 the number of death sentences for the year had dropped to 125. Since 1973, more than 120 Americans have been released from death row as a result of exonerations, and a few highly publicized cases have focused public attention on the possibility of errors in the system. The "discovery of innocence" refers to the shift in public attention away from the traditional morality-based discussion of the issue toward a new topic: The possibility that the justice system, dealing as it does with thousands of cases every year, could potentially make mistakes, sending the wrong person from time to time to death row or even, tragically, to the gallows.

In this book, we offer an explanation of one of the most dramatic and unlikely policy reversals in modern times. After all, even today a solid majority of Americans support the death penalty, and few politicians are anxious to appear "soft on crime." Further, those who stand to benefit most directly from an abolition of capital punishment are often notorious killers, brutally insensitive to the lives of others. As convicted felons, they do not have the right to vote. The collection of activists who have campaigned for changes in death penalty laws is made up largely of public defenders, criminal defense attorneys, and a few student-dominated organizations in law and journalism schools at a small number of universities. A majority of Americans continually report support for the concept of a sentence of death for those convicted of murder, even though many states never impose the death penalty and the vast majority of murderers never face a death sentence in spite of their crimes. Further, the constellation of forces traditionally cool to the idea of death penalty reform includes many politically powerful actors, including prosecuting attorneys and attorneys general as well as the U.S. Department of Justice and a majority of the members of the U.S. Supreme Court. Nothing of what we report in this book should be taken to imply that politicians are willing to appear soft on crime or that Americans have suddenly changed their moral views away from the belief that the biblical eye-for-an-eye attitude toward heinous crime is entirely appropriate. Most Americans have such moral views. And yet, things have changed.

Social and political trends are not particularly favorable to the innocence movement: Different religious traditions have differing views on capital punishment, with many abolitionists basing their views on the moral teachings of their church, be they Catholics, traditional Protestants, Jews, or members of other faith communities. But many members of other faiths strongly support an eye-for-an-eye biblical interpretation, including members of many of the fastest-growing religious communities in America. The number of Americans affiliated with evangelical Protestant denominations has sharply increased over the past thirty years, while affiliations with traditional liberal denominations have declined. The post-9/11 war on terror has justified many restrictions on civil liberties and the rights of those accused of crimes, and the federal government has sought the death penalty in several high-profile cases, including that of al-Qaeda sympathizer Zacarias Moussaoui (unsuccessfully) and Washington-area sniper John Muhammad (successfully). Finally, for much of this period, the president has been a former governor of Texas who during his time as governor commuted only one death sentence while presiding over the nation's most active death chamber; more than 150 inmates were put to death in Texas during the years that George W. Bush was governor, more than any other governor in U.S. history (Gross et al. 2005).

And yet, despite many reasons why this trend may be surprising, the death penalty debate has been completely transformed over the past ten years. The new innocence frame diverts attention away from theoretical and philosophical issues of morality to focus simply on the possibility of errors in the criminal justice system. No matter what one thinks about the death penalty in the abstract, this new argument goes, evidence suggests that hundreds of errors have occurred in spite of safeguards designed to guarantee that no innocent people are executed. As attention has shifted from the long-dominant morality argument to the innocence argument, other concerns have risen as well: Is the death penalty effective? Is it racist? Is it worth its high financial cost? Is life without parole a more appropriate sentence? Could we design a set of judicial procedures that would guarantee no errors?

FRAMING, THE STATUS QUO, AND POLICY CHANGE

We aim to understand and demonstrate why the new innocence argument has been so effective in changing U.S. public opinion and public policy. In doing so, we tether our discussion to a theoretical understanding of the politics of attention more broadly. And we will develop new methodologies for studying issue-definition along the way. The death penalty, like abortion, is a moral issue on which most Americans' views are solidly fixed. What is more, a consistent majority of Americans are in favor of the death penalty when queried about it in the abstract. But the death penalty, like any other issue of public policy, is multifaceted. It includes questions of morality, efficacy, constitutionality, fairness and equity of its use, and so on. We trace media coverage of the issue back to 1960 and show dramatic shifts over time in which of these arguments has been most prominent. We chronicle the unprecedented rise in attention to the innocence frame beginning in the mid-1990s and show, statistically, how this shift in the nature of public discourse has driven changes in public opinion and in policy outcomes. Further, by understanding how the death penalty has been reframed, we illustrate the importance of framing and attention-shifting in American politics more generally and show how these factors affect not only public opinion, but the direction of public policy as well. American constitutional law concerning the death penalty is being transformed by a shift in attention. Public opinion is shifting because of the rise of a new frame. Public policy, measured by the number of death sentences imposed, has already been transformed.

We demonstrate how the structure of political conflict surrounding the death penalty has been transformed by a self-reinforcing process that is likely to continue in the future. A "tipping point" has been reached where changes in public understanding have begun to induce further changes in policy, which in turn reinforce those same changes in public understanding. Studies of tipping points and social cascades are fundamental to many areas of social science, ranging from models of residential segregation to cultural fads to momentum associated with candidates for office during a political campaign (see Gladwell 2002 for a popular overview of work on these topics and Schelling 1971 and 1978 or Granovetter 1978 for classic citations from economics and sociology). The death penalty illustrates these ideas well. Beginning in the mid-1970s, a self-reinforcing process generated greater and greater acceptability of the death penalty for almost thirty years as Americans became more and more accustomed to capital punishment. Then a new cascade began in the 1990s, following a similar process but with opposite results: The new focus on innocence has generated public doubt, official caution, powerful individual stories of exoneration, and fewer death sentences, all in a self-perpetuating cycle.

Tipping points and social cascades are by their nature unpredictable, but the continued operation of a system of self-reinforcement allows us to conclude with some predictions about future developments. Increased attention to "innocence" may well be questioned by some, but it will continue to dominate the discussion, with the effect of lowering, for the foreseeable future, the number of death sentences nationwide. Powerful forces of momentum ensure that the current decline in death sentences will continue. The impact of these changes on public opinion has been more difficult to observe, because public opinion at the aggregate level is highly inertial. Most Americans do not think that much about the death penalty, and when they do think of it, they tend to do so in abstract, theoretical terms. (Juries, by contrast, are faced with anything but a theoretical question; this helps explain why juries – expressed through the death sentences they deliver – have changed their behavior in response to the innocence argument much more quickly than public opinion in the abstract – as evidenced in national polls.)

Beyond offering a critical analysis of the evolution of the death penalty debate over time, ours is the first book-length treatment of the dynamics of attention-shifting, following on the work of Bryan Jones and Frank Baumgartner in *The Politics of Attention* (2005). They argued that when dealing with multidimensional and highly complex issues of public policy, political institutions will be affected by over-attention to the status quo definitions of the issue, which inevitably will be incomplete rather than comprehensive. Policies shift not smoothly in response to changing social inputs, but in a disjointed manner associated with threshold effects, information cascades, and shifts in the focus of attention. Policies are often stable for decades as the status quo is reinforced by an established way of thinking about the problem, but when new dimensions arise, policies can change sharply, not just incrementally. Here, we look at one case in great detail. We want to know about the substance of the case first, and our book focuses on the developments of the death penalty debate over the past forty-five years. But we also provide some general lessons about the nature of political change in America along the way.

Kenneth Arrow (1970) won the Nobel Prize for work that showed that politics may be inherently unstable because of the multiple possible methods of aggregating opinion and the intransitivities of individual opinions. Even such things as the order in which alternatives are presented can cause outcomes to shift in surprising ways. Arrow's Paradox is that social outcomes can shift dramatically even if underlying preferences do not change. Our work is closely related to these complex social and economic theories because we do not believe that Americans have suddenly shifted their opinions about the moral justifications associated with capital punishment. On the moral dimension, some strongly oppose the death penalty, believing that two wrongs do not make a right; others strongly support it, believing that a dreadful crime merits a like punishment. A majority of Americans has consistently supported the second moral view of things. But the moral way of considering the issue is not the only way to think about it; there are other important dimensions of evaluation – such as whether it works effectively as a deterrent to crime; whether it is equally and fairly applied; whether it is worth the high cost; whether it isolates America internationally; and whether indigent defendants get sufficient resources to defend themselves, considering the adversarial nature of U.S. criminal procedures and the desires of prosecutors to seek the death penalty in high-profile cases. Certainly there are many other elements of the debate as well.

The point is that the death penalty, like other issues, is multifaceted. For this reason, an individual might hold views leading to support of the death penalty while recognizing aspects of the issue that might point in the other direction. This apparent ambivalence is not unusual; in fact, Arrow explored the implications of exactly such multidimensionality in political debate in his highly theoretical work about "cycling." By *cycling*, he meant that if a political leader could present the same questions for debate in different order or with different points of comparison (e.g., have the vote focus on different dimensions of evaluation), then often no clear and consistent outcome is possible, at least theoretically. Since the demonstration of this paradox, political scientists have focused on understanding the causes of the stability in social outcomes that we do observe.

One of the most important ideas here is Ken Shepsle's concept of the "structure-induced equilibrium" (see Shepsle 1979 and Shepsle and Weingast 1981, 1987). He explained how the institutional design of politics, especially the powers of important gatekeepers such as committee chairs in Congress, induce or create stability in public policy outcomes even if the underlying issues about which political debate occurs are highly complex and multidimensional. In fact, despite what Arrow demonstrated, most policies (including the death penalty) are quite stable most of the time; we do not see "cycles" very much in practice. The structure of the U.S. judicial system, with its adherence to rules of precedence and accumulated case law, induces great stability in judicial outcomes in a similar manner; indeed the concept of *stare decisis* is designed to do exactly that. But stability need not be permanent.

Occasionally, in fact, we see important instances in which policies flip from one seemingly stable equilibrium to another. William Riker explored many such examples in his various works. One of the most important ways in which Riker believed that debates could be affected was when a political leader introduced a new dimension of debate. Riker provided examples of powerful rhetorical strategies by which individual U.S. senators were able to alter the votes of their colleagues by convincing them that a given vote was not really a vote about what it seemed or had been presented, but instead was "really" about the Senate's independence from the president, for example. If one can focus attention on one aspect of the debate rather than another, Riker demonstrated, then one really can create important changes in political outcomes (see Riker 1980, 1983, 1984, 1986, 1988, 1990, 1996).

There are many theoretical reasons to expect that policies – especially those on such a highly charged moral issue as the death penalty – will be quite stable. However, as the above works make clear, stability is not the only possible outcome; framing matters as well, and if the issue can be reframed, then outcomes can change dramatically. In general, when stability is the norm, aggregates move slowly, but even when stability is the dominant feature of individual opinions, aggregate opinion can move in a meaningful way and the effects of framing can be quite large. The apparent puzzle here is simply resolved. When a small number of citizens are attuned to shifting dimensions of debate inherent in policy frames, aggregate opinions can shift in a systematic way. When many do not change their opinions but a few do so in tandem, the signal in the aggregate is created solely by those few responding to new frames. We explore some of these points in greater detail in Chapter 6 on public opinion.

It is easy to state that framing matters in theory, but hard to isolate and measure the precise impact of framing on actual policy outcomes. In fact, the evidence is mixed about who can frame, how resistant individuals are cognitively to accepting new frames when these are presented, how long frames last, and what kinds of issues are most easily reframed. There is, of course, a voluminous literature on these topics. Most framing research has been conducted at the individual level. For example, psychologists have studied how people respond when alternatives are presented in terms of the possibilities of gains versus losses (see Kahneman and Tversky 1985 and Quattrone and Tversky 1988). Political scientists have looked at source credibility as an important factor determining who can frame a debate most effectively and have investigated many other factors that determine whether or not framing effects will occur and, if so, the strength, persistence, and sources of these effects (see Berinski and Kinder 2006; Druckman 2001a, 2001b, 2004; Druckman and Nelson 2003; Gilliam and Iyengar 2000; Nelson et al. 1997). Cognitive psychologists have long noted the remarkable ability of individuals to refuse to consider or to discount new information that contradicts rather than reinforces their existing attitudes, concluding that cognitive dissonance is indeed a powerful force (see Festinger 1957 and Lord et al. 1979).

Although these studies motivate our work in important ways, our analysis is different because we examine the process and effects of framing at the system rather than at the individual level. Throughout our discussion, we maintain a firm awareness of the individual experience – what it has been like for individual citizens to witness the evolution of the death penalty debate over the years – but our primary interest is in understanding how redefinition occurs at the system level, as well as what effect this framing has on opinion and policy formation in the aggregate. From the aforementioned studies rooted in political psychology (and from a few but important framing studies already conducted at the system level, such as Wood and Doan 2003), we have strong reason to believe that framing matters. Yet there are many unanswered questions about the processes by which and how much it matters. Our analyses are designed to answer at least some of these questions.

REFRAMING CAPITAL PUNISHMENT

Each of the theoretical perspectives outlined above suggests that attention to issues of innocence should have been around "in the background" for some time before capturing public attention, coming to the fore of the public agenda suddenly with a bang rather than slowly. We will demonstrate this transformation, tracing the capital punishment debate in America for more than forty-five years of its history. In doing so, we offer a detailed look at how even in this "hardest case" of an issue so entrenched in history and public opinion, information cascades can produce a dramatic redefinition of even a familiar issue.

Just as we expect from the theoretical literature above, we find that public discussion of the death penalty tends to be simplified, focusing during some periods on one aspect of the issue and during others on a different aspect. Morality and constitutionality issues have most commonly dominated discussion, even though there are many possible elements of debate on the issue. Deterrence issues have sometimes been prominent in the debate; at other times they have been only background considerations. Sometimes the two sides of the debate have directly argued along the same dimension, with one arguing, for example, that capital punishment deters crime and the other side saying it does not. At other times the argument has been more cacophonous, with supporters raising a given argument and opponents raising objections based on entirely different perspectives or dimensions. Individual elements of the innocence debate have been around for decades, but in the 1990s they suddenly came to dominate. In this sense, the death penalty, in its confusing complexity, is pretty much like most other complex social issues about which Americans argue politically. Our arguments are never complete, never comprehensively rational, but rather reflect the incomplete and partial nature of debate that stems from various political entrepreneurs attempting as best they can to affect the debate given changes in the stream of information coming in from forces beyond their control.

In our detailed analysis of the rise of the innocence frame, we show that this new frame is 1) unprecedented in its strength compared with previous understandings of the issue, 2) powerful in its effects on public opinion as well as on policy outputs, and 3) *more* powerful in these effects even than underlying social trends, such as the murder rate or other reasonable rival explanations. Our substantive point is to understand the death penalty, and our theoretical point is to understand the nature of policy change. Policy change often stems from attention-shifting. The practical consequences of this fact for those interested in the death penalty debate are fundamental: As long as attention continues to focus on issues of innocence, trends will continue toward less and less public support and official sanction of the practice.

If attention were to shift to other topics, the tone of discussion could easily tip back in a pro–death penalty direction, as it did in the 1970s and 1980s. In particular, the morality question reinforces a dimension of the death penalty that leads individuals to discount the practical questions of the functioning of the criminal justice system and to rely on abstract, theoretical, or philosophical reasoning to reach a conclusion. One practical implication of our study is simply that the topic of discussion determines its tone. If political leaders and activists focus attention on problems associated with the details of how trials are actually conducted and the imperfections likely to be inherent in many cases, this frame reinforces a message that practical considerations, not theoretical concerns, are a relevant dimension of consideration. Focusing attention on practical effects rather than abstract morality frames the debate. Along the practical dimension, most Americans can easily see many problems, even though along the moral dimension they support the death penalty. Shift the dimension and you shift the attitude. It's that simple.

Well, it's not really as simple as all that. Political debates are not controlled by any single actor, so saying that one can shift public attitudes by altering the dominant focus of attention may well be true (and our analysis strongly points to this conclusion), but this is easier said than done. Many leaders would like to shift attention from one topic to another, on all kinds of political issues. But few have the power single-handedly to do so. Opponents fight back. The audience shows resistance. The agenda shifts to another issue entirely, so efforts to focus attention come to nothing. In sum, there are many difficulties associated with reframing a debate, and most efforts to do so fail. But the death penalty has been reframed nonetheless. The innocence frame has upended the previously dominant constitutionality and morality frames from previous decades. So, although reframing is rare and may be difficult, it does occur and we will explore the process of how this one particular reframing process unfolded over the past decades.

We develop new methods for the study of issue-definition and framing and believe that these techniques can be used widely across fields in political science. We go into considerable detail in describing exactly how we coded media coverage systematically to trace attention to various component arguments, and we develop new techniques to determine which arguments "resonate" or gain greater attention than others. We show the similarity of media coverage across ten different media outlets, and we link our data on media coverage and framing to statistics on the severity of the underlying problems, public opinion, and policy response using multivariate time series analysis.

We hope to make two important methodological contributions to the literature. First, we develop new methods for measuring and analyzing framing and issue-definition over time. Second, armed with these new measures, we demonstrate statistically the impact of these framing variables on aggregate-level public opinion measures and on actual public policy outcomes. In both cases, we do so with appropriate controls for potential alternative explanations of these changes, and we use the most up-to-date statistical techniques. Most studies of framing effects have been much shorter in their time coverage and have not used such a broad range of information as we incorporate. Further, they have not shown the powerful statistical results we show about the impact of framing on actual policy outcomes. The methodological innovations we develop here may well be applicable in other cases, but we develop them first and foremost because they help us answer the substantive and theoretical questions with which we start; namely, has the U.S. debate about the death penalty been transformed, and why?

GOALS AND STRUCTURE OF THE BOOK

This book is not about what one Chicago lawyer, Governor Ryan, a single journalist or exoneree, or even a small number of innocence projects have created, but about how these things came together to be more than the sum of the parts. We focus not on how individual Americans respond but on how media framing, violent crime rates, and the actions of hundreds of separate actors working in isolation and in tandem behind the scenes came together to change how Americans collectively view the death penalty and how the nation has responded, collectively, to these new interpretations. As such, we study not just the pieces but the whole. We study the effects of framing on Americans' collective opinions and their willingness to sentence their fellow citizens to death. Most studies of this topic focus on individual attitudes not developments at the collective, or system, level. The two are obviously related, but there are also important differences in focus. In any case, our focus is collective, on the system as a whole, not individual.

Our goals here are fourfold. First, we want to understand the evolution of the death penalty debate; we want to know what has happened and why and to speculate about the future development of the death penalty debate. Along the same lines, we want to understand the linkages between those debates and discussions that go on within professional communities such as the legal community, in this case with broader public discussion, and finally how these debates affect political leaders, public opinion, and ultimately public policy. Our second goal is to draw some lessons about the causes of opinion and policy change more generally. This includes theoretical lessons about where change comes from as well as practical lessons for policy advocates about what types of arguments, or frames, are more effective than others. One paradox of our study of the death penalty that should be lost on no one is that many abolitionists are motivated by a moral view that capital punishment is wrong. Our study suggests that they will make little headway in the debate as long as they lead with this argument, however. Ironically, their greatest success has come by changing the subject to a different dimension entirely. Thus, the study has important theoretical and also practical lessons for those interested in understanding, or even causing, policy change. Our third goal is a broader understanding of the power of social groups in American democracy. In many ways, the death penalty should never have been reframed. The constituency standing most to benefit from policy change is hardly an appealing or powerful one politically; the constellation of actors pushing for policy change includes none of the most powerful corporations in America, none of the traditional power bases in American politics, and is not particularly wealthy; public opinion for most of recent history has been against them; and politicians have been jittery about how to respond to them. And yet this group has achieved major successes. This puzzle merits significant attention, and we will return to this issue in the conclusion. Finally, our fourth goal is to develop new methodologies for the study of policy change and issue-framing and to demonstrate how such studies need not rely only on qualitative or anecdotal assessments, but how we can combine such approaches with more comprehensive, systematic, and statistical techniques. The following chapters explore these topics in detail.

Chapter 2 traces the evolution of capital punishment since 1945. We give special focus, first, to the period surrounding the 1972 to 1976 moratorium – the time between the Supreme Court's 1972 *Furman v. Georgia* (408 U.S. 238) decision effectively outlawing capital punishment and its 1976 *Gregg v. Georgia* (428 U.S. 153) decision reinstating the punishment – and, second, to the post-1994 period during which, as we will show, the innocence frame has come to dominate the death penalty debate. We chronicle the shifting political landscape of the death penalty debate, marking landmark events and Supreme Court decisions. We provide descriptive statistics on the annual numbers of capital convictions, death row inmates, executions, and exonerations over time, mostly in charts and figures. We assess the geographical and racial distributions of these numbers as well as the ratio of federal to state cases. We also give a brief description of how public opinion has shifted over time. The chapter focuses on the chronological development of the debate and is designed to provide the basic background information associated with the issue so that the reader understands, up front, the history of the issue and in particular how trends in the number of death sentences, the size of death row, the number of executions, and the level of public support have varied over time. Later chapters systematically analyze these trends.

Chapter 3 gives detailed treatment to the rise of the innocence frame. We track national trends while paying special attention to events in Illinois, where the organizations that would come to be known as innocence projects took root. Some of the first of these groups were housed at Northwestern University, representing a unique intersection between academic research and hands-on legal aid and journalism clinics. And it was in large part because of the innocence projects that in 2000 Illinois governor George Ryan – a former death penalty advocate who had become convinced of the system's fallibilities – imposed the nation's first executive moratorium on executions and in 2003 commuted the sentences of all inmates on that state's death row. Events in Illinois had tremendous resonance nationally and helped create the national surge of attention that we document to issues of innocence. We bring together into a single chronological narrative the following: high-profile sentencing verdicts, executions, and exonerations; landmark Supreme Court rulings; public events relevant to death penalty debate; and the growth of various advocacy groups and legal projects associated with the "innocence movement." We show that one type of organization in particular – the "hands-on" legal and journalism clinics centered in a few law and journalism schools – played a pivotal role in generating public interest in the questions of innocence. Academics and specialists had been documenting these issues for decades but were never successful in generating the degree of public concern with the issue as that which occurred during the 1990s. We show a steady growth, but no spikes, in exonerations over time. We document a dramatic rise in mobilization around the issue during the 1990s, even though there were cases of exoneration in earlier decades. We review media coverage of each of more than 120 exonerees and demonstrate that their stories have become compelling news, although they once were not. In fact, the average number of stories published about each exoneree has expanded greatly over the years; this increased attention to each exoneree, rather than a greater number of exonerees, explains most of the rise in overall attention to the issue and illustrates nicely the threshold and self-reinforcing effects of the rise of the innocence frame.

Chapter 4 documents the rise of the innocence frame through a comprehensive review of the content of the 3,939 articles on capital punishment appearing in the *New York Times* since 1960. Ours is the first systematic study of issue-definition to apply such detailed coding to such a large dataset. Using a comprehensive list of 65 potential arguments that can be made about the death penalty, we trace the shifting foci of attention over time across seven main dimensions of debate: efficacy, morality, constitutionality, fairness, cost, the mode of execution, and international concerns. The data we collect show clear shifts in the framing of capital punishment over this time period, from the moral and constitutional frames of the 1960s and 1970s to the innocence frame of the last decade and others in between. Of all the frames, the innocence frame is the single most powerful in terms of amount of attention; thus, we expect it to have the greatest impact on the political system. Across the entire dataset, we find that the dimension a given news story employs consistently predicts that story's tone (pro–death penalty, anti–death penalty, or neutral). Stories focusing on moral arguments, for example, are usually pro–death penalty, whereas almost all stories on the fairness dimension have an anti–death penalty tone. Similarly, stories mentioning the victim of a capital crime are predominantly pro–death penalty, whereas stories about the defendant are generally anti–death penalty. The frame determines the tone of the debate and, as we demonstrate in Chapters 6 and 7, respectively, the tone of the debate has significant influence on public opinion and public policy.

In addition to our review of forty-five years of coverage in the *New York Times*, we corroborate our findings with computer-based searches of ten major newspapers from 1980 to the present. This analysis demonstrates that 1) the coverage in the *Times* is broadly consistent with the amount of coverage in a range of papers (including the *Washington Post, Miami Herald, Houston Chronicle, Pittsburgh Post-Gazette, Seattle Times, Boston Globe, Chicago Sun-Times, Denver Post*, and *San Francisco Chronicle*); 2) all these papers show a surge in attention to the innocence frame just as we documented with the *Times*; and 3) many of the more locally focused papers exhibit spikes and declines in coverage associated with local cases, with the *Times* and the *Post* better reflecting national trends.

Chapter 5 offers a theoretical discussion of the mechanisms of issue-definition and a new methodology to match. We argue that *saliency* (how often a given set of arguments is used) is only one of three key components of the issue-definition process. Also important are *resonance* (how many individual arguments move in tandem over time) and *persistence* (how long the frame lasts). We develop a new statistical approach, evolutionary factor analysis (EFA), to take these components into account. The method involves factor analyzing our set of sixty-five basic arguments within moving time windows to isolate those arguments in each window that dominate that historical period. When there are no patterns to which arguments are used in conjunction with other arguments, the debate is diffuse, cacophonous. When, on the other hand, use of one argument tends systematically to be accompanied by use of specific other arguments, then we can identify statistical patterns of resonant themes in the debate.

Indeed, the data show consistent patterns associated with the dominant foci of attention throughout the historical period of study, including periods when morality and constitutionality were the dominant frames. Further, our method gives us an indication of the power of an argument because we can measure its resonance, salience, and persistence. Through this method, we see that the innocence frame is not only the most salient of all the frames in the modern history of the death penalty debate, it is also the most resonant and the most persistent. We also demonstrate that although this frame is driven by a few core arguments regarding wrongful conviction, calls for a moratorium, and the availability of DNA evidence, several other arguments that have been raised – unsuccessfully – at other points in time are now finding traction in the death penalty debate by "piggybacking" on the innocence frame.

Thus, our technique allows us to see the reemergence of perennial debates, such as the argument that the system has a significant racial bias or that the system harbors tremendous geographical arbitrariness and perverts the equal protection of the laws by making criminals in some jurisdictions liable to a death sentence, whereas those guilty of the same crimes in other areas of the country are not. Our analysis of resonance allows us to show that these arguments, made unsuccessfully in isolation, grew to constitute a more coherent cluster with the rise of the innocence frame. The resulting cluster of arguments is more convincing because of its resonance than any of the individual arguments would be taken alone. These methods allow a re-creation of the substance of the debate and help to explain why the new innocence frame is so powerful. It is powerful, in part, because it is not entirely new. Rather, it gives a coherent overall structure to a number of arguments that have, in fact, been around for decades.

Chapter 6 builds a model of public opinion, showing how aggregate levels of public support for the death penalty have changed over time since 1960 and how these changes relate to argumentation, framing, and the discovery of innocence. We discuss individual-level opinions, but our focus is on public opinion in the aggregate. Individual opinion is highly stable on moral issues such as the death penalty, and we do not expect to see much change in individual opinions measured over time. However, as attention shifts and citizens – even in small numbers – respond at the margins, their responsiveness imparts a signal that is reflected in overall trends. As such, public opinion moves systematically over time as cues about the appropriateness of the death penalty ebb and flow. We focus on this variation in aggregate public opinion in Chapter 6. Although demographic characteristics and environmental conditions distinguish opinions among citizens, they change only slowly over time and thus do not explain variation in opinions over time. To explain variation in public opinion over time, we turn instead to sources that leverage over-time variation, namely, evolving media frames and violent crime rates. Our analysis is based on a comprehensive review of more than 250 national surveys, the most complete compilation of such surveys so far assembled. We use a sophisticated mathematical algorithm (explained in Appendix B) to incorporate as many survey questions as possible into our series, even those using slightly different question wordings, creating a more complete and robust time series for public opinion. (As long as each question wording was itself asked multiple times over the series, the algorithm allows us to combine these into a single indicator of attitudes over time.) Controlling for relevant political background variables as well as for the number of homicides, we analyze public opinion over the past twenty years, examining quarterly patterns in public opinion in the period of dramatic change in opinion. The analysis shows clearly the impact of the tone of media coverage. This framing effect is over and above the actual number of exonerations, the number of homicides, and other control variables. We use media coverage as an indicator of the nature of public discussion, so it makes sense that as people discuss the issue in different ways, focusing on one dimension of the debate or another, public opinion would shift in response. The increase in public support for the death penalty during the 1980s and the early 1990s was clearly associated with increased pro–death penalty news coverage, and the shift in this coverage since the mid-1990s, a result of the rise of the innocence frame, is clearly and powerfully linked with declining public support.

In Chapter 7, we shift our attention to a broad and longer-term perspective, analyzing public policy since the early 1960s. We use the annual number of death sentences as the best single indicator of the state of public policy in this area. This number has ranged widely across the period from 1960 to the present, generally declining from 1960 to 1972, fluctuating tremendously during the period surrounding the reinstatement of capital punishment in 1976, growing inexorably during the late 1970s through the mid-1990s, and declining precipitously since then. It is the single best indicator of the state of capital punishment in America, reflecting the actions of juries as well as the strategic decisions of prosecutors as they elect to bring capital charges partly with respect to their likelihood of winning the case. As in Chapter 6, our focus here is on the willingness of Americans collectively to sentence others to death. Rather than analyze the decision of juries in individual cases, we develop a statistical model to predict the annual number of death sentences, including appropriate controls, such as those for the number of homicides, the number of exonerations, the number of death sentences, and levels of public support in the previous year. Whereas idiosyncratic factors can explain the outcomes of particular jury trials, these effects cancel when we aggregate to the annual level, and the systematic effects of attention to innocence or homicide rates, which change over time, explain the variation in the number of death sentences handed out each year. Our question is whether framing effects remain apparent even after controlling for these other factors, and our results demonstrate that they do. The substantive effect of shifts in framing indicate that media effects alone account for a decline of more than 100 death sentences per year in recent years; the number attributable to declining homicide rates is about one quarter as much. The effects on opinions are equally impressive and exert additional indirect effects on sentences.

Chapter 8 concludes the book. The death penalty debate has been transformed over the past ten years by a rediscovery of some old arguments. As public attention has focused on the question of "innocence," aided by increased public understanding of problems in police crime labs, DNA testing, and significant publicity associated with cases in which inmates have been exonerated often after having served more than a decade on death row, public opinion and public policy both have shifted. The death penalty is in decline. All this comes at a time of a war on terror, during the presidency of George W. Bush, and with many national leaders expressing strong support for the morality of capital punishment. Morality is no longer the main focus of discussion, however; errors and imperfections in the system have replaced morality and constitutionality as the central points of attention.

We conclude with a discussion of the future of the death penalty and with reflections on the causes of policy change more generally. Like any issue, the death penalty elicits concerns on many dimensions, in this case about morality, constitutional procedure, race, class, fairness, and other issues. The theoretical perspective used throughout this book reflects a bounded-rationality view on the policy process emphasizing the expectation that, at any given time, political leaders and members of the public will focus their attention on a small subset of the complex and disparate set of questions associated with any policy. The death penalty debate illustrates this model of attention-shifting perfectly. Although it is not clear that any of those promoting the new innocence frame could ever have controlled or predicted its development, there is no surprise whatsoever that, once the new frame became so dominant, public opinion and public policy would respond. That is how American democracy works. In fits and starts, we move from one direction in public policy, justified by a given set of understandings of the underlying problem, to another. Policy advocates toil away within their respective professional communities, attempting to gain greater attention to their preferred ways of viewing the issue, attempting to reframe the debate. Occasionally, through the combined efforts of many, and with a little luck, they succeed. The model of attention-shifting that we have followed here, with its emphasis on the impact of framing on the subsequent opinion and policy response, is central to how policies are made and revised in all areas of American government. For capital punishment in America, the discovery of innocence may portend its own death sentence.

2 THE DEATH PENALTY IN AMERICA

THE MODERN ERA of capital punishment in the United States dates from the reinstatement in 1976 of state death penalty laws invalidated by the Supreme Court in 1972. During the moratorium period, state legislatures around the nation revised their legislation and procedures in an effort to pass constitutional review. Today more than 3,000 convicted criminals sit on the various death rows around the country. The revival of the death penalty in the modern era reflects in some ways a return to longstanding American traditions of justice, as the United States (like most Western countries) has a long history of capital punishment. There are, however, important differences between the modern and the pre-moratorium death penalty. In this chapter we look at some long-term trends in the use of capital punishment. We review the chronology of the use of the death penalty since 1800 and more specifically since 1976, we look at its geographical distribution internationally and across the fifty states, we assess the racial breakdown of those executed, and we present other basic background information. Later chapters focus more specifically on public understandings and media framings of capital punishment; our goal in this chapter is simply to lay out the historical context for the current debate.

LONG-TERM TRENDS IN THE UNITED STATES AND WORLDWIDE

The United States has a long history of capital punishment, as do most Western countries. We reached a peak in our application of the death penalty shortly before World War II, and after that period, in parallel with many other Western countries, the incidence of capital punishment declined precipitously. After reaching a maximum of 197 in 1935, executions dropped sharply until the 1960s, when they disappeared completely even before the Supreme Court's *Furman* decision barring executions in 1972. In contrast to other countries, however, which permanently

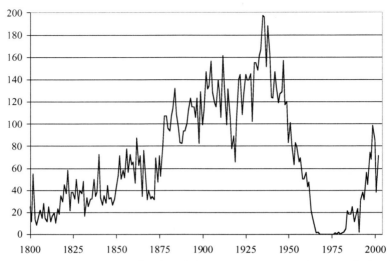

Figure 2.1. Executions in the United States, 1800 to 2002. (*Source:* calculated from Espy and Smykla 2005.)

abolished the death penalty, we have seen a resurgence in executions since the Supreme Court's *Gregg* decision reinstating the death penalty in 1976. And, as we will see, although a small handful of U.S. states account for the vast bulk of sentences and executions nationwide, still the majority of states – thirty-eight out of fifty – maintain the death penalty as a legal option and have prisoners on death row. So even though many states rarely execute prisoners, these thirty-eight death rows constitute an important policy statement. In this sense, the United States differs quite dramatically from other Western countries, and increasingly so. Further, geographic differences within the United States have grown, increasingly distinguishing a small number of states that have amplified their use of the death penalty from the vast majority of states within the United States that have either entirely abandoned or dramatically reduced their use of capital punishment. These trends have made the modern death penalty quite different from its historical cousin. Figure 2.1 shows the number of executions in the United States from 1800 to 2002.

Stuart Banner (2002) provides the most complete history of use of the death penalty in America, going back to colonial times. He shows in particular how the penalty was used differently in the South and in the northern states. Crimes of morality were more often historically punished by death in the North, economic crimes more often in the South (including, of course, those related to slavery). Since 1800, we can see a general rise in the use of the death penalty across the United States that parallels the growing national population. The numbers of executions have never been huge, considering the size of the U.S. population, the number of crimes, or

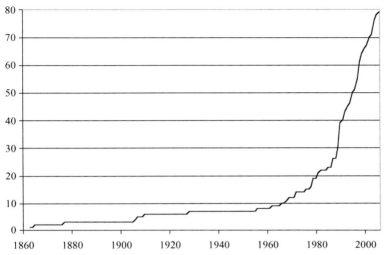

Figure 2.2. Cumulative number of countries having abolished the death penalty, 1863 to 2006. (*Source:* calculated from Amnesty International 2006.)

the number of lesser sentences. The series fell dramatically from its 1935 peak of 197 until the early 1960s, until there were no executions at all by the mid-1960s. This decline marks a period of significant doubt over the constitutionality of the penalty. Although there were death sentences during this time, they were not carried out until after the constitutional issues were resolved in 1976. There were no executions whatsoever in the United States from 1968 to 1977.

International trends paralleled the declining U.S. use of the death penalty in the post–World War II era. Use of the death penalty declined throughout the Western world, and abolition developed apace. Since 1970, dozens of Western countries have outlawed capital punishment, including Finland and Sweden (1972), Portugal (1976), Denmark (1978), Luxemburg and Norway (1979), France (1981), the Netherlands (1982), Australia (1985), Germany (1987), Ireland (1990), Switzerland (1992), Italy (1994), Spain (1995), Canada and the United Kingdom (1998), Greece and Turkey (2004), and Mexico (2005) (Amnesty International 2006). As of 2006, Amnesty International reports that eighty-seven countries have no death penalty; eleven maintain it only for extraordinary crimes, such as in military tribunals; twenty-eight retain the death penalty officially but have not executed anyone in more than ten years and have clear policies against it; and seventy-one maintain the death penalty as a regular judicial sanction. Among the eighty-seven countries having abolished the death penalty, the bulk of these formal decisions came in the 1990s. Figure 2.2 shows cumulative growth in the number of countries having abandoned the death penalty over time.[1]

The sharp rise in international movement away from the death penalty in the 1980s and 1990s is clear. In fact, the actual use of executions declined much earlier than did formal abolition: Fifty of the eighty-seven countries having abolished the death penalty had not carried out any executions since before 1980, even though the bulk of the formal abolitions came more recently. At the time of its 1998 abolition, the United Kingdom had not executed anyone since 1964; in Ireland, no one had been executed since 1954; in Sweden, no one since 1910. Among Western countries, the trends against imposition of capital punishment are almost universal. Of thirty members of the Organization of Economic Cooperation and Development (OECD), just three maintain the death penalty: the United States, Japan, and South Korea. Among European countries (including Russia and the former Soviet states), only Belarus is among the seventy-one countries maintaining regular judicial executions.[2] Abolition of the death penalty is also a requirement of membership in the European Union.[3] The United States, too, was part of this broad international trend toward abolition until the reinstatement and growth of executions after 1976. In this sense, the modern death penalty differs substantially from the historical one. Before 1976, U.S. death penalty trends fit in well with those of similar countries; now, the United States stands alone among Western nations.

THE GEOGRAPHY OF THE MODERN U.S. DEATH PENALTY

The death penalty has never been a common or standard penalty for even the most terrible crimes in the United States. Of the thousands of murders committed each year, only a minute fraction see the murderer charged with a capital offense (and, of course, only a fraction of those are sentenced to death, and only a fraction of those are actually executed). Even this relatively rare use of the penalty was on its way to oblivion, as Figure 2.1 makes clear, after World War II. Many states abandoned it, even those that had made extensive use of it in previous decades. Considering the geographic disparity in the use of the death penalty in our country, most states in the United States remain fully in line with international trends. However, geographic and racial disparities in application of the death penalty in the United States have always been powerful, and they are even more so today. The modern era of the death penalty, since 1976, shows striking breaks from the past in several ways. The United States as a whole no longer fits international trends. Yet within the nation, capital punishment has grown increasingly geographically distinct as national consensus about its use has splintered.

Across the fifty states, the death penalty ranges from the unconstitutional to the theoretical to the routine.[4] Michigan, for example, declared capital punishment unconstitutional in 1847, shortly after it became a state in 1837; no one has been executed there for a state crime, ever. Twenty-one states have not executed a single individual since 1976. And more and more state legislatures are moving to limit the death penalty or strike it from the books altogether. Illinois is perhaps the best-known example; the state gained national attention in 2000 when then-governor George Ryan placed a formal moratorium on the death penalty. But abolitionist activity has been brewing in many other states as well. In 2004, New York's death penalty laws were declared unconstitutional by the state supreme court, and the state legislature has made no move toward constitutional revision; the state is effectively abolitionist. In 2006, the New Jersey state legislature imposed a formal moratorium on executions in that state. In 2006, legislatures in at least eighteen states considered legislation to repeal capital punishment or to impose a moratorium on executions; for the first time, there is a serious possibility of actual abolition or repeal of the death penalty in several states, including Maryland and New Jersey.

Of course, death sentences are not the same as executions. Most of those individuals initially sentenced to death are not executed because, through appeal, they have their sentences changed to life in prison; because, through appeal, they gain a new trial and are subsequently acquitted or sentenced to a lesser penalty; because they die of natural causes; or – rarely – because they are exonerated or their sentences are commuted by the governor. The states differ quite dramatically in what happens to inmates after they are sentenced to death and put on death row. All death penalty convictions are automatically reviewed by federal courts, and the federal appeals process invalidates a large percentage of the initial verdicts, finding flaws in either the original trial assessing guilt or in the second, penalty phase; these procedures apply to all states, but of course the level of reversal is higher in some states than in others. Sixteen states and jurisdictions, including Maryland and Connecticut, have the death penalty on the books but have fewer than twenty inmates on death row; this number includes New York – where the death penalty was ruled unconstitutional in 2004 but where one man still lives on death row – as well as New Hampshire – where the death penalty is legal but death row is empty. Thirteen states have more than 20 but fewer than 100 individuals on death row, and ten have more than 100 death row inmates. Even in this last group, there is substantial variation in actual use of the death penalty: Pennsylvania and California have hundreds of people on death row (228 and 657, respectively) but have carried out just three and thirteen executions since 1976. Ohio similarly has a "theoretical" death penalty, with 192 persons on death row, but only twenty-four executions in the modern era. At the other end of the spectrum, a few states have executed large numbers of inmates in the modern era: Texas (379);

Table 2.1. *Size of death row by jurisdiction, as of October 1, 2006*

State	Inmates	Ranking
A. States and jurisdictions with more than 100 inmates on death row		
California	657	1
Florida	398	2
Texas	392	3
Pennsylvania	228	4
Alabama	192	5
Ohio	192	5
North Carolina	184	7
Arizona	124	8
Tennessee	108	9
Georgia	107	10
B. States and jurisdictions with 21 to 99 inmates		
Oklahoma	89	11
Louisiana	88	12
Nevada	79	13
Mississippi	66	14
South Carolina	66	14
Missouri	50	16
U.S. federal government	44	17
Kentucky	39	18
Arkansas	37	19
Oregon	33	20
Indiana	24	21
Idaho	20	22
Virginia	20	22
C. States and jurisdictions with 1 to 19 inmates		
Delaware	18	24
Illinois	11	25
New Jersey	11	25
Kansas	9	27
Nebraska	9	27
Washington	9	27
U.S. military	9	27
Utah	9	27
Connecticut	8	32
Maryland	8	32
South Dakota	4	34
Colorado	2	35
Montana	2	35
New Mexico	2	35
Wyoming	2	35
New York[a]	1	39
D. States and jurisdictions with no inmates on death row		
Alaska, District of Columbia, Hawaii, Iowa, Maine, Massachusetts, Michigan, Minnesota, New Hampshire,[b] North Dakota, Rhode Island, Vermont, West Virginia, Wisconsin		
Total for all states	**3,344**	**53**

[a] In 2004, New York's state death penalty statute was declared unconstitutional.

[b] New Hampshire is the only state with the death penalty but no inmates currently on death row.

Source: DPIC 2006b.

Table 2.2. *Executions by the ten biggest death row states, 1976 to 2006*[a]

State	Number on death row	Executions since 1976
Texas	392	379
Florida	398	64
North Carolina	184	43
Georgia	107	39
Alabama	192	35
Ohio	192	24
Arizona	124	22
California	657	13
Pennsylvania	228	3
Tennessee[b]	108	2

[a] Six of the 11 biggest execution states are not among the 10 biggest death row states: Virginia (98 executions), Oklahoma (84), Missouri (66), South Carolina (36), Louisiana (27), and Arkansas (27).
[b] Tennessee executed Robert Glen Coe on April 19, 2000, and Sedley Alley on June 28, 2006, both by lethal injection.
Source for death row data: DPIC 2006b.
Source for execution data: DPIC 2006c.

Virginia (98); Oklahoma (84); Missouri (66); and Florida (64). These five states, in fact, account for an absolute majority of the entire number of executions since 1976; Texas alone is responsible for more than one third (36 percent). Table 2.1 shows the size of death row across the fifty-three jurisdictions,[5] and Table 2.2 shows the number of executions among those states with the largest death row populations.

The geographical peculiarities of the death penalty in the modern era have changed many of the dynamics and arguments associated with it. Because the vast bulk of capital cases occur only in certain states, concerns about safeguards often come from outside observers not located in those states. Can we be sure that all those Texas convictions were free from error? Do Texas judicial officials expect to be told by outside officials how to run their justice system, or appreciate outside commentary? States' rights arguments intermingle with moral concerns increasingly in the modern era.

Figure 2.3 shows the number of executions in the modern era by state. A total of 1,057 executions took place from 1977 to 2006, the period covered here, and the figure shows that more than one third of them (36 percent) were in Texas. Virginia, with the second highest number of executions, accounts for 9 percent. Most states, in fact, have little or

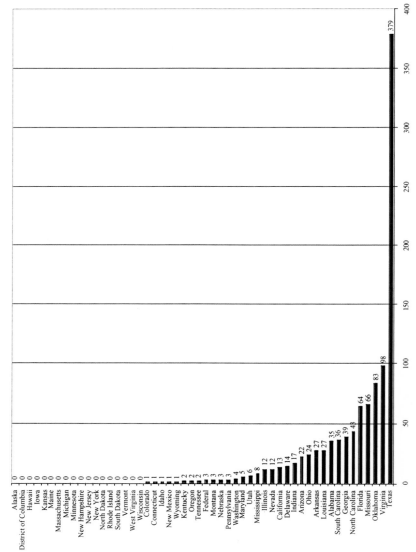

Figure 2.3. Executions by state, 1977 to 2006. (*Source*: calculated from DPIC 2006c.)

no use for the death penalty. Eighteen states (including the District of Columbia) have not executed a single person during this time, and the median number of executions by state is less than three. For this reason, it is largely inaccurate to say that the United States has bucked international trends. A few states make substantial use of the death penalty (Texas chief among them), but for the most part the judicial systems of the U.S. states have either completely abandoned capital punishment or nearly so.

Of course, many Americans live in states with active death chambers, and some states have expanded, rather than reduced, their use of executions since 1976. Figure 2.3 shows the extreme concentration of executions in the modern era in just a few states of the South. In fact, the states of the South are the only group that has executed such large numbers of people since 1976. During earlier historical periods, the situation was quite different, as states in all regions of the country were much more likely to execute criminals (and Figure 2.1 shows that the death penalty was much more common before World War II; these numbers include executions in many northern states).

The death penalty has long been geographically distinct. However, in the modern period it has become increasingly so. Many states with long histories of the death penalty and hundreds of executions carried out have virtually abandoned the practice in the modern era. New York, for example, executed 1,130 individuals from 1608 to 1976, but none since 1976. Similarly, in Pennsylvania, 1,040 were executed in the state's history up to 1976, but only 3 in the modern era. Other states with dramatic declines similar to these include Ohio, 438/24; New Jersey, 361/0; Massachusetts, 345/0; and California, 669/13. In fact, comparing the numbers of executions in the post–World War II period to those of the post-1976 period shows that forty-three states (including the District of Columbia) showed a decline in or an equal number of executions. Eight states, on the other hand, bucked this trend. Table 2.3 shows these figures.[6]

Table 2.3 shows that four states dramatically counter the general national and international trend toward fewer executions: Texas, Oklahoma, Virginia, and Missouri. These four states are, of course, among only five in the nation to have executed more than sixty individuals in the modern era.[7] Four additional states – Delaware, Indiana, Arizona, and Montana – also executed more people between 1976 and 2006 than in the earlier period, but the changes are less dramatic. The eight states listed in Table 2.3 are the only ones to have increased the number of executions; every other state has dramatically reduced or completely abandoned the practice. The modern death penalty is perhaps most different from the historical one in this simple geographic peculiarity. Most states have virtually abandoned the practice, but a few have embraced it more forcefully.

We can summarize the geographic distribution of the death penalty with a simple graphic. Figure 2.4 shows the percentage of those executed by

Table 2.3. *States with an increase in executions between 1945 and 1975 and 1976 and 2006*

State	Number of executions		Difference
	1945–1975	1976–2006	
Texas	144	379	235
Oklahoma	20	83	63
Virginia	51	98	47
Missouri	23	66	43
Delaware	2	14	12
Indiana	8	17	9
Arizona	15	22	7
Montana	0	3	3
Total for all 53 states and jurisdictions	1,566	1,057	−509

Source for 1945–1975 data: calculated from Espy and Smykla 2005.
Source for 1976–2006 data: DPIC 2006c.

region, for three historical periods: from colonial days until 1944, from 1945 to 1975, and in the modern period.

The South has always led the nation in capital punishment, but the geographic disparities have grown over time. From the beginning of U.S. history until World War II, just less than 60 percent of all executions were in the South, with 22 percent in the Northeast, and 11 and 9 percent, respectively, in the Midwest and West. The percentage of executions in

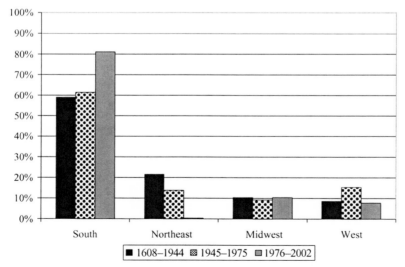

Figure 2.4. Percentage of executions by region during three historical periods. (*Source:* calculated from Espy and Smykla 2005.)

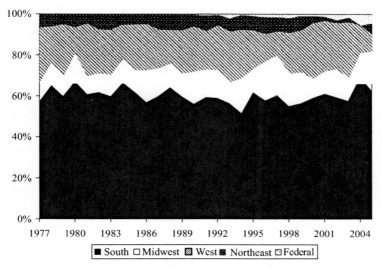

Figure 2.5. Death sentences by region, 1977 to 2005. Sentencing values for 2006 were not yet available at time of publication. (*Source:* calculated from DPIC 2006d.)

the northeastern states declined from 22 to 13 to 2 percent in successive periods, whereas that in the South increased from 59 to 61 to 80 percent. Figure 2.5 shows the consistency of these trends as they relate to death sentences, and Figure 2.6 shows that they are even stronger with regards to executions.

Race and geography go hand in hand in the United States, so there should be no surprise that race plays a major role in these questions as well. We consider this issue next.

RACE

Racial disparities in the application of the death penalty have always been part of the debate. Although African Americans make up roughly 11 percent of the U.S. population, they have constituted 50 percent of all individuals executed from 1800 to the present. Figure 2.7 shows the number of executions from 1800 to 2002 by race.

Whether we consider the modern era or take a longer-term perspective, racial disparities in the application of the death penalty have been powerful and consistent. A total of 13,716 individuals have been executed in the United States since 1800. Of this total, 6,713 or 48.9 percent were black, 5,677 or 41.4 percent were white, and 1,326 or 9.7 percent were of other or unknown races. The percentage of blacks among those executed was consistently in the area of 40 to 60 percent throughout the period

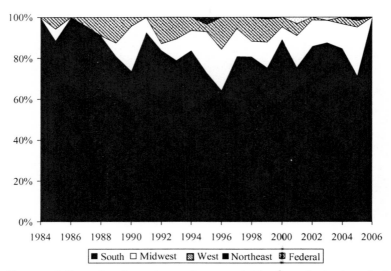

Figure 2.6. Executions by region, 1984 to 2006. The figure begins in 1984 because there were very few executions between 1977 and 1983 and none at all in two of those years; percentage calculations were impossible or unstable. (*Source:* calculated from DPIC 2006c.)

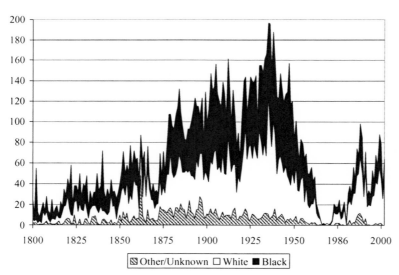

Figure 2.7. Executions by race, 1800 to 2002. (*Source:* calculated from Espy and Smykla 2005.)

from 1865 to 1960. Since 1980, the percentage of blacks has fluctuated between 25 and 50 percent of the total.

Race affects the debate not only because of who is executed, but even more so because of the differential likelihood of facing capital charges depending on the race of the victim in the crime. In a carefully conducted study of murder convictions in California covering the decade of the 1990s, Glenn L. Pierce and Michael L. Radelet calculated the rate of death sentences per 100 murders of victims of different races. The rate for murders of non-Hispanic whites was 1.745. That means that just under 2 percent of murders of white victims led to a capital conviction (we will see in the next section that only a minority of convictions typically lead to execution). Comparable figures for blacks and Hispanics were 0.471 and 0.369 – less than one half of 1 percent odds. Killers of white victims, in other words, were more than 3.5 times as likely to receive a death sentence as those who killed a black or a Hispanic individual (Pierce and Radelet 2005, 20). These differences held up when the authors controlled for factors such as the presence of aggravating and mitigating circumstances: Capital punishment rates were much higher, of course, where several aggravating circumstances were present, but the racial disparities remained. Further, their study noted substantial geographic disparities – juries in some counties were much more likely to impose a death sentence than were others; race effects were prevalent throughout the state, however.

California has the largest death row in the United States. The powerful race-of-victim findings that resulted from this comprehensive study of murders and capital sentences during the 1990s reflect important and long-lasting trends in the application of the death penalty. As the study rests on very recent information in a state outside the South, its results make clear that one cannot assume that racial disparities are limited to one region of the country or represent only a historical reality no longer of relevance. The trio of geographic disparities, race-of-victim effects, and race-of-defendant effects has been a fundamental part of the debate for as long as there has been capital punishment in America.

Pierce and Radelet focused on the disparities of application of the death penalty based on the race of the victim. Their study also shows another important element of the debate: Even for convicted murderers, getting a death sentence is akin to being struck by lightning. It is very rare. Executions, as we will see in the next section, are rarer still.

DEATH SENTENCES, EXECUTIONS, AND DEATH ROW

Between 1976, when the death penalty was reinstated by the Supreme Court, and the end of 2005, 7,177 individuals were sentenced to death in the United States and 1,004 were executed. At the end of 2005, 3,373 individuals were on death row, a slight decline from the maximum of almost 3,600 in 2000. Many of these prisoners may be executed eventually, but most will not. The majority of those sentenced to death see their convictions or their sentences retried because of serious errors in their trials – more than two thirds, in fact. Capital sentences go through a two-stage review process, with automatic federal review of state court decisions. In a comprehensive analysis of death sentences from 1973 to 1995, James Liebman and colleagues found that of all the cases that had been fully reviewed (i.e., not counting the cases still pending at the time of their research), only 32 percent of the death sentences were confirmed and carried out. Sixty-eight percent were "so seriously flawed that they had to be reversed and sent back for a new trial of guilt or punishment" (Liebman et al. 2002).

In this section, we briefly review the numbers associated with sentencing, death row populations, and executions. Although the three series are logically linked to one another, there are important differences among them, as the Liebman study makes clear. One way to start is to consider what happens after a homicide. Liebman and colleagues analyzed the outcomes following arrests for murder from 1973 to 1995 in those states that have the death penalty, showing the following breakdown:

331,949 homicides[8]
300,257 homicide arrests
118,992 murder convictions (181,265 other outcomes, including convictions of lesser crimes)
   5,826 death sentences (113,166 other outcomes)
     358 affirmed (3,119 still under review at time of study; 2,349 reversed)
     350 executed (286 of those above plus 64 who were executed without full court review; 11 others were released, 6 were granted clemency, and 55 were still on death row or unknown)

Any one study, even a large and careful one such as the Liebman group's work, may not be perfectly accurate, as it is difficult to establish clear figures for the final outcome of each of hundreds of thousands of criminal arrests across all the jurisdictions of the United States. Therefore, we may not want to rely completely on the precise numbers found in this study. Still, the general tendencies are indisputable and can be confirmed in other ways. For example, during the modern era from 1976 to 2004, the annual number of homicides nationally ranged from a low of about 15,000 in 1999 to a high of just under 25,000 in 1993, but the number of executions was never greater than 98. Overall, there were approximately 577,322 homicides from 1976 to 2004, and 944 executions. The rate, 1.6 executions per 1,000 homicides, is significantly higher than that reported by Liebman and colleagues (350 executions for 331,949 homicides, or closer to 1.1 per 1,000). This discrepancy could be a result of the fact that more than half the cases in the Liebman study were still pending – see the breakdown given above. Still, whether the rate is 1.1 or 1.6 per 1,000, these are low numbers indeed.

Death Sentences

Death is an extremely rare form of punishment, even for those convicted of murder. Perhaps more surprisingly, it is rare even for those having received a death sentence. However, as we will see, trends could point toward greater numbers of executions in future years because the cumulative number of death sentences over the years has caused the numbers of inmates on death row to swell considerably, and many of those who finally exhaust all appeals will not have their sentences overturned or receive new trials. (It should be noted in all of this that the typical outcome of new trials – which often consider sentencing only, not the original finding of guilt – is that the prisoner is sent to the general prison population, off death row, but not exonerated. Exonerations are another story, discussed later.)

The death penalty is rare, but in a large country with tens of thousands of homicides, hundreds of death sentences are sometimes handed down annually. Figure 2.8 shows the annual number of death sentences nationally, and also the remarkable concentration of these sentences in just five states. During most years, these "top five" states equal the combined output of the other forty-five states in the union, and the trends are highly similar over time. The total number of death sentences has ranged significantly from year to year in the modern era. The number steadily rose during the 1970s and 1980s from 137 in 1977 to more than 300 per year, reaching a peak in 1996 at 317. Since then, the number has declined regularly, dropping to 128 by 2005. Federal involvement in the death penalty, as the figure makes clear, is a very small proportion of the total. In any case, we can see important trends up and down in the use of the death penalty nationwide. Even though use of the death penalty differs from state to state, the figure makes clear that trends over time have been similar whether we look at the national totals or limit ourselves to the five most active states.[9]

Figure 2.9 shows the numbers of death sentences nationally, the resulting size of the total death row population, and the number of executions annually.

Figure 2.1 shows the dramatic decline in executions from the 1930s to the 1960s. But even during this period, capital sentencing continued in many states. As Figure 2.9 shows, the number of death sentences hovered around 100 per year during the 1960s before declining sharply and temporarily after the 1972 invalidation of state capital laws. As soon as the

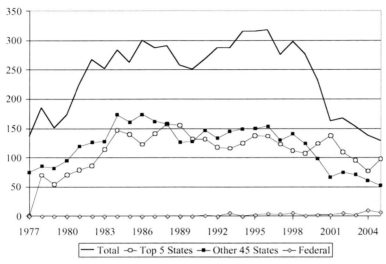

Figure 2.8. Total death sentences compared with sentences in the "top five" states, sentences in the other forty-five states, and federal sentences, 1977 to 2005. In descending order, the five states with the most death sentences between 1977 and 2005 are Texas (882), Florida (806), California (775), North Carolina (428), and Alabama (386). The correlation between the trend for the top five and the other forty-five states is r = 0.78. (*Source:* calculated from DPIC 2006d.)

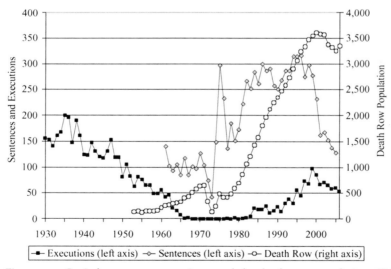

Figure 2.9. Capital sentences, executions, and the death row population. (*Primary source:* Snell 2005.)

laws were revised, however, a surge in death sentences followed, with a momentary spike in 1975 and a longer-term upward trend so that during the 1980s and 1990s in the United States there were 300 or so death sentences annually. This was, of course, in a smaller number of states than in earlier periods, so it was clearly much more common in certain jurisdictions. Finally, the death sentencing series shows a sharp decline beginning in the mid-1990s so that by 2005 the number of annual death sentences had returned to 125, the lowest figure in the modern era.

This book is largely about explaining these trends. The United States bucked international trends and reversed its own forty-year pattern when executions began again, and death sentences increased, steadily, for more than two decades. Beginning in the mid-1990s, however, and continuing until today, these trends have reversed again. Is this a momentary blip or a return to historical and international norms? Is this an historic shift in the direction of public policy, or a temporary interruption of a trend soon to be reinstated? These are questions to which we return throughout this book. However, before asserting that the change we are witnessing is monumental, we must look at executions, not just sentences. These trends are quite different.

Executions

The numbers of executions have always been substantially lower than the numbers of death sentences for the reasons discussed earlier. Further, Supreme Court decisions completely blocked all executions during certain periods, and as noted already, there were none at all from 1968 to 1976. This stay of executions did not apply to initial sentences, however, as the states continued to send people to death row even when there were no executions. Still, Figure 2.9 clearly shows a gradual rise in yearly executions from 1977 onward so that by 1998, there were ninety-eight executions, the highest annual total in the modern period. These numbers have declined by about one third since then; the modern numbers, whether at their high or low points, stand in sharp contrast with the 197 executions in the United States in 1935 (see Figure 2.1).

Death Row

The total population of death row has reached historic highs in the modern era. The series reached an early peak of 642 in 1971 before declining during the moratorium period to a low of 134 in 1973. Since that date, it increased regularly to a maximum of 3,593 in 2000 before declining modestly since then. Declines in the overall size of death row have come mostly from appeals sending individuals into the general prison population for terms of life. Still, the data make clear that with thousands of inmates on death row, as compared with only a few hundred before the modern era, executions could well return to their pre–World War II levels, or surpass these figures.

In 2003, 267 people were released from death row, the largest number of people since 1976, and the population of death row declined to 3,374. The bulk of the 2003 releases, 91 percent in fact, resulted from the decision of Illinois governor George Ryan, once a strong supporter of the death penalty, to empty that state's death row completely, commuting the sentences of 167 prisoners to life in prison and exonerating four others (Associated Press 2004). Governor Ryan's decision was the result of rising doubts about the accuracy and validity of the judgments in many cases. We look at exonerations next.

EXONERATIONS

As the above discussion should make clear, there is a large gap between being sentenced to death and actually being executed. Yet only a small minority of those individuals who avoid execution are actually released from prison completely exonerated. The vast majority are not exonerated but have their sentences *reversed* or *invalidated*. This means that appellate courts deem that there were such serious problems in either the original trial determining guilt or in the separate trial determining that the crime merited the death sentence that the court invalidates the decision, sending it back to the lower court for a new trial. This new trial may or may not lead to the same outcome, and often such a decision is a setback for prosecutors who either do not seek the same penalty or cannot get it after correcting the errors that led to the death sentence in the first place. For example, a reversal may come because prosecutors withheld exculpatory evidence, or because of problems in crime lab handling of allegedly damaging evidence. Either the penalty phase of the trial or the original conviction may be overturned. If the original conviction is overturned (as happened with the case of Kirk Bloodsworth, discussed in the opening pages of this book), prosecutors may or may not seek the death penalty in a second trial. However, the defendants whose sentences are reversed are hardly out of the justice system: They simply avoid the death penalty (for the time being, at least) and face another trial.

Executive clemency, or *commutation*, is a second route out of death row. Procedures differ from state to state, but all states have some procedure by which the governor (acting alone or on the basis of a recommendation from a pardon board) has the authority to grant clemency. This action commutes a death sentence to a lesser sentence of life in prison; the inmate is not released. From 1976 to 2006, 229 prisoners have received clemency (DPIC 2006a).

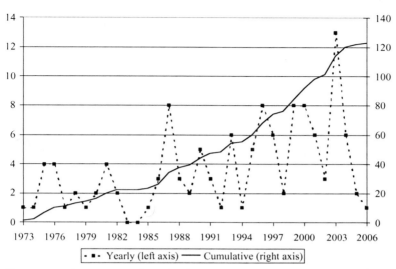

Figure 2.10. Exonerations from death row, 1973 to 2006. (*Source:* calculated from DPIC 2006e.)

Exoneration is different from reversal or commutation. Exoneration is going free. This action occurs only in cases in which the courts or the governor determine that the defendant was not in fact guilty of the crime for which he or she was convicted. DNA evidence has been used in many cases to prove conclusively that a convicted inmate could not have been the person responsible for a crime. Only a minority of those released from death row since 1976 have been released because of DNA evidence, however. More common are problems with eyewitness testimony, prosecutorial misconduct, false testimony, and other causes. This relates to problems with the initial trial for guilt, not the second, penalty phase. Exonerees are those found to have been innocent after having been found guilty once through a flawed trial and then additionally sentenced to death in a second trial. One hundred twenty-three people have been exonerated in the modern era, as of March 2007. Figure 2.10 shows the number of exonerations over time.

There have been exonerations for as long has there have been criminal sentences; sometimes mistakes are made. In fact, exonerations are often used by supporters of the death penalty as evidence that the system works, because if the person was innocent and deserved to be freed, the exoneration demonstrates that, in spite of years that may have been lost in prison for a crime the person did not commit, at least the ultimate sanction was never applied. The numbers of exonerations are indicated in Figure 2.10 on the left-hand scale; they are typically just a few cases per year. There were fewer than five exonerations per year until 1987, then a gradual increase until twelve exonerations occurred in 2003. Fewer have occurred in the past few years. The right-hand scale of the figure and the solid line show the cumulative number of exonerations since the modern era, a total of 123. The exonerated have become a powerful symbol of the dangers of errors in the justice system. Many of these men and women spent years on death row before being shown not only to have had bad attorneys or to have suffered from some technical imperfection in their trial, but indeed to have been completely innocent of the crimes of which they were accused, investigated, convicted, and sentenced to die. We look in greater detail at the trends in exonerations in Chapter 3.

A glance at the cumulative numbers of exonerations in the United States shows the period of most rapid increase to be in the late 1990s. However, the data also make clear that the absolute numbers are not huge, and there has been no sharp spike in the numbers over the years. A few people have been found innocent every year since the beginning of the modern system, though with little notice paid. Public and media attention to the question of "innocence," however, spiked sharply in the mid- and late 1990s, a fact explored in greater detail in other chapters.

One reason for the rise in attention to questions of innocence could be the arrival of DNA evidence on the scene.[10] Such evidence seems so compelling, so objective, so scientific and certain that it has led to many dramatic reversals in capital cases. Of course, DNA evidence is not available in all cases (often there is no biological evidence related to the murderer), and not all reversals are the result of DNA. Still, in the public mind, DNA may play a special role. The most careful study of exonerations done to date, one covering not only capital cases but all criminal exonerations from 1989 to 2003, found in fact that DNA was involved in fewer than half. Samuel Gross and colleagues (Gross et al. 2005) studied all exonerations for which they could find information (noting that as there is no central source for information across the entire criminal justice system, they probably underestimate the total number of exonerations, many of which may have been done without public comment simply by dismissing charges). They identified a total of 340 exonerations, distributed over time as shown in Figure 2.11. Fewer than half were related to DNA, even in the later years, when DNA testing became more common.

The first DNA-related exonerations were in 1989. David Vasquez was an unemployed former high school janitor with an IQ below 70 who falsely confessed to a 1984 rape and murder after intense police interrogations in Virginia. Shortly after this, Gary Dotson, who served more than ten years in prison or on probation for a 1979 rape that had not, in fact, occurred, was exonerated by Illinois authorities (Warden and Radelet 2008). There were few DNA-related exonerations in the early years, and relatively few exonerations of any type until about the mid-1990s, when the annual numbers (both capital and noncapital cases) reached twenty

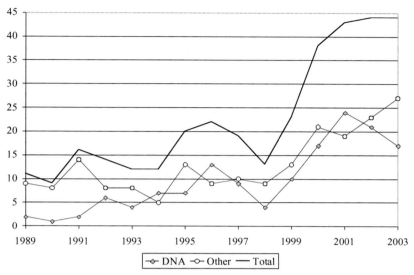

Figure 2.11. Exonerations (DNA and otherwise), including noncapital cases, 1989 to 2003. (*Source:* Gross et al. 2005, note 10.)

for the first time. After 2001, there were more than forty exonerations each year, just under half of which were DNA related. DNA is most commonly used in rape cases: Of 121 exonerations for the crime of rape, 105 were DNA related. In murder cases, including capital murder cases, DNA evidence is not always available, but there are substantial numbers of exonerations nonetheless. Among 205 murder convictions leading to exoneration, just 39 were based on DNA evidence. For capital murder cases, the total in this study was 74, of which just 13 were DNA related (see Gross et al. 2005, table 1). Two things are clear: DNA is important, and DNA remains only a partial explanation of the rise in the number of exonerations in the 1990s and beyond. Now, public reaction to the idea of exonerations is a different story and may well have been more affected by DNA-related cases than the Gross study indicates was merited. The DNA cases provided compelling and easily understood evidence that a serious error had been made. Somehow the scientific value of the DNA evidence seems to put it in a different category in the public mind, irrefutable and objective.

COST

The costs associated with having a death penalty are enormous, surprising, and increasing. Each time there is a movement to improve the reliability of the death penalty system, costs of trials increase. Compared to noncapital first-degree murder trials, capital trials last longer, involve larger teams of lawyers on both the defense and prosecution sides, involve more expert witnesses, are more likely to see the juries sequestered, and so forth. Further, capital trials are followed by a second trial, the penalty phase. After being sentenced to death, death row inmates are housed in high-security installations typically with only one inmate per cell and a higher ratio of guards to inmates. The system is highly inefficient in that most of those initially sentenced to death are later transferred to the general prison population after their convictions are overturned on appeal because of procedural problems in the initial trial or the penalty phase (as we saw in the study by Liebman and colleagues). So the typical outcome of a death penalty trial is that the costs of the initial trial are much higher than those of a noncapital murder trial; a second trial is required, which may or may not lead to a death sentence; if sentenced to death, the inmate is housed in a much more expensive facility for several years; and then he or she is transferred to the general prison population or retried.

Many studies have been done of the additional costs of capital punishment beyond that of other murder trials, and the cost *per execution* typically has been estimated on the order of $2 million or more. Most of these costs are "up-front" costs associated with the trial, but even the incarceration tends to be more expensive for a death row inmate than what it would cost to sentence that person to prison for forty years because of the higher costs associated with death row facilities. Of course, the total cost per execution depends substantially on how many executions a state actually carries out. Texas performs a high number of executions per death sentence; California, on the other hand, has executed only 13 people since 1976 but has more than 600 people housed in an extremely expensive facility. Each of those people was the subject of a trial that cost millions more than a normal noncapital murder trial. Estimates have put the extra cost of the California system at approximately $100 million per year. In New Jersey, there have been 197 capital trials since 1982, resulting in sixty death sentences. Fifty of these were reversed on appeal, leaving ten individuals on death row, none of whom have been executed. (In 2006, New Jersey established a moratorium on executions, based on fears of problems in the system, so the entire modern experience with capital punishment in that state may lead simply to many trials, much expense, and no executions.) The total cost of these trials and the extra incarceration costs, above those costs associated with noncapital trials, was estimated at $253 million since 1983. (The figures in this paragraph come from the Death Penalty Information Center.) Whatever the precise numbers (and the numbers here, based on journalistic reports or state commissions, should not be taken as completely accurate but only as broad estimates), the numbers are staggering. Considering that it generally costs less than $150,000 to

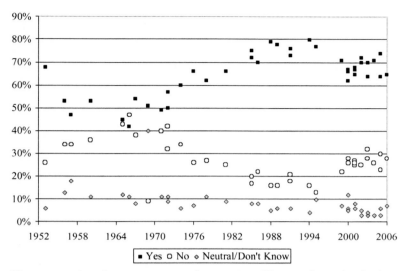

Figure 2.12. American responses to the question, "Do you favor the death penalty in the case of murder?" 1953 to 2006. (*Source:* Gallup Organization public opinion surveys conducted November 11, 1953, to May 5, 2006.)

hire and train a new police officer, and less than that to employ one in each subsequent year, the additional cost of having the death penalty is equivalent to thousands of police officers nationwide. Interestingly enough, in our analysis of 3,939 *New York Times* stories about capital punishment, we find that only twenty mentioned arguments of cost on either side of the debate (see Chapter 4).

PUBLIC OPINION

The American public has a longstanding and substantial aggregate level of support for the death penalty. Figure 2.12 shows a simple compilation of Gallup surveys on the question, "Are you in favor of the death penalty for persons convicted of murder?" This question was asked thirty-nine times from November 1953 to May 2006, making it the single most consistent time series on the question. Some years had more than one survey, some had none, but the figure shows clear trends for the three series shown: support, opposition, and no opinion.

Public opinion reached a minimum of support for the death penalty in 1966, when just 42 percent of Americans indicated they were in favor, and this level of support reflected the low levels of usage of the death penalty at that time. From that period, public support increased steadily throughout the late 1960s and 1970s, when crime and fear of crime rose among the American public, and into the 1980s and 1990s, when support reached 80 percent. Since the mid-1990s, public support for the death penalty has declined slightly. We have much more to say about public opinion surveys and how the questions are worded and give more detailed estimates of the state of public opinion over time in Chapter 6. Still, as a practical matter, it is clear that the bulk of Americans are comfortable with the death penalty. In fact, given that the Gallup question refers to those "convicted of murder" (and not only those guilty of the most heinous murders), one might conclude that Americans would support even more executions than currently take place. (Few Americans probably realize just how rare capital punishment is, even for those convicted of murder.) On the other hand, it is true that significantly lower numbers report support for the death penalty when told by the person doing the survey that life with no option of parole is a possible alternative punishment. The figure shows the numbers opposed to the death penalty and those who report having no opinion as well. The numbers with no opinion do not vary in any meaningful way over time, so we do not focus on them here. The numbers opposed mirror the numbers in favor, so in later chapters we focus on the difference between these two series as the simplest gauge of public opinion: Net support started out substantially pro–death penalty in the 1950s; declined to virtual parity in the 1960s; grew to unprecedented levels in the 1970s, 1980s, and through the early 1990s; and has declined somewhat since 1994.

Most Americans understand the death penalty as a theoretical question, and they view it from a moral perspective. Some strongly disagree with the concept of retribution, basing their views on feelings of forgiveness and mercy, or on the conviction that the state should not have the authority to "play God." Others equally strongly support the punishment, seeing it as just deserts for those who commit murder. Those who support the death penalty and those who oppose it are alike in that they often base their views on biblical or religious teachings. Along the moral or religious dimension, there are more supporters than opponents of capital punishment, by a substantial margin. We explore changes in public opinion in detail in Chapter 6, but we trace important differences in how the death penalty has been framed in several of the following chapters. During most of the period covered in our book, public support for the death penalty has been increasing. However, although the bulk of Americans continue to support the death penalty, in recent years a small but important reversal of this long-term trend has been apparent. Substantial ambiguity remains about the future course of public opinion on this matter. Only about one half of Americans express support for the death penalty as opposed to life without parole when they are presented with this alternative possibility. Further, as we show in great detail in Chapter 6, as attention to the question of innocence has risen, support has declined. As the framing of the issue shifts away from the constitutionality and morality dimensions that have traditionally dominated discussion of the issue and toward the innocence question, public opinion changes may be much more substantial in the future. No one likes the idea of executing the wrong person.

CONCLUSION

This chapter lays out some basic facts about long-term trends relating to the death penalty and its application in America. Many of the series discussed, from public opinion to sentencing to executions, indicate that recent history can be divided into three key periods: before 1972; from the reinstatement until the mid-1990s; and the period since approximately 1995. We explore the reasons for these historical breaks, particularly the last one related to the rise of the innocence argument, in each of the chapters to follow.

The data presented in this chapter could include a number of surprises to those not already familiar with the history and details of the death penalty in the United States. Perhaps most surprising is the relative rarity of the death penalty's application: Fewer than one half of 1 percent of all homicides in the United States result in an execution. It is clearly an exceptional policy not a standard punishment by any means for the crime of murder. Further, the rate of capital punishment is vanishingly small in most states, even lower than the national average would imply, because so many states have either abolished the penalty or impose it so rarely that it is a true statistical rarity. To the extent that these numbers might surprise many Americans, given the level of popular support for capital punishment, we might conclude that many people would probably support a dramatic expansion of the punishment.

Yet what we observe in the United States is not a dramatic expansion of the death penalty at all. Many trends militate for increased use of the death penalty: the global war on terror, the Republican dominance of national politics in recent elections, the rise of evangelical religious affiliations, continuing fear of crime. On the other hand, Americans have increasingly been exposed to stories about justice miscarried, about arbitrary differences in the application of the death penalty, about the release of more than 120 individuals from death row after having served years in prison for crimes they did not commit, and about other flaws in the system. Many abolitionists have argued for decades about the flaws in the American capital punishment system, and during the 1950s and 1960s, these opponents made great progress as the death penalty became rare, rarer, and finally disappeared altogether. Yet the death penalty has retained significant support among most Americans, who have rejected the theoretical and moral arguments of the abolitionists. Something is different about the more recent arguments associated with the concept of innocence. These new arguments do not challenge Americans' general support for the death penalty in theory. Rather, they point to another dimension of the issue: whether the system works without error. The next chapter traces in detail the beginnings and development of what can be loosely called the "innocence movement."

3   A CHRONOLOGY OF INNOCENCE

AMERICANS DISCOVERED INNOCENCE in a wave of attention that started in the mid-1980s and reached a peak in the late 1990s. In this chapter, we review developments that led to this outcome. We know from the previous chapter that, although there are somewhat higher numbers of exonerations now than there were in the 1970s and 1980s, the increase was not radical. Attention to the concept of innocence, on the other hand, has spiked dramatically. Why attention to a concept would spike even while the underlying facts have changed only slowly is an interesting puzzle. To answer the puzzle, we look in some detail at threshold effects and social cascades.

Here, we investigate how the innocence frame came to dominate public debate. We begin by offering a meticulous chronology as presented in five separate lists. We first review developments among the most important organizations and institutions involved in the movement, especially the so-called innocence projects at many law and journalism schools; then we look at key events in Illinois, where many of the innocence arguments first gained attention; trace noteworthy events elsewhere in the country; consider federal government actions; and finally look at important Supreme Court rulings. We examine these developments in relatively stark detail to understand when the innocence frame took root, how it developed, and how it came to flood the death penalty debate. Was there a prime mover of sorts, perhaps a powerful lobbying group or a network of journalists pursuing a political agenda? Or did something change within the system itself – in how death sentences are assigned or carried out – giving objective cause for concern where none previously existed? Our research refutes both these explanations.

Rather, we find that the unprecedented level of attention paid to the innocence frame in recent years is the product of many independent but mutually reinforcing elements working in a positive feedback system. We see that events, organizational efforts, governmental actions, and media framing have moved in unintended tandem to break the death penalty debate wide open, exposing a new dimension of innocence and redefining the debate. We offer a broad discussion of these many moving political parts, which together explain the rise of the innocence frame. None of these events alone would have been sufficient to create the momentum that we see. Rather, in a mutually reinforcing process in which each change made subsequent changes more likely, a cascade of social change has occurred, due not to any single factor but to the combination of many. Many observers might think, for example, that the current wave of attention to innocence would have been impossible without, or can be explained simply by, the decline in homicides and violent crime that the United States was fortunate enough to experience in the period since the 1980s. Others might suggest that Governor Ryan's actions, or the development of DNA evidence, or trends in popular culture subsequent to the O. J. Simpson trial and its minute and highly publicized depiction of police handling of evidence, or some other single factor played a crucial role. Our argument is that none of these factors alone could have caused the shift in attention we observe, though all were contributing elements. In a social cascade, the whole is much greater than the sum of the parts.

The innocence frame is a prime example of a social cascade, on the order of fashion trends, epidemics, and sudden restaurant popularity, amenable to models of networked behaviors similar to what scholars have observed in these disparate areas, as we discussed in Chapter 1. We trace the roots of the death penalty cascade back to the quiet yet potent efforts of legal aid innocence projects that took root in universities in New York and Chicago in the 1980s. To these lawyers and law students (as well as journalists and journalism students) working to exonerate wrongfully convicted defendants, the concept of innocence was old hat long before President Reagan left office. By 1987, scholars Hugo Bedau and Michael Radelet had published an article in the *Stanford Law Review* entitled "Miscarriages of Justice in Potentially Capital Cases," and indeed by that year thirty-four individuals had been exonerated from death row since the reestablishment of the death penalty in 1976. The timing of these journalism-based projects, coming just after Woodward and Bernstein broke the Watergate story and caused a president to leave office, is certainly not coincidental. Some of the motivation here was not so much to uncover innocent individuals as it was to investigate and to uncover official misconduct wherever it could be found. If that happened to be in the local police department as occurred in Chicago, fine. In fact, therefore, we can trace some of the rise of the innocence movement to Watergate, but no one could argue that Watergate was a cause. Rather, in a positive feedback system, the causes can be extremely complex.

Despite the beginnings of the innocence projects in the years shortly after the reinstatement of the death penalty, our chronology shows that it would be more than a decade before the innocence frame would grab hold. Attention, after all, is not proportional to urgency. Public focus shifted to the question of innocence only after a nexus of political forces pushed it in that direction. Before the innocence frame would penetrate social consciousness, it would take the establishment of another eighty legal clinics under the Innocence Project model, the exonerations of another two dozen innocent defendants from death row, the concerted effort of D.C. lobbyists, several more academic publications, and many, many national news stories. At some point in the mid-1990s, however, these elements coalesced. And once past a critical threshold, the innocence frame took public attention by storm, exploding onto the agenda and dominating the debate.

At that point, one thing just seemed to lead to another. Starting with Kirk Bloodsworth in 1993, new DNA technology led to an increased number of exonerations, and combined with the "CSI effect," the role of DNA testing in capital cases became common knowledge by the mid-1990s. As we discussed in Chapter 2, DNA is hardly the whole story; in fact, only a small minority of those exonerated from death row have owed their freedom to DNA testing. But increased attention to issues of DNA evidence, the discovery of evidence fabrication in several crime labs across the country, TV attention to such problems after the O. J. Simpson trial – these and other related events combined to prepare the ground for critics to call other procedural elements into question. Psychologists call this effect "priming" – making the listener ready to hear a given argument in a certain way by introducing elements of it ahead of time – and clearly, Americans were primed to be attuned to innocence arguments during the 1990s.

By the year 2000, when 134 *New York Times* articles focused on issues of innocence and fallibility in the death penalty system, the American public was well-versed in such concepts as prosecutorial misconduct, inadequate representation, evidence suppression, "dry labbing" (the most egregious form of scientific misconduct that can occur in a forensic laboratory, in which crime lab technicians fabricate results in support of police suspicions without ever testing the evidence), and "jailhouse snitch" testimony. And the Innocence Project–type legal clinics embedded in universities across the country came to play a pivotal role in garnering public interest in the questions of innocence that academic scholars had been asking for decades. In Illinois, with police corruption and evidence tampering coming to light in Chicago and the investigative work at the Center on Wrongful Convictions and the Medill Innocence Project at Northwestern University pushing the innocence frame to the forefront of discussion, Republican governor George Ryan – previously a staunch supporter of the death penalty – imposed a statewide moratorium on executions in 2000 and then commuted all death sentences to life in prison before leaving office in 2003. The U.S. Supreme Court followed suit, ruling the death penalty unconstitutional in the case of mentally retarded defendants in 2002 and in the case of minors in 2005. The start of the new millennium has seen a lower percentage of Americans who support the death penalty than has been witnessed since the *Furman* moratorium in 1972 and a dramatic decline in jury decisions to impose the death penalty in capital trials. In observing the innocence frame unfold, we have witnessed a social cascade on a national scale.

In this way, the innocence frame is much more than a bit of rhetoric or spin. It is a cultural shift embodied by declining trends in sentencing rates, executions, and public support and by a list of exonerated individuals that continues to grow. Mostly, this shift is embodied by the commonality that the innocence frame has acquired. Today, few Americans would be shocked, as they were in the mid-1990s, to consider that there may be innocent men and women sitting on death row. Certainly it is a familiar concern in state legislatures around the country, one no longer easily dismissed as the argument of extreme left-wingers or of those who are hopelessly "soft on crime." The argument is taken seriously across the board, part of mainstream concern. This was not always the case. The newfound familiarity of the innocence frame means that today's journalists can more easily write about flaws in the death penalty system than they did a decade ago. The terms are already acquired, the cultural framework already established. The public is primed. The stories "write themselves," fitting in easily with widely understood cultural frames. In the past, the same story might have been isolated, an interesting human interest or crime story, but of no larger significance. That all changed in the 1990s.

After discussing the chronology of the rise of the innocence frame, we turn to a focused look at these journalistic trends. We reiterate our argument that the innocence frame has developed as a social cascade by showing that media attention to exonerations has risen with a speed disproportionate to the number of exonerations themselves. The exoneration rate has increased over the last three decades, due in part to advances in DNA testing and other crime lab technologies that help uncover wrongful convictions but, we argue, also as a result of the new political climate of the innocence frame, which brings attention more readily to flaws in the system. Still, the rate of media attention to exonerations has increased much more dramatically. As we will show, exonerated defendants today receive more than ten times the number of stories, per individual, than those who were exonerated before 1991.

As is typical in many public policy disputes about highly complex issues, the national conversation about the death penalty is not and never has been comprehensive, and the rise of the innocence frame has not been challenged substantially. That is, although there have been some counterarguments that the problems are not really very serious or that the movement is a front for abolitionists searching for winning arguments, there has been relatively little "push-back," or retaliation, from the pro–death penalty movement. Despite several high-profile capital cases like John Muhammad (the Washington-area sniper) and Zacarias Moussaoui (the al-Qaeda sympathizer), the innocence frame has continued to gain traction in the national debate, even during the war on terror; the historical situation is not favorable, after all, to a "soft-on-crime" approach. Compared with other public policy issues over which powerful social cascades have developed, this is not surprising. Nuclear power became unpopular in the 1960s and 1970s in a similar manner; the smoking industry has been severely challenged by a wave of attention to issues that are inherently negative for it. In both cases, countervailing arguments virtually disappeared (see Baumgartner and Jones 1993 for several illustrative examples of "waves of enthusiasm" or "waves of criticism" affecting these and other industries). So although it may seem surprising at one level that there has been little push-back challenging the innocence movement, in fact that is often how social cascades work. We focus our attention so completely on one aspect of a complex issue that other perspectives are virtually drowned out.

A TRADITION OF WRONGFUL CONVICTION

Issues of innocence are not new in America. According to the Northwestern School of Law's Center on Wrongful Convictions, "the first documented wrongful conviction case in the United States (not counting the Salem witch trials) came to light in 1820, when the purported victim of a murder for which two men had been sentenced to death in Vermont turned up alive and well in New Jersey" (2007). In the nearly two centuries since, hundreds of additional cases have been uncovered. In 1932, Yale law professor Edwin Borchard documented sixty-five wrongful convictions in his book *Convicting the Innocent*. And in their 1992 book *In Spite of Innocence*, professors Michael L. Radelet and Hugo Adam Bedau and nonfiction writer Constance E. Putnam detailed more than 400 twentieth-century cases. We saw in Figure 2.10 that 123 people in twenty-five states have been released from death row since 1973 in light of evidence of their innocence.

Yet until the mid-1990s, issues of innocence did not catch the public's eye. Was this lack of attention the result of an uninterested or uncaring public? We do not believe so. Rather, the wrongfully convicted are a small and unsympathetic constituency, what Anne Schneider and Helen Ingram call "deviants" (1993). It was not that the public did not care about innocent people being imprisoned or even executed in the 1970s, 1980s, or earlier, but negative stereotyping of criminal defendants conspired with basic ignorance to produce mass-level denial about the fallibilities of the American justice system. Criminal defendants just are not appealing targets for most Americans' affections or concerns. Criminals proclaiming their lack of guilt are nothing new, after all. But most Americans assume that the justice system works pretty well, and if some mistakes are uncovered, that is good news for the exonerated individual but not more broadly significant than that.

All this changed in the mid-1990s. Within a few short years, the innocence frame came to dominate the death penalty debate, and with it came newfound attention to the defendants themselves. As we show in Chapter 4, sympathetic descriptions of individual defendants, their hardships, and their extenuating circumstances came to be as prominent in articles about innocence as sympathetic descriptions of the victims had been in articles about "eye-for-an-eye" retribution. Exposed to a virtual flood of information about the risk of executing an innocent individual, the public slowly began to see things from another point of view.

THE RISE OF THE INNOCENCE FRAME

The following sections provide tables chronicling the events and developments that have been instrumental in transforming attention in the American death penalty debate to issues of judicial error, wrongful conviction, and (potentially) wrongful execution. We give one table each for major organizational activities, major events specific to Illinois, major national events, key federal government actions, and landmark Supreme Court rulings. To construct these chronologies, we began by drawing up a rough timeline of events related to the death penalty from numerous books and articles on the subject, as listed in our bibliography. Then, working from these rough timelines, we searched the Internet for additional details about the events we had listed or additional events to include. We worked as systematically and exhaustively as possible to ensure that our chronologies represent a comprehensive illustration of how the innocence frame began and developed. For example, when we turned from reading books and articles to browsing Web sites, we started with a list of Web sites we knew we should investigate based on our reading and general knowledge of the death penalty debate. We explored each of these Web sites not only for information relevant to our chronologies but also for references to additional Web sites (or books or articles). Then we browsed these additional resources, again looking both for information and for yet additional resources. We followed each branch of our reference trail in this way until it ran dry or produced only repetitive information. As the reader can imagine, this process involved reviewing scores of Web sites. Some, of course, were more credible than others, and we were careful to collect information only from sites hosted by a reputable organization or institution. By far, the most challenging chronology to compile was the table of major organizational activities. By following the process described above, working outward in a growing network of organizations referenced between Web sites, we finally developed a fairly cohesive understanding of the innocence project community (though we cannot claim that it is completely exhaustive). On each organizational Web site, we paid particular attention to the group's founding date and organizational mission, as well as to the dates of actions mentioned in the books and articles we had read. Of the many sources we used to construct these five chronologies, we have recorded only the principal books, articles, and Web sites in our bibliography. We have not cited each source individually because the information presented in all these chronologies is publicly available and we are reporting facts and dates rather than interpretations. These lists should be taken as our own compendia of relevant facts and developments over time, taken from many sources.

We organize our discussion of these venues in this order (focusing in turn on major organizational developments, Illinois events, national events, governmental actions, and Supreme Court rulings) because it helps us tell the story of how the innocence frame has developed. The innocence frame, as we understand it, began to take shape in academic research and volunteer activism that, although noteworthy, went all but unnoticed. Meanwhile, through the concerted efforts of pivotal scholar activists such as David Protess, Rob Warden, and Lawrence Marshall, the innocence frame came to penetrate a key state – Illinois. Some of the first organizations that would come to be known as innocence projects took root here, and provided the momentum for the cascade of redefinition that would not stop at the state lines. In addition to organized educational efforts, this cascade was fueled by the Chicago police torture and abuse scandal still tormenting Illinois in the late 1990s and an unlikely governor who had no particular interest in issues of innocence before becoming concerned about problems under his watch but who nevertheless became the national symbol for the changing social understanding of the debate. These changes in Illinois provoked a surge of national attention to wrongful conviction, not only by the public but also by Congress and even former Texas governor George W. Bush. Finally, the innocence frame is undoubtedly responsible, at least in part, for landmark decisions restricting the death penalty offered by a decidedly conservative Supreme Court. Each of the changes in this reframing sequence reinforced the others; the events are not separable from one another. We present them separately here for clarity of exposition, but each development in the changing death penalty debate was unmistakably the product of many self-reinforcing elements, as is typical in a positive-feedback process or social cascade.

Within each chronological table, for the sake of context we have included major events of general importance to the death penalty debate, such as landmark Supreme Court cases from as early as 1968. However, these tables do *not* capture the history of capital punishment in the United States, broadly speaking. Instead, the chronologies offer a focused look at the major factors that together led to a groundswell of concern about fallibility in the death penalty system. We have been as systematic as possible in compiling this chronology, but still these tables represent nothing more than yearly snapshots of the death penalty debate as described by available sources, and snapshots of only the "major" events at that. For example, in our table chronicling the national developments concerning the innocence frame, we show no record of major exoneration cases highlighting prosecutorial misconduct and crime lab evidence fabrication before the 1990s. This is not to say that such cases did not occur. Rather, it means that those earlier cases did not garner enough interest or attention to carry them onto any of the historical resources we consulted in compiling this chronology. And because our effort here is not to document all the historical facts but rather to document the development of a social cascade, we believe our chronology is a fair portrayal of the rise of the innocence movement. Even within the scope of this specific endeavor, our chronology tables report only a fraction of the innocence movement developments and events that have occurred since the late 1990s. Sadly, there are simply too many cases of wrongful convictions, evidence mishandling, evidence fabrication, and other errors in the system – too many to fit in our tables and too many, period. Descriptions of all 123 exoneration cases since 1976 alone would take up more space than we have here. In the end, faced with hundreds and hundreds of items that could be included in these tables, we have used our best judgment to report the most significant (and thus, usually the most egregious) items.[1]

Organized Efforts: The Unique Role of Legal Aid Clinics

We begin with a chronology of the innocence frame in organizations, shown in Table 3.1. As noted earlier, the academic community developed discussion of the innocence frame many years ago. American scholars have been writing about questions of fallibility in the death penalty system since at least 1932, to no real public effect. With a modicum of D.C. lobbying firms on either side of the death penalty debate – and very small ones, at that – there was simply no one to bring the message to the American public. Table 3.1 shows events related to the innocence frame in terms of the organizations involved – their creation, significant growth, and events. It begins in 1983.

Table 3.1. *The growth of the innocence movement, 1983 to 2006*

1983	The first of what will come to be known as the innocence projects, Centurion Ministries is founded in Princeton, New Jersey, by former executive and now minister James McCloskey. Centurion Ministries is a nonprofit organization dedicated to identifying prison inmates who are innocent and freeing them from prison and clearing their names. To date, Centurion Ministries has helped exonerate more than 14 innocent individuals, most from life sentences or death row.
1985	The MacArthur Justice Center is created as a nonprofit public-interest law firm at the University of Chicago Law School, working through litigation and education to raise public awareness of the fallibility of the death penalty system.
1988	Peter J. Neufeld and Barry C. Scheck (later cofounders of the Innocence Project) become involved in studying and litigating issues regarding the use of forensic DNA testing. This work leads in part to a National Academy of Sciences study on forensic DNA testing as well as important state and federal legislation setting standards for the use of DNA testing. In addition to their work with the Innocence Project, Neufeld and Scheck will both gain national attention for legal assistance they provide in individual criminal trials. In 1997, Neufeld will represent Haitian immigrant Abner Louima, who was assaulted and tortured by New York City police officers after being arrested outside a Brooklyn nightclub. Also in 1997, Scheck will serve as lead lawyer in the murder defense of British au pair Louise Woodward. Scheck will become even more well-known for his role as one of the lawyers on O. J. Simpson's "dream team" legal defense team.
1990	The Death Penalty Information Center is launched in Washington, D.C., as a nonprofit organization offering capital punishment analysis and information to the media and the public.
	Equal Justice USA is launched as a national anti–death penalty organization building on several years of work by the Quixote Center, a faith-based social justice center located in Brentwood, Maryland.
1992	Barry C. Scheck and Peter J. Neufeld create the Cardozo Innocence Project, a nonprofit legal clinic housed at the Benjamin N. Cardozo School of Law at Yeshiva University. To date, the Cardozo Innocence Project has helped exonerate eight innocent individuals, most from life sentences or death row.
	Richard Dieter takes over as executive director of the Death Penalty Information Center.
	Northeastern University Press publishes *In Spite of Innocence*, written by Michael Radelet and Hugo Adam Bedau, profiling 23 cases since 1900 in which innocent people were executed in the United States.

(continued)

Table 3.1 *(continued)*

1993	Representative Don Edwards, chair of the House Judiciary Subcommittee on Civil and Constitutional Rights, asks Richard Dieter and the staff of the Death Penalty Information Center to work with the senior staff of the subcommittee to prepare a report on the dangers of executing innocent people. This study includes discussion of 48 cases of individuals being exonerated from death row on the basis of evidence in the prior 20 years.
1997	The Innocence Project Northwest is founded as a legal clinic dedicated to freeing wrongfully convicted individuals. The clinic consists of volunteer students and attorneys who have helped secure the release of 11 innocent people in Washington. In 2002, the program becomes part of the University of Washington School of Law's Clinical Law Program, providing investigation and litigation training to students.
	The American Bar Association (ABA) calls for a moratorium on executions until policies are implemented to minimize the risk that innocent persons may be executed. In its announcement, the ABA focuses on issues of unequal application, specifically racial disparities and inadequate defense.
	The Death Penalty Information Center releases a further update of the 1993 report by the House Judiciary Subcommittee on Civil and Constitutional Rights, this time detailing a total of 69 cases in which innocent individuals have been exonerated from death row.
1998	The Wisconsin Innocence Project is founded at the Frank J. Remington Center at the University of Wisconsin Law School. Co-directed by law professors Keith Findley and John Pray, the program includes approximately 20 law students working under the supervision of attorneys to investigate and litigate claims of innocence by prisoners in Wisconsin and elsewhere.
	The United Nations Commission on Human Rights calls for a moratorium on the death penalty, a statement the commission will repeat nearly annually from this point forward.
	Northwestern University School of Law hosts a National Conference on Wrongful Convictions and the Death Penalty, in which 28 individuals exonerated from death row meet to share their stories with 1,200 assembled lawyers, as well as with a much larger public audience via the international media coverage paid to the event.
1999	Journalist Rob Warden and professor and attorney Lawrence C. Marshall cofound the Center on Wrongful Convictions at Northwestern School of Law as a hands-on litigation group working to uncover mistakes made in death penalty convictions and sentencing. The center also works to help exonerated individuals make the transition into free society.
	Professor David Protess establishes the Medill Innocence Project at the Northwestern School of Journalism as a hands-on body of investigative research working to uncover and document flaws in the death penalty system.

After a visit to Missouri in which Pope John Paul II calls for the abolition of the death penalty and pleads for mercy in the case of Darrel Mease, pro–death penalty Missouri governor Mel Carnahan commutes Mease's sentence from death to life in prison.

The United Nations Commission on Human Rights again calls for a moratorium on the death penalty and, in particular, a ban on executing juvenile and mentally retarded defendants.

2000   Across the country, the "pioneer" innocence projects (Centurion Ministries, the MacArthur Justice Center at the University of Chicago Law School, the Cardozo Innocence Project at Yeshiva University, the Wisconsin Innocence Project at the University of Wisconsin Remington School of Law, the Innocence Project Northwest at the University of Washington School of Law, the Center on Wrongful Convictions at Northwestern University's School of Law, and the Medill Innocence Project at Northwestern University's School of Journalism) continue to attract attention. Across the country, legal communities begin to form innocence projects of their own under this same model. Within five years, some 80 programs across all 50 states and the District of Columbia will be in place, specifically focused on providing legal assistance to defendants whose innocence can be proven by DNA evidence or other newly discovered exculpatory evidence.

Barry Scheck, Peter Neufeld, and Pulitzer Prize–winning *New York Times* reporter Jim Dwyer publish their nonfiction book *Actual Innocence: Five Days to Execution, and Other Dispatches from the Wrongly Convicted* (New York: Doubleday).

Columbia University Law School releases a report entitled "A Broken System: Error Rates in Capital Cases, 1973–1995" documenting serious procedural errors in 68 percent of completed death penalty appeals.

At a conference in Virginia, Illinois lawyers involved in death penalty appeals explore the possibility of seeking clemency for all death row prisoners.

2001   Innocence projects continue to develop across the country. For example, the Northern California Innocence Project is founded at the Santa Clara University School of Law. At the clinical program, students and law professors work together within an educational framework to exonerate indigent California prisoners who have been wrongfully convicted.

The Center on Wrongful Convictions releases a report documenting how mistaken or perjured eyewitness testimony has helped send 46 innocent Americans to death row.

In Missouri, work by a journalism class at Webster University uncovers that prosecutors in the case against death row inmate Richard D. Clay had allowed a key witness to mislead the jury. Based on this evidence, a federal judge orders a new trial for Clay.

(continued)

Table 3.1 *(continued)*

2002	Innocence projects continue to develop around the country. For example, Lionel H. Frankel founds the Rocky Mountain Innocence Center, seeking the exoneration and release of innocent inmates in Utah, Nevada, and Wyoming.
	The Center on Wrongful Convictions reports that false confessions have led to 26 innocent people being convicted of murder in Illinois since the 1950s, and that 28 innocent individuals have been sentenced to death based on false jailhouse-snitch testimony.
	In Indiana, Larry Mayes is freed from prison after spending 21 years behind bars when the Innocence Project at Benjamin Cardozo Law School secures his release. Mayes marks the 100th inmate freed from prison as a result of DNA testing. "This DNA revolution," says Peter Neufeld, cofounder of the Innocence Project, "it's made clear our criminal justice system is not as reliable as we always thought it was." Rev. Jesse Jackson, after visiting with death row prisoners at the Pontiac Correctional Center, calls for blanket clemency.
2003	Louisiana death row inmate John Thompson is exonerated due to the legal help of the Philadelphia law firm of Morgan Lewis. Two partners at the firm, J. Gordon Cooney, Jr., and Michael L. Banks, provided pro bono services. Over a 15-year period, the firm spent $1.7 million in legal work and expenses and involved 90 lawyers and support staff in Thompson's defense. Even with top legal counsel, Thompson had come close to being executed in 1999 before it was discovered that a piece of evidence had been withheld from the defense since 1985. According to the Philadelphia Bar Association's Volunteers for Indigent Defense, there is an enormous need for lawyers to provide pro bono services.
	The Innocence Project and the Cardozo School of Law and the Centurion Ministries of New Jersey arrange for DNA tests in the cases of three men, Dennis Halstead, John Kogut, and John Restivo, who had been imprisoned for nearly two decades for the 1985 rape and murder of 16-year-old Theresa Fusco. After the tests show that semen found on the victim's body was from another man, all three defendants are released.
	Timothy Howard and Gary Lemar James are released after spending nearly 25 years in prison, including time on Ohio's death row, for their convictions in a 1976 robbery and murder. They were released after their defense attorneys, in conjunction with Centurion Ministries, provided new evidence in the cases, including fingerprints, witness statements, and polygraph results that were not available when Howard and James were sentenced to death during the original trial.
	The American Civil Liberties Union (ACLU) releases a report calling for the state of Virginia to place a moratorium on all executions until the capital punishment system can be reformed.
2004	The Symposium on Wrongful Convictions is featured in the summer 2004 *Drake Law Review*, with articles discussing wrongful convictions,

how victims' families cope with the news of a wrongful conviction, and how wrongful conviction may be rectified for those who are innocent, and specific looks at the Illinois and North Carolina commissions investigating capital punishment. Authors of these articles include Hugo Bedau, Michael Radelet, Thomas Sullivan, and Steven Drizin.

The Center for Law and Justice at the University of Cincinnati, which is home to the Ohio Innocence Project, hosts an Innocence Week. The week's events include a presentation by Scott Hornoff, who was wrongfully convicted of murder in Rhode Island; another by Barry Schneck, a DNA expert; and performances of the play *The Exonerated*.

Northwestern University law professor Steve Drizin and University of California, Irvine (UC Irvine), criminologist Richard Leo conduct a study of 125 exoneration cases in which the wrongly convicted had falsely confessed, finding that minors and mentally impaired defendants are more likely to do so. This supports previous findings by the *University of Chicago Law Review*, which found that among those mentally impaired, only 27 percent understood the ramifications of their confessions and that they were unlikely to know procedures or in which tactics police can or cannot engage. To ensure that false confessions do not occur, experts suggest that suspects be tape recorded at all interviews, possibly reducing the number of false confessions by 90 percent.

Bruce Dallas Goodman is exonerated after spending 19 years in prison after the Rocky Mountain Innocence Center reexamines DNA evidence in the case and reveals that Goodman could not have been the killer. The new DNA tests indicate that two other men, neither yet identified, are responsible for the brutal rape and murder in 1984 of Goodman's girlfriend, Sherry Ann Fales, crimes for which Goodman spent 19 years in prison.

2005 Innocence projects continue to develop around the country. For example, the Oregon Innocence Project is formed as a law clinic at the University of Oregon. Run by volunteer law students, the clinic offers legal research and investigative services to wrongfully convicted inmates.

The University of Cincinnati's Center for Law and Justice, home of the Ohio Innocence Project, hosts an Innocence Week aimed at drawing attention to wrongful convictions. Activities include a presentation by Scott Hornoff, a Rhode Island police officer wrongly convicted of murder and finally released after being cleared through DNA analysis; performances of the award-winning play *The Exonerated*; and a talk by DNA expert Barry Scheck of the Innocence Project at Yeshiva University.

Rob Warden, executive director of the Center on Wrongful Convictions at Northwestern University School of Law, publishes a book entitled *Wilkie Collins's The Dead Alive: The Novel, the Case, and Wrongful Convictions*, in which he discusses the first instances of exoneration in the United States and others that have followed.

(continued)

Table 3.1 (continued)

	Professor Samuel Gross and colleagues of the University of Michigan Law School publish an article analyzing patterns of false convictions in the United States (Gross et al. 2005). The paper examines 340 exonerations between 1989 and 2003 and finds that a significant number of individuals who were wrongly convicted were also sentenced to die. The researchers conclude that capital defendants are more likely to be convicted in error and that false convictions are more likely to be detected when defendants are on death row. The study also shows that the leading cause of wrongful conviction is perjury, followed closely by false confessions; that almost all of the juvenile exonerees who falsely confessed were African Americans; and that 90 percent of all exonerated juvenile defendants were African American or Hispanic. The authors conclude that "any plausible guess at the total number of miscarriages of justice in America in the last fifteen years must run to the thousands, perhaps tens of thousands, in felony cases alone."
2006	In Washington, D.C., a panel on the application, morality, and constitutionality of the death penalty is hosted by the Pew Forum on Religion and Public Life in conjunction with the Federalist Society and the Constitution Project. The panel features former Texas district attorney Samuel Millsap, Jr., counselor to the head of the Drug Enforcement Administration William Otis, attorney Kenneth Starr, and director of the Equal Justice Initiative in Alabama Bryan Stevenson.
	In Washington, D.C., the sixth annual Forensic Science and Law Conference, "Justice for All," features national experts discussing the causes of and solutions to wrongful conviction. The event is co-hosted by the D.C.-based Justice Project, Duquesne University, and the Cyril H. Wecht Institute of Forensic Scientific Law.
	The journal *Scientific American* publishes an article examining the extent to which television programs about forensic science, such as *CSI* have altered the expectations of jurors in criminal trials. Researchers Simon Cole and Rachel Dioso from the UC Irvine, argue that there is nothing but anecdotal evidence of a "CSI effect," although forensic shows may certainly have increased the demand on forensic laboratories to review criminal evidence.
	University of California, Los Angeles (UCLA) hosts a "Faces of Wrongful Conviction" conference, featuring individuals exonerated from California's prisons and death row.

Table 3.1 shows that the 1980s saw a new kind of organization appear on the national scene. A handful of journalistic research and legal aid organizations were founded, most within the institutional structures of major research universities, and all with the specific purpose of providing research and/or legal assistance to wrongfully convicted defendants

serving long sentences or waiting on death row. Almost all these organizations – which we will hereafter call the innocence projects, collectively – were founded by attorneys or professors of law or journalism with extended networks of legal or journalistic resources. The location of these innocence projects within the context of major universities provided each legal clinic with an ample supply of bright, energetic, and dedicated young volunteers who gained invaluable experience and in some cases course credit in exchange for the time and talent they devoted to the clinic.

This unique arrangement served to meet the staffing needs of the innocence projects, but it did something even more important as well. It put a fresh, earnest face on the innocence frame, and if forced to identify a single element that has had the greatest impact on the rise of the innocence frame social cascade, we would point to this one. News that college students have helped to free an innocent man from prison tells a fundamentally different story than news that high-powered attorneys have accomplished the same feat. When lawyers win their clients' release, the public may assume that some ploy was involved; people may assume that the defendant was guilty, even if the charges were dropped. For example, many white Americans think that O. J. Simpson's high-priced legal team "got him off." This is not typically the reaction when an underfunded, overworked, inexperienced, and unpaid group of students unearths clear evidence that an obscure inmate sitting for years in a state penitentiary was convicted erroneously or, even better, identifies the guilty party and brings a real criminal to justice by obtaining a confession. And if unfunded student-led organizations are able to find mistakes in the system, the public must wonder how many more mistakes might there be that simply have not been unearthed for lack of looking?

Student-led innocence projects are newsworthy for additional reasons. For one, they tend to be focused on cases right there in the same city or state. They and those who work with them may be on a mission to unearth injustices, but no one can say they are self-interested; their actions cannot be dismissed as self-serving, as the arguments of a defense attorney, a defendant, or members of a defendant's family could be. The defendant is not the focus; the system becomes the focus. Now, it seems clear that journalism students may be interested in unearthing injustices, and law students may similarly engage in a crusade. But these crusades, as covered by the local media, are altruistic efforts to uncover mistakes and injustice; no one claims they are self-serving. And if a student-led organization convincingly demonstrates to the satisfaction of a judge that prosecutors made a significant error, this is newsworthy indeed if only for the David and Goliath aspect of the unfunded student organizations poking holes in a case on which police and prosecutors may have spent millions of taxpayer dollars. Injustice uncovered is an interesting story. True crime sells papers.

Table 3.1 shows how these innocence projects developed, one by one, and then at the turn of the century caught on like wildfire across the country. Today, there are at least eighty loosely affiliated Innocence Project–like organizations across all fifty states and the District of Columbia. Together, these organizations have been responsible for the release of dozens of wrongfully convicted individuals serving time in prison or waiting on death row. In fact, beyond advances in DNA technology, the spread of the innocence projects may be one of the most significant causes of the increased rate of exonerations.

Illinois: A Tidal Wave of Activity

Two of the first and most influential innocence projects were founded in Illinois, both at Northwestern University: the Center on Wrongful Convictions at the School of Law and the Medill Innocence Project at the School of Journalism. Together, these groups contributed to the release of more than ten innocent individuals in Illinois during the 1990s, and several more to date. Moreover, they launched concentrated efforts to educate the public about issues of innocence, making the state of Illinois "ground zero" in the innocence debate. Table 3.2 chronicles the events that gave rise to the innocence frame in Illinois.

At the same time that the Northwestern innocence projects were taking root, the city of Chicago suffered one of the worst scandals in its history with the revelation that Chicago police commander Jon Burge and several of his subordinates had routinely tortured prisoners, using methods ranging from electric shock to Russian roulette to obtain false murder confessions that in some cases led to capital convictions and death sentences.

It was on this wave of innocence project activism and police scandal that conservative governor George Ryan came to reconsider his position on the death penalty. In 2000, Governor Ryan declared a moratorium on executions in the state and called for an investigation into the Illinois death penalty system, saying that no one else would be executed on his watch until he could be certain that there was no chance of executing an innocent person. And in 2003, directly before leaving office, he offered blanket clemency to all 167 inmates on Illinois's death row. In both actions, the governor's decision was based in large part on the work of Larry Marshall and his students at the Center on Wrongful Convictions and David Protess and his students at the Medill Innocence Project.

As Table 3.2 shows, the work of the Northwestern groups, the changing political climate in Illinois in the wake of the police torture scandal, and Governor Ryan's moratorium and mass clemency decisions offered an uncoordinated but jointly powerful surge of activity that brought national focus to the innocence frame.

Table 3.2. *Innocence developments in Illinois, 1980 to 2006*

1980	John Wayne Gacy is sentenced to death after being convicted of raping and murdering 33 boys and young men in Cook County, Illinois, 29 of whom were found buried beneath Gacy's house.
1983	Indicative of the national trend beginning around this time, Illinois adopts lethal injection as its mode of execution in lieu of the electric chair.
1987	Darby Tillis and Perry Cobb become the **first two** death row prisoners in Illinois to be exonerated (and the 28th and 29th nationally) following the 1977 reinstatement of the death penalty.
1989	New forensic DNA technology is used to prove that Illinois death row inmate Gary Dotson did not commit the rape of which he had been convicted a decade earlier. Dotson's conviction had been gained on the basis of fabricated testimony by the supposed victim and false forensic testimony that appeared incriminating.
	Protestors accuse Chicago police commander Jon Burge and several subordinates of torturing prisoners to obtain false murder confessions, some leading to death sentences. The reported methods of torture include beatings, electric shock to the ears and testes, Russian roulette, and suffocation under typewriter covers.
1990	After abandoning his appeals, Charles Walker becomes the first person to be executed in Illinois since 1962. He had been sentenced to death in St. Clair County for murdering a young couple in 1983.
1993	A secret Chicago police internal report surfaces cataloging more than 50 instances of "methodical" and "systematic" torture by Jon Burge and his subordinates in Illinois.
1994	John Wayne Gacy, the "Clown Killer," is executed by lethal injection in the first involuntary execution in Illinois, 17 years after the state reinstated the death penalty. A virtual media circus surrounds the execution as large groups gather for "execution parties" outside the penitentiary. The execution itself proves problematic when the state's new $24,900 lethal injection machine malfunctions, mixing the chemicals in such a way that they solidify. The execution is prolonged as a result, and it takes 27 minutes for Gacy to die. Gacy's last reported words: "you can kiss my ass."
	Joseph Burrows becomes the **third** person to be exonerated from Illinois's death row (and the 61st exoneree nationally) when the key witness for the prosecution admits to committing the murder of which she accused Burrows.
1995	In spite of evidence gathered by journalism students at Northwestern University indicating that he may be innocent, Girvies Davis is executed in Illinois.
	Codefendants Rolando Cruz and Alejandro Hernandez become the **fourth** and **fifth** individuals to be exonerated from Illinois's death row (and the 58th and 59th exonerees nationally). Cruz, represented in part by a volunteer legal team led by Lawrence C. Marshall (cofounder of

(continued)

Table 3.2 *(continued)*

	the Center on Wrongful Convictions at Northwestern), is exonerated first. His acquittal is based on DNA evidence and the confession of a sheriff's officer who admitted to having lied during two previous trials when he claimed that Cruz had made an incriminating statement about the crime. After Cruz is exonerated, prosecutors drop all charges against Hernandez.
1996	Three former prosecutors, one now a state circuit judge, are indicted for obstructing justice in their prosecution of Rolando Cruz and Alejandro Hernandez, both now exonerated.
	Verneal Jimerson and Dennis Williams, the two men sentenced to die in the "Ford Heights Four" case, become Illinois's **sixth** and **seventh** defendants to be exonerated from death row (and the 62nd and 63rd exonerees nationally). Due in large part to the research efforts of students and professors at Northwestern University, the defendants are exonerated after DNA evidence and the confessions of the real perpetrators establish their innocence.
	Gary Gauger becomes the **eighth** person to be exonerated from Illinois's death row (65th nationally) when an appellate court holds that police lacked probable cause to arrest him for the murders of his parents, crimes for which Gauger had served nine years thus far in prison.
	Carl Lawson becomes the state's **ninth** Illinois exonerated prisoner (67th nationally) when forensic testing discredits the state's case against him.
1999	The *Chicago Tribune* publishes a five-part series entitled "Trial & Error/How Prosecutors Sacrifice Justice to Win" documenting hundreds of examples of prosecutorial misconduct in Cook County.
	Within 48 hours of execution, Anthony Porter becomes Illinois's **10th** exonerated death row prisoner (78th nationally) after a legal team including Larry Marshall and students at the Northwestern School of Law win a reprieve from the Illinois Supreme Court, making it possible for Northwestern professor David Protess and several of his undergraduate students at the Medill School of Journalism to reinvestigate Porter's case. Porter's innocence is established beyond doubt when Paul Ciolino, a private investigator working with the Protess group, obtains a video-recorded confession from the man responsible for the murder for which Porter had been convicted.
	Steven Smith becomes the **11th** person to be exonerated from Illinois's death row (79th nationally) when the Illinois Supreme Court reverses his conviction and bars a retrial, saying that the prosecution's star witness in the case is not believable.
	The Cook County Board settles civil claims arising from the Ford Heights Four case for $36 million, the largest civil rights settlement in U.S. history. The county board approves state attorney Dick Devine's request to hire Gino L. DiVito, a former top assistant state attorney, to investigate how the innocent men known as the Ford Heights Four were wrongly sentenced to death in that case.

Andrew Kokoraleis dies by lethal injection after Governor George Ryan denies clemency on the eve of the execution.

Ronald Jones becomes the state's 12th exonerated death row prisoner (81st nationally) when DNA exonerates him of the rape and murder for which he had been sentenced to death.

The *Chicago Tribune* publishes a series entitled "The Failure of the Death Penalty in Illinois" exposing how dubious evidence, racial discrimination, and incompetent legal defense have affected scores of Illinois capital cases.

2000   As a result of growing public and elite concerns about flaws in the capital punishment system – prompted in large part by the work of professors and students at Northwestern Law School and School of Journalism – Governor George Ryan declares a moratorium on executions in the state, saying that the ban will be in effect until he can be morally certain that no innocent person will face execution in Illinois.

Steve Manning, a former Chicago cop sentenced to death on the word of a jailhouse informant with a reputation for lying, becomes the state's 13th exonerated death row prisoner (85th nationally).

The *Chicago Tribune* publishes a poll showing that support for the death penalty among Illinois voters has declined to 58 percent from 63 percent a year earlier. In 1994, support stood at 76 percent. This dramatic drop in support is indicative of the national trend.

Governor Ryan announces a Commission on Capital Punishment to study flaws in the administration of the Illinois death penalty and to recommend measures for reform. After its investigation, the commission will eventually recommend more than 80 reforms to the death penalty system.

The *Chicago Tribune* publishes the first of a two-part investigative series examining four individuals who were executed despite evidence of their innocence, including incriminating evidence pointing to other suspects, inadequate legal representation, and the use of testimony from jailhouse snitches. Of all 682 executions in the United States since 1976, the *Tribune* assesses that 120 individuals were executed despite their claims of innocence.

2001   The Capital Litigation Trust Fund is established, providing funding for defense attorneys to pay investigative costs and hire independent forensic experts in capital cases.

In a plea bargain arrangement that will later result in his release, former death row prisoner Darrell Cannon agrees to abandon claims that he was tortured by Jon Burge's officers. The *Chicago Tribune* later discloses that state attorney Dick Devine has offered deals to additional death row prisoners, promising release for defendants who abandon allegations of police torture.

Lawyers handling capital appeals for the Office of the State Appellate Defender agree to launch an effort seeking clemency for all Illinois death row prisoners.

(continued)

Table 3.2 *(continued)*

	Groups interested in pursuing blanket clemency hold a series of closed-door meetings at the Chicago Office of the State Appellate Defender's Capital Litigation Division.
	The *Chicago Tribune* publishes a series exposing coerced, fabricated, and otherwise tainted confessions in 247 Cook County murder cases from 1991 to 2001.
2002	Through amendatory veto power, Governor George Ryan strikes a death penalty provision from an antiterrorism bill and in its place adds reform measures recommended by the Governor's Commission on Capital Punishment. The Illinois House of Representatives then overrides the antiterrorism bill veto that Ryan used.
	The Illinois Supreme Court establishes regulations for defense lawyer conduct in capital cases, sending a clear message to prosecutors that carrying out justice, not winning convictions, should be their goal.
	Governor Ryan tells reporters that he is contemplating commutations for all of Illinois's death row inmates.
	Indicative of many local papers, an editorial in the *Chicago Sun-Times* criticizes blanket clemency, saying it "ignores the reality that each case must stand on its own facts."
	The *St. Louis Post-Dispatch* publishes poll results indicating that voters in Illinois are divided almost exactly in half around the issue of blanket clemency.
	Governor Ryan receives an open letter, signed by more than 650 Illinois attorneys, urging him to grant clemency to the state's nearly 160 death row inmates.
	Governor Ryan receives another letter urging him to commute the sentences of all state death row inmates; this time the letter comes from 21 former state and federal judges, including former Criminal Division presiding judge Richard J. Fitzgerald, former U.S. Court of Appeals chief justice and White House counsel Abner J. Mikva, and former chief justice of the Illinois Supreme Court Moses Harrison.
	In the first of two such meetings, Governor Ryan meets with murder-victim survivors who urge him not to commute death sentences.
	During a conference on wrongful convictions at Northwestern School of Law, death row exonerees and advocates of death penalty reform join together to complete a 14-hour-long "Dead Man Walking" journey, comprising one-mile relay segments, from the Statesville Correctional Center's execution house to the State of Illinois Building in Chicago. Participants call on Governor George Ryan to grant clemency to all state death row prisoners.
	Four prisoners convicted of a 1997 torture murder are released in Chicago after prosecutors uncover evidence that their convictions were based on coerced confessions and false testimony by a police informant.

In a speech given at the University of Illinois School of Law, Governor Ryan offers pardons based on innocence to death row inmates Rolando Cruz, Gary Gauger, and Steven Linscott. Ryan notes that Cruz and Gauger were among the cases of innocence that prompted the governor to declare a moratorium on the state's death penalty in 2000. Ryan also expresses puzzlement over the families of victims who, as he says, feel entitled to have someone executed.

2003   On the steps of the Northwestern University School of Law, Governor Ryan announces his decision to offer blanket clemency to all 167 death row inmates, commuting 163 of the sentences to life in prison. He grants complete pardons based on innocence to the remaining four men – Aaron Patterson, Madison Hobley, Leroy Orange, and Stanley Howard – who represent the 14th through 17th death penalty exonerations in Illinois (103rd to 106th nationally). These four men are members of the "Death Row 10," a group of Illinois death row prisoners who say they were victims of police torture. The four men claim their innocence and say they confessed only after former Chicago police commander Jon Burge and his detectives beat them, pointed guns at them, subjected them to electric shock, and nearly suffocated them with typewriter covers placed over their heads. In his speech, Ryan offers special thanks to professors Larry Marshall and David Protess and their students at the Northwestern University Law School Center for Wrongful Convictions, along with investigator Paul Ciolino, for going "above the call" to help spare the lives of 17 men wrongfully accused and sentenced to death.

The Chicago City Council finance committee approves a wrongful conviction settlement of $2.2 million to be awarded to exonerated death row inmate Ronald Jones. Jones spent 14 years on Illinois's death row before DNA tests proved he did not commit the 1985 rape and murder of which he had been convicted; he was pardoned in 2000 by former Illinois governor George Ryan.

The *Chicago Tribune* releases a report arguing that once a wrongly convicted defendant has been exonerated of a crime and released from death row, police and prosecutors rarely pursue new leads and new suspects in the unsolved case. The report offers evidence from court records that shows that police charged a new suspect in just 10 of the dozens of cases in which an alternate suspect was identified in a case in which the defendant was exonerated, and in 3 of these 10 cases the crime was solved not by police but by defense attorneys, private investigators, or student organizations. This low number, the report argues, reflects not only the difficulty of pursuing cold cases but also the reluctance of authorities to admit error and pursue alternate suspects. "In some of those cases," the report states, "police did not take even the simplest investigation step – entering genetic profile evidence into a database to identify the real attacker."

(continued)

Table 3.2 *(continued)*

2004	The Northwestern University School of Law releases a report analyzing 51 cases in the United States in which persons were wrongfully executed based on testimony from witnesses who are not credible. The book, *The Snitch System: How Snitch Testimony Sent Randy Steidl and Other Innocent Americans to Death Row* from the Center on Wrongful Convictions, argues that convictions based on such testimony is the number one cause for wrongful death penalty convictions, accounting for 45 percent of all such cases.
	The *Chicago Tribune* releases a five-part series on forensic science and wrongful convictions. Part of the series investigates how scientific developments in fire investigations have raised doubts about the credibility of expert testimony at the heart of several criminal cases, including capital trials. The report discusses the case of Ernest Willis, recently freed from Texas's death row after spending nearly 20 years in prison for a 1986 fire that experts now agree could not have been arson. Although new advances in fire investigation allow for more accurate interpretation of crime scene evidence, fire experts say that some arson investigators are resistant to incorporating new science into their methodology and, as a result, continue to offer expert testimony based on outdated theories. Another part of the series traces how flaws in evidence testing analysis and sloppy criminal lab procedures can often lead to wrongful convictions. The investigation includes findings from a review of 200 DNA and death row exonerations nationwide over the past 20 years, showing that in 55 cases with 66 defendants (more than a quarter of the cases studied), original forensic testing or testimony was flawed. For example, the investigation finds that, in many cases, fingerprinting identification is so subjective that even experienced examiners can make large mistakes and that there are no standardized guidelines by which forensic dentists (called to testify in cases in which bite marks are left on crime victims) are required to measure their rate of error.
2005	Former Illinois death row inmate Steven Manning is awarded $6.6 million in a civil lawsuit against two FBI agents, Robert Buchan and Gary Miller. The jury finds convincing evidence that the agents framed Manning, their one-time informant and a former Chicago police officer, in the murder of a trucking firm executive and in the kidnapping of two Missouri drug dealers.
2006	The *Chicago Tribune* publishes an investigative report on the case of Carlos DeLuna, who was executed in Texas in 1989 despite his continued claims of innocence and despite evidence that a second man, Carlos Hernandez, bragged about committing the crime. ABC's *World News Tonight* also covers the story.
	The *Chicago Tribune* prints an editorial by David A. Schwartz, who had served as the last defense attorney for death row inmate Girvies Davis before Davis was executed in Illinois in 1995. Schwartz claims that

Davis only confessed to the murder for which he was on death row after police threatened to kill him. The editorial also notes the differences between fighting a wrongful conviction a decade ago and today. Schwartz writes, "Timing is everything, of course, and former Gov. George Ryan's decision in 2003 to empty Illinois' Death Row came too late to save my client and friend, Girvies Davis, who was put to death on May 17, 1995. By the time I got involved in the case, 15 years after the trial and five months before the execution, nothing short of finding the real murderer would have saved (Girvies) Davis' life. Our criminal justice system admits mistakes only when it has to, and belated attempts to cast doubt on a verdict are usually swept aside, regardless of merit, unless the defendant can actually prove his innocence."

The Nation: Taken by Storm

As Table 3.3 shows, by the time Governor Ryan instituted a moratorium on executions in Illinois, the rest of the country was quickly becoming aware of the innocence frame. In 1993, Kirk Bloodsworth became the first death row inmate to be exonerated by means of DNA testing, and his story was followed by a growing number of captivating accounts of wrongful conviction across the country. Additionally, the last decade has seen several revelations of blatant and malicious evidence fabrication and evidence suppression by prosecuting attorneys and, perhaps most disturbingly, by crime lab scientists.

The innocence frame gained momentum in the late 1990s, and had saturated the death penalty debate by 2000. National attention and activity surrounding the innocence frame did not go from zero to saturation gradually, but explosively. After Governor Ryan placed a moratorium on executions in Illinois, other states began to jump on board. In the past five years, many states have formed commissions to investigate the potential for wrongful conviction in their death penalty systems, several state legislatures have considered new bills restricting the death penalty or eliminating it all together, and police departments across the country have begun to adopt mandated procedures to ensure fairness in evidence collection and processing, and in witness identification procedures. Although public opinion on specific questions about support for the death penalty is slow to move, as we discuss in Chapter 6, the general mood regarding the fallibility of the death penalty system is substantially different from what it was in the early 1990s, before the cascade of the innocence frame. We can see throughout this process that events in one state affected those in other states. News stories led to official commissions. These commissions, when they reported their findings, lent credence to the new frame. Events can be seen to ricochet, each one reinforcing the next. The death penalty is not mostly a federal issue, but the federal government was affected as well.

Table 3.3. *Innocence developments in the nation, 1973 to 2006*

1973	David Keaton becomes the first individual to be exonerated from death row in the modern era of the death penalty when the actual killer in Keaton's case is identified and convicted.
1977	In Utah, Gary Gilmore is executed by firing squad, ending the U.S. moratorium on executions. Beyond his historical role as the first person to be executed in the modern era of the death penalty debate, Gilmore gains public notoriety and the execution receives unprecedented levels of media attention. Like many after him, Gilmore is a "volunteer" for the death penalty, having instructed his lawyers not to file appeals.
1980	Jerry Banks becomes the 15th death penalty exoneree after his defense attorneys discover new exculpatory evidence that they claim was known to the state all along. After being released from prison, Banks's wife divorces him and he commits suicide. His estate wins a wrongful conviction settlement from the county for the benefit of his children.
	Larry Hicks becomes the 16th person to be exonerated from death row. Hicks is spared only two weeks before his scheduled execution when a volunteer attorney helps secure him a stay. The Playboy Foundation becomes interested in Hicks's claims of innocence and supplies funds for a reinvestigation of evidence, which shows that Hicks had a solid alibi at the time of the crime and that the eyewitness who testified against him was lying. Hicks is acquitted and released.
1981	Charles Ray Giddens, an 18-year-old African American, becomes the 17th exoneree after the Oklahoma Court of Criminal Appeals finds that the prosecution's star witness was unreliable and that the all-white jury in Giddens's case took only 15 minutes to decide their verdict.
	Johnny Ross, a 16-year-old African American who was sentenced to death for the rape of a white woman, is exonerated after investigations by the Southern Poverty Law Center show that Ross's blood type does not match semen found in the victim. Ross had confessed to the crime after being beaten by police, and his trial lasted only a few hours.
1982	In Texas, Charles Brooks becomes the first person in U.S. history to be executed by means of lethal injection. Sentenced to death for killing a car mechanic, he also gains public attention as the first person executed in Texas since 1964.
1989	James Richardson becomes the 40th person to be exonerated after spending two decades behind bars. Richardson had been convicted and sentenced to death in 1969 for the poisoning of one of his children. Prosecuting attorneys had argued that Richardson committed the crime to obtain the resulting insurance money, even though no insurance policy existed. Later investigation revealed that the neighbor who had been caring for Richardson's children had a prior homicide conviction and had also confessed the crime to individuals who later testified against him. Richardson received a new hearing after this new evidence prompted then–Dade County state attorney General Janet Reno to overturn his conviction.

1993 In Maryland, Kirk Bloodsworth becomes the 49th individual to be exonerated from death row since 1973 and the first American having faced a sentence of death to be exonerated as a result of DNA evidence. Because of the unprecedented use of DNA technology and likely in part because Bloodsworth is a former marine, this exoneration captures significant public attention. Based primarily on the testimony of faulty eyewitness identification, Bloodsworth had been convicted and sentenced to death for the rape and brutal murder of a nine-year-old girl. After subsequent DNA testing proves his innocence, he is released from prison, where he had been for eight years. In 2003, the real perpetrator of the girl's rape and murder will be identified, already in prison for another sexual assault.

1997 In Pennsylvania, a state district court overturns the conviction of Lisa Lambert after discovering 25 separate instances of prosecutorial misconduct, including perjury by police officers, the destruction of exculpatory evidence, the fabrication of incriminating evidence, and witness intimidation. Lambert, who was raped in prison, is released. But she will be returned to prison in one year after an appeals court rules that the federal judge had no jurisdiction in the state trial.

1998 In Florida, retiring state supreme court justice Gerald Kogan reports having "grave doubts" about the guilt of some individuals executed in Florida.

Kentucky becomes the first state to pass legislation outlawing the use of race as a factor in capital sentencing. This legislation mirrors the Racial Justice Act passed by the U.S. House of Representatives in 1990 and again in 1994 but defeated both times in the Senate. Kentucky's new law allows a capital defendant to cite statistical evidence to show that race influenced the decision to seek the death penalty in his or her case.

In Ohio, DNA evidence taken from the exhumed body of Dr. Sam Sheppard, implicated in the murder of his wife in 1954, shows compelling support for Sheppard's innocence. In one of the most sensational trials of the century, the prosecution had sought the death penalty, but Sheppard was sentenced to life in prison. Later his conviction was overturned and he was acquitted at retrial. The case was the basis for a popular TV series and the movie *The Fugitive* starring Harrison Ford.

In Texas, Karla Faye Tucker is executed by lethal injection despite international protest. Tucker is the second woman to be executed since the reinstatement of the death penalty in 1976 (Velma Barfield was put to death in North Carolina on November 2, 1984). Convicted of two brutal murders in 1983, Tucker became a Christian while in prison and, according to many religious leaders, lived the 14 years between incarceration and execution as a transformed individual.

1999 Oklahoma executes Sean Sellers, 16 at the time of his crime, provoking a swell of opposition within the United States and from the

(continued)

Table 3.3 *(continued)*

	international community. Sellers is the first individual to be executed in the past 40 years for crimes committed before the age of 17. With Sellers's execution, the United States joins only four other nations who were executing juveniles at the time of the crime in the 1990s: Iran, Pakistan, Saudi Arabia, and Yemen.
2000	In Florida, Frank Lee Smith is exonerated through DNA evidence for the 1985 rape and murder of an eight-year-old girl for which he was convicted. Smith's exoneration comes 11 months after he died of cancer on death row.
	In Louisiana, Michael Graham and Albert Burrell are exonerated after spending 13 years each on death row. All charges are dropped against the murder codefendants after DNA tests reveal that blood found at the victim's home did not belong to Burrell or Graham. With no other physical evidence in the case, questionable witness testimony, and prosecutorial misconduct in the original trial, current prosecuting attorney Dan Grady says that the case "should never have been brought to [the] grand jury." In dismissing all charges, the attorney general's office states that "prosecutors would deem it a breach of ethics to proceed to trial." Later, the trial attorneys appointed to defend Burrell will be disbarred for other reasons.
	In Texas, DNA results and other corroborative evidence uncovered by law students at the University of Wisconsin's Innocence Project show that codefendants Christopher Ochoa and Richard Danziger are innocent of the 1998 rape and murder for which they were both sentenced to life in prison. Texas district judge Bob Perkins, who ordered Ochoa's release, says the men "suffered a fundamental miscarriage of justice." While in prison, Danziger suffered permanent brain damage incurred during a brutal beating when another inmate wearing steel-toed shoes kicked him in the head.
	In Virginia, mentally retarded death row inmate Earl Washington is exonerated after DNA tests prove that he could not have committed the 1982 rape and murder for which he was committed.
2001	In Alabama, a state appeals court awards a new trial to death row inmate James Lewis Martin, Jr., after concluding that prosecutors withheld exculpatory evidence, including the facts that a key witness gave a statement under hypnosis and that another witness identified someone other than Martin in a police lineup.
	In Arizona, state supreme court justices call for legislation allowing judges to consider any "residual doubt" on their part when considering a death sentence.
	In Florida, the state supreme court overturns the capital conviction of Joseph Ramirez, which was based on what the court calls the "extraordinary claim" of a police technician, who testified that he could identify Ramirez's knife as the murder weapon to the exclusion of every

other knife in the world. The court also criticizes the trial judge for improperly disregarding the jury's recommendation of a life sentence.

In Florida, circuit judge Daniel Perry orders a new trial for death row inmate Rudolph Holton, saying that prosecutors inadvertently withheld police reports and other exculpatory evidence. Since Holton's first trial, additional tests have been performed on a hair found on the victim, a hair that was used at trial to link Holton to the crime, and the new tests now show that the hair is not his. Additionally, witnesses who testified against Holton at his trial recant their testimonies and admit to lying.

In Maryland, U.S. District Court Chief Judge J. Frederick Motz overturns death row inmate Kevin Wiggins's murder conviction and death sentence based on insufficient evidence and inadequate representation.

In Mississippi, an investigation opens into the case of death row inmate Kennedy Brewer, who was convicted and sentenced to death in 1995 for raping and murdering the three-year-old daughter of his girlfriend. The investigation is prompted by DNA tests showing that Brewer is not a match for semen removed from the victim's body.

In Missouri, work by a journalism class at Webster University uncovers that prosecutors in the case against death row inmate Richard D. Clay had allowed a key witness to mislead the jury. Based on this evidence, a federal judge orders a new trial for Clay.

In New Jersey, state attorney general John J. Framer, Jr., mandates changes in police lineup procedures, making New Jersey the first state in the country to implement such changes.

In Oklahoma, Timothy McVeigh, one of the two men convicted of the Oklahoma City bombing that killed 168 people on April 15, 1995, is executed by lethal injection at the U.S. federal penitentiary in Terre Haute, Indiana, after dropping all of his existing appeals.

In Oklahoma, a federal court overturns the death sentence of Alfred Brian Mitchell after discovering that Oklahoma City police chemist Joyce Gilchrist gave false and misleading testimony at trial. On September 25, Gilchrist is fired for laboratory mismanagement and flawed casework analysis. Later that month, a federal grand jury subpoenas evidence from 10 additional murder cases in which Gilchrist was involved, and the Oklahoma State Bureau of Investigation (OSBI) begins its own review of her work. In nine of the cases, the defendants have already been executed. Among other findings from the investigation is the discovery that Gilchrist's testimony concerning crime scene sperm in the 1982 trial of Malcolm Rent Johnson – testimony that was central to the prosecution's case – was based on slides that contained no sperm at all. This finding comes 18 months after Johnson was executed. In October, the OSBI also reviews the work of former agency serologist Kenneth Ede, previously criticized for his work on two death penalty cases, after a DNA test contradicts testimony he gave in a

(continued)

Table 3.3 (continued)

	1983 murder trial. Eventually, the OSBI reviews all 371 cases on which Ede worked. Additionally, the Oklahoma City Police Department asks the task force to review 10 other cases handled by another former police chemist, the late Janice Davis.
	In Pennsylvania, U.S. district judge J. Curtis Joyner overturns the conviction of death row inmate Otis Peterkin after finding that the trial judge acted improperly by admitting hearsay evidence and inflammatory and inappropriate statements by the prosecution. Judge Joyner also criticizes Peterkin's defense attorney for failing to investigate a purported alibi witness and, during the penalty phase of the trial, for declining to offer any character evidence on Peterkin's behalf.
	In Virginia, death row inmate Robin Lovitt mounts a challenge against his conviction after DNA materials that Lovitt says could exonerate him, including the murder weapon, are destroyed by an official at the Arlington County Circuit Court clerk's office to clear up space in the office.
2002	In *United States v. Quinones*, federal district court judge Jed Rakoff rules that the federal death penalty is rendered unconstitutional, because the demonstrated risk of executing an innocent person violates substantive due process. The U.S. Court of Appeals for the Second Circuit later reverses Rakoff's decision, concluding that a change in constitutional interpretation "is a change that only the Supreme Court is authorized to make." In 2003, the Supreme Court denies the case certiorari.
	In Arizona, Ray Krone is released from prison, becoming the 100th person exonerated from death row. This milestone exoneration gains considerable media attention and heightens public concerns about flaws in the capital punishment system.
	In Florida, prosecutors drop all charges against Juan Roberto Melendez, who had spent 18 years on Florida's death row, after a circuit court judge finds that prosecutors in the original trial withheld critical evidence and used the testimony of two witnesses whose credibility was later challenged with new evidence.
	In Florida, a federal judge grants a new trial to death row inmate Billy Kelley, denouncing the prosecutor for his "habit of failing to turn over exculpatory and impeachment evidence." Kelley was assisted with his appeal by constitutional law expert Laurence Tribe of Harvard Law School.
	In Indiana, Larry Mayes is freed from prison after spending 21 years behind bars when the Innocence Project at Benjamin Cardozo Law School secures his release. Mayes marks the 100th inmate freed from prison as a result of DNA testing.
	In Kentucky, Larry Osborne is exonerated from death row after the state supreme court reverses the conviction, concluding that the trial court allowed inadmissible hearsay testimony from a witness who died

before the original trial and, therefore, could not be cross-examined. Osborne was 17 at the time of the double homicide for which he was originally convicted.

In Maryland, Bernard Webster becomes the first inmate to be exonerated under the state's new DNA law (and the 115th person nationwide whose conviction has been overturned by DNA evidence) after spending 20 years in prison for a rape he did not commit.

In Michigan, both the defense attorneys and the prosecutors in the case of prison inmate Eddie Joe Lloyd present exculpatory DNA evidence in support of Lloyd's exoneration. Lloyd, a paranoid schizophrenic, was in a mental institution when he falsely confessed to the murder of Michelle Jackson to, he says, smoke out the real killer.

In Mississippi, Kennedy Brewer is granted a new trial based on DNA evidence that DNA samples taken from the victim are not a match to Brewer but instead to two unknown suspects.

In Minnesota, David Brian Sutherlin is exonerated after spending 17 years in prison for a rape that DNA testing now proves he did not commit. Sutherlin represents the nation's first exoneration based on DNA evidence initiated by a prosecutor.

In Montana, the FBI releases a report revealing that the former director of the state's crime laboratory, Arnold Melnikoff, misidentified a critical piece of hair evidence in the state's case against Jimmy Ray Bromgard. Bromgard spent 15 years in jail for the crime that DNA evidence now proves he did not commit. Peter Neufeld of the Innocence Project at the Benjamin N. Cardoza School of Law in New York City states, "This conceivably will be the biggest crime lab scandal in the country. He was the top guy in the state." Melnikoff has spent the past 13 years working as a forensic scientist for the Washington State Police. Authorities are now reviewing all cases in which Melnikoff provided forensic analysis. In New York, *Newsday* releases the results of an examination of inmates in New York City who had been wrongfully convicted of murder.

In New York, state justice Charles Tejada dismisses all charges against the five defendants, now ages 28 to 30, who were convicted of the Central Park Jogger rape and attempted murder. An 11-month-long examination of DNA evidence in the case confirms that another man, convicted murderer and serial rapist Matias Reyes, committed the crime. Reyes, serving time in prison for other rapes, confessed to the crime and says he acted alone. The defendants, after 5.5 to 12 years in jail for a crime they did not commit, are released.

In North Carolina, a Bertie County judge throws out the 1998 murder conviction of death row inmate Alan Gell and orders a new trial after concluding that prosecutors withheld exculpatory evidence from defense attorneys. The ruling marks the first case in which a state superior court judge overturned a death sentence after only hearing arguments from lawyers.

(continued)

Table 3.3 *(continued)*

In North Carolina, state supreme court chief justice I. Beverly Lake, Jr., convenes the North Carolina Actual Innocence Commission, comprising the state's top legal authorities. The group is charged with reviewing the danger of wrongful convictions in the state judicial system and considering possible corrective measures, including a review for claims of innocence beyond the normal appeals process.

In Texas, the state court of criminal appeals rules unanimously to overturn the 1987 murder conviction of death row inmate Damon Richardson, finding that prosecutors failed to disclose evidence that would have "severely undermined" the credibility of the prosecution's key witness and failed also to turn exculpatory evidence over to the defense.

In Texas, CBS local television station KHOU broadcasts an investigation series, developed by reporters David Raziq and Anna Werner, examining the accuracy of the Houston Police Department's crime lab (Harris County, in which Houston is located, has overseen more executions than any other county in the nation). The series uncovers multiple instances of sloppy or inaccurate lab work, raising doubts about the guilt of defendants convicted on the basis of evidence processed in the lab. By the end of the week of the multipart investigative series, the Houston Police Department announces plans to ask an independent team of scientists to audit the lab and its procedures. The resulting audit reveals disturbing flaws in the lab, including a serious lack of education and qualification on the part of the lab technicians, repeated incorrect tagging of samples, improper handling of samples that might have resulted in contamination, and possible contamination incurred when a section of the lab's roof had leaked into sample-containment areas. Within a month, the Houston Police Department closes the DNA section of its laboratory. Soon after the lab is closed, reporters Raziq and Werner are contacted by the mother of Josiah Sutton, who has spent 25 years in prison for a rape conviction based on DNA evidence processed through the Houston lab. With the help of DNA expert Bill Thompson of UC Irvine, Raziq and Werner analyze the lab's DNA report in Sutton's case and find glaring mistakes. The Houston Police Department agrees to retest the DNA evidence, and the results offer conclusive proof of Sutton's innocence. Sutton will be released from prison in March 2003 and granted a full pardon in 2004.

In Virginia, the state supreme court rules unanimously to deny petitions for posthumous DNA testing in the case of Roger Keith Coleman, who was executed in 1992 despite doubts of his guilt. The petitions for DNA testing were launched by several organizations, including *The Virginian-Pilot, The Washington Post, The Boston Globe, The Richmond Times-Dispatch*, and Centurion Ministries, a New Jersey organization that investigates innocence claims. The court writes, "Certainly, the right to test evidence in a criminal case has not been historically extended to the press and the general public."

In Washington, the U.S. Court of Appeals for the Ninth Circuit overturns Gary Benn's 1988 conviction and death sentence after finding that prosecutors improperly failed to disclose discrediting information about a jailhouse informant who testified against Benn.

Five fatal shootings committed in a period of 15 hours in Montgomery County, Maryland, mark the first deaths in a series of apparently random shootings that struck panic in the Washington, D.C., area – the shootings will come to be known as the beltway sniper attacks. By October 24, when police apprehend snipers John Muhammad, 41, and Lee Malvo, 17, the toll will stand at ten dead and three injured. Lee Malvo will be given several life sentences without parole, and John Muhammad will receive the death sentence in Virginia as well as additional sentencing in Maryland.

The play *The Exonerated* opens at off-Broadway's 45 Bleecker Theatre in New York City. The script is the compilation of excerpts from interviews that playwrights Jessica Blank and Erik Jensen conducted with individuals exonerated from death row, profiling six stories of wrongful execution and, later, rebuilding. Aided by a rotating cast of household-name actors, the play receives rave reviews.

2003   In Alabama, at the third trial for this crime, a jury acquits death row inmate Wesley Quick of the 1995 double murder for which he was sentenced to death in 1997.

In Florida, new DNA evidence casts doubt on the guilt of death row inmate Michael Rivera, who was sentenced to death in 1987 for the murder of an 11-year-old girl.

In Florida, the state supreme court has suspended the previously set October 1 deadline by which inmates would have to request DNA testing of evidence that might prove their innocence before the evidence would be destroyed. The court passes the ruling by a vote of four to three. The deadline for DNA testing will be suspended while the Court considers the constitutionality of the deadline.

In Iowa, Governor Tom Vilsack grants a reprieve to Terry Harrington, who has spent 26 years in prison for a crime it now seems he did not commit.

In Louisiana, new DNA evidence casts doubt on whether Ryan Matthews, a juvenile on death row, is in fact guilty of the crime for which he was sentenced to death, killing Tommy Vanhoose in 1997.

In Maryland, prosecutors charge Kimberly Ruffner with first-degree murder in the 1984 rape and murder of nine-year-old Dawn Hamilton. These charges come a decade after Kirk Bloodsworth was exonerated after spending nine years in prison, including time on Maryland's death row, for the crime. Ironically, the two men interacted frequently in prison during a period when Bloodsworth was not on death row; in fact, Ruffner's cell was directly over Bloodsworth's. In 2004, Ruffner will be sentenced to life in prison, a sentence he will begin serving after he

(continued)

Table 3.3 *(continued)*

completes the time he is currently serving for a similar attack in the same area committed just three weeks after Bloodsworth was arrested for Dawn Hamilton's murder.

In Massachusetts, district attorneys from several Massachusetts counties criticize Governor Mitt Romney's goal of reinstating the state's capital punishment system as a "foolproof" mechanism. A news investigation reports that Boston's Suffolk County is responsible for the second highest number of wrongful convictions in the nation, second only to Chicago. Scientists are also critical of Governor Romney's assertion that the death penalty system could be made infallible. Theodore D. Kessis, founder of Applied DNA Resources in Columbus, Ohio, and a faculty member at the Johns Hopkins School of Public Health in Baltimore, says that "like anything that involves humans, there is always the possibility of error in DNA testing."

In New York, former governor Mario Cuomo writes a letter to the editor of the *New York Times* urging New Yorkers to rethink the death penalty in light of the exonerations of John Kogut, Dennis Halstead, and John Restivo after spending 18 years in prison for a rape and murder they did not commit. "If New York had the death penalty in the 1980s," Cuomo writes, "[these three men] would most likely have been executed years before DNA evidence in their case proved their innocence. In light of the ever-growing number of exonerations of the wrongfully convicted, New Yorkers should once again ask themselves if the death penalty is worth the enormous risk it poses of executing the innocent."

In New York City, Republican mayor Michael Bloomberg reiterates his opposition to the death penalty: "The death penalty I've always had a problem with, because too many times in the past you've seen innocent people incarcerated and, tragically, every once in a while they've been executed. And until you can show me that the process never would ever convict somebody that later on we find out was innocent of a crime, murder is murder no matter who does it, and I think we as a society can afford to incarcerate people."

In North Carolina, for the second time in four months, a state judge throws out a death row inmate's murder conviction after finding that prosecutors or police withheld exculpatory evidence.

In North Carolina, the *Charlotte News & Observer* publishes an investigative series criticizing state prosecutorial misconduct that it claims led to a number of wrongful convictions and noting that prosecutors who withhold evidence often receive minimal or no punishment. Among the capital cases reviewed in the series is that of Alan Gell, who was sentenced to death in 1998 when the state attorney general's office withheld a tape recording of the state's star witness admitting to fabricating her story as well as other witness statements indicating that Gell was in jail at the time of the murder. The investigative report also discusses the case of Charles Munsey, who in

1999 won a new trial after his attorneys revealed that the Wilkes County district attorney withheld evidence showing that the jailhouse informant serving as the state's star witness was in fact never in the prison where Munsey purportedly confessed to him. Before his new trial arrived, Munsey died in prison. Former superior court judge Tom Ross, who reversed Munsey's conviction, is quoted as follows: "From my perspective as a lawyer and judge, the adversarial system has gotten to the point where winning is more important than justice."

The North Carolina Actual Innocence Commission, composed of judges, police, prosecutors, and defense attorneys, recommends new procedures for state law enforcement agencies geared toward ensuring the accuracy of eyewitness identification and preventing wrongful convictions. Recommendations include requiring police to show eyewitnesses suspect photos or lineup participants one at a time instead of as a group and requiring that the police officers in charge of the lineup not know which participant is the suspect.

In Ohio, the state parole board recommends to Governor Bob Taft that he grant clemency to death row inmate Jerome Campbell after the board concludes that the jury in Campbell's case was not given all relevant evidence to consider. This marks the first instance in which the board has recommended clemency since Ohio resumed executions in 1999.

In Texas, in an op-ed article, former FBI chief and federal judge William Sessions calls on state legislators to pass a measure introduced by Senator Rodney Ellis of Houston to create an Innocence Commission, charged with examining the Texas criminal system and developing measures to safeguard it against wrongful conviction. The state senate passes the legislation.

In Texas, the district attorney's office reports that it may be forced to ask for pardons in the cases of several defendants (one capital murder case and seven other cases) whose convictions rested in large part on DNA evidence – DNA evidence that was tested by the Houston Police Department's crime lab and destroyed. Under heat of mounting criticisms about poor laboratory conditions and careless practices, the Houston Police Department shut down the DNA division of its crime lab in December 2002. As prosecutors and police work to retest DNA evidence in nearly 400 cases originally analyzed by the Houston Police Department's DNA division, these 8 cases in question are among 21 that are feared missing. Also in 2003, the *Houston Chronicle* publishes a report based on examination of personnel records at the discredited DNA lab. The report states that none of the analysts who worked in the lab, including the former head of the lab, James Bolding, met the national standards of education or background experience.

The PBS program *Frontline* presents an investigative documentary on what happens to wrongfully convicted individuals after they have been exonerated from death row and reenter society, many with no financial or transitional assistance.

(continued)

Table 3.3 *(continued)*

2004	In California, the state senate passes legislation to establish the California Commission on the Fair Administration of Justice, a collection of experts charged with examining the state's criminal justice system to determine why wrongful convictions have occurred. The commission will be responsible for making recommendations to the legislature and governor regarding what safeguards should be put into place to improve the system.
	In California, an article in the *San Francisco Chronicle* called "Innocence Lost" reports that California wrongfully convicts more innocent persons than any other state criminal system and laments the number of chances state lawmakers have had to prevent such mistakes from occurring but have ignored.
	In California, the Conference of Delegates of the California Bar Association, comprising some 450 attorneys, calls for a moratorium on the state's death penalty until an investigation can be conducted to determine whether the capital punishment laws in California are fairly administered.
	In Indiana, Governor Joseph Kernan commutes the death sentence of Darnell Williams to life in prison after the former prosecutor who sent Williams to death row and one of the jurors in the case together file suit in federal court asking for a stay of Williams's execution until new DNA testing can be performed. Although DNA results were inconclusive, Governor Kernan commutes Williams's sentence because of doubts about Williams's involvement in the case and Williams's low IQ, just above the threshold for defining mental retardation. Students at Northwestern University Law School also contributed work leading to the commutation decision.
	In Louisiana, an analysis of the state's capital punishment system shows that more inmates are exonerated than are executed. From 1999 to 2004, 6 cases had convictions dismissed and only 3 were actually executed out of a total of 22. Lawyers for two of those executed, in fact, were disbarred. A Louisiana State University law professor, Stuart Green, was surprised. "That 27 percent of all capital convictions led to exonerations is shocking. I can't see how any criminal justice system can tolerate that level of error, particularly in the matter of the death penalty. It is unacceptable." Based on these findings, attorneys and legal experts push Governor Kathleen Blanco and other state lawmakers to authorize a review of the death penalty and put a hold on executions in the meantime.
	In Massachusetts, Louis Greco, an inmate who died nine years previously while waiting on death row, is finally exonerated by authorities after the justice department found FBI information claiming Greco and his codefendants had been convicted on perjured testimony.

Massachusetts's "Foolproof Death Penalty" is entered into the *New York Times Magazine*'s yearly acknowledgment of "the absurdly wide range of human originality."

In Missouri, former Missouri Supreme Court chief justice Charles Blackmar repeats his stance against capital punishment after the recent exoneration of Joseph Amrine, who spent 17 years on death row. He claims that even a very small percentage of mistaken convictions do not warrant keeping the death penalty as an option.

In Nevada, Roberto Miranda, a Cuban native who spent 14 years on the state's death row before being exonerated in 1996, settles a civil rights lawsuit for $5 million against Clark County, the public defender's office, and two former Las Vegas police detectives. Miranda's suit argued that public defenders violated his civil rights by offering him woefully inadequate representation after Miranda (who speaks Spanish) performed poorly on a polygraph examination conducted in English, and that police withheld exculpatory evidence during his trial. Although the first federal judge to hear the suit threw out the case saying that Miranda could not sue the county or the public defender's office regarding grievances about his representation, the U.S. Court of Appeals for the Ninth Circuit later reinstated the case and the U.S. Supreme Court declined to review that court's ruling, thus opening the possibility for like lawsuits in the future.

In New Jersey, Governor Richard Codey calls for a moratorium on executions and the creation of a commission to decide if the state's capital punishment system is economical, just, and consistent with "evolving standards of decency." The state legislature considers legislation to this same effect.

In North Carolina, Alan Gell is exonerated after spending nine years in prison (including four on death row), when the jury in his retrial acquits him of all charges. Gell had been convicted originally based on testimony by two teenage girls, testimony that was later called into question by a tape recording of one of the girls admitting to fabricating her story and by contradictory testimony offered by as many as 17 witnesses who say they saw the victim, Allen Ray Jenkins, alive during days following the date on which the girls claimed Gell had committed the murder (and during which time Gell was in jail on a charge of vehicle theft). Following Gell's release, the North Carolina State Bar gives written reprimands to two former assistant attorney generals for withholding evidence that could have prevented Gell's wrongful conviction, although an investigative panel concludes that the mistakes made were unintentional.

In the property room of the closed-down Houston Police Department crime lab DNA division, investigators begin sorting through 280

(continued)

Table 3.3 *(continued)*

unopened and mislabeled boxes of evidence that were discovered nearly a year earlier. Some of the evidence may be part of the 379 cases in which prisoners convicted in Harris County have requested the retesting of DNA evidence, hoping new tests will establish their innocence. In a case in which investigators find new evidence in these cases, prosecutors would have to report to the court that some of the evidence previously thought to be lost or destroyed is available after all. An investigatory panel also concludes that the number of crime lab cases to be reexamined, originally estimated at around 360, is actually closer to 5,000 to 10,000, a number that almost certainly would include capital murder trials from Harris County.

In Texas, state legislators and the Houston chief of police, Harold Hurtt, call for a moratorium on executions in cases from Harris County. In response, four of the state's largest newspapers publish editorials in support of halting executions. Judge Tom Price, a 30-year Republican veteran on Texas's highest criminal court calls for a limited moratorium on executions while investigations are conducted into the cases of inmates on the state's death row who were convicted using evidence processed in the Houston Police Department's DNA crime lab. Former FBI director William Sessions and former Texas Court of Criminal Appeals judge Charles Baird, members of the Constitution Project's Death Penalty Initiative, also call for a moratorium on capital punishment, citing fears of executing an innocent person.

Ernest Ray Willis is exonerated from death row after a federal judge throws out his capital conviction, finding "strong reason to be concerned that Willis may be actually innocent" and criticizing prison guards in West Texas for incorrectly administering antipsychotic medication to Willis during the trial to treat Willis's chronic back pain, medication that the judge says impeded Willis's ability to defend himself. The judge also holds Willis's defense attorneys responsible for providing inadequate representation during the trial.

Bill Kurtis, investigative reporter for A&E television, publishes a book entitled *The Death Penalty on Trial: Crisis in American Justice*, which chronicles his transition from being a death penalty advocate to a staunch opponent of capital punishment.

Scott Christianson analyzes the errors made by New York state's criminal justice system in his new book entitled *Innocent: Inside Wrongful Conviction Cases*. Specifically, he looks at issues such as misidentifications, perjury by witnesses, poor attorney counsel to the defendant, false confessions, and systematic misconduct.

Tim Junkin releases a book entitled *Bloodsworth: The True Story of the First Death Row Inmate Exonerated by DNA*, detailing the events that led to Bloodsworth's conviction, death sentence, and eventual exoneration from death row.

Sister Helen Prejean, author of *Dead Man Walking*, publishes a new book in which she details the fundamental elements of capital punishment throughout the history of the United States.

The *Chicago Tribune* releases the results of an independent investigation into the case of Cameron Willingham, executed in Texas earlier in 2004 for the deaths of his three children in a 1991 house fire that prosecutors claimed Willingham set intentionally. The report states that four national arson experts who reviewed evidence from the case have concluded that the original arson investigation was flawed, having been based on arson theories that have since been repudiated by scientific advances. The report quotes arson expert Gerald Hurst as saying, "There's nothing to suggest to any reasonable arson investigator that this was an arson fire. It was just a fire." Willingham's defense attorneys presented expert testimony detailing the new arson investigation to the state's highest court and to Texas governor Rick Perry before Willingham's execution, but no stay was granted. Some of the Texas jurors who convicted Willingham were troubled to hear the investigation's findings. Dorinda Brofofsky, one of the jurors, said, "Did anybody know about this prior to his execution? Now I will have to live with this for the rest of my life. Maybe this man was innocent." Less than a year after Willingham's execution, Ernest Willis would be exonerated from Texas's death row because of arson evidence presented by some of the same experts who had appealed for a stay of execution in Willingham's case – experts note that evidence in the two cases is nearly identical.

2005   In Georgia, the state board of pardons and paroles issues a formal pardon to Lena Baker, the only woman executed in Georgia during the 20th century, after concluding that her execution was "a grievous error, as this case called out for mercy." An African American, Baker was tried, convicted, and sentenced to die in a single day in 1944 by an all-white, all-male jury. She was convicted of murdering her white employer, Ernest Knight, a man who Baker says she shot in self-defense after he locked her in his gristmill and threatened her. Baker was electrocuted in 1945, and the Cuthbert paper reported her execution under the headline "Baker Burns." Today, Baker's last words are displayed with her picture near the electric chair in which she died, which has been retired to a museum at Georgia State Prison in Reidsville. Her last words: "What I done, I did in self-defense, or I would have been killed myself. Where I was I could not overcome it. God has forgiven me. I have nothing against anyone. I picked cotton for Mr. Pritchett, and he has been good to me. I am ready to go. I am one in the number. I am ready to meet my God. I have a very strong conscience."

In Indiana, outgoing governor Joe Kernan grants clemency to Michael Daniels and calls for a state examination into whether Indiana's sentencing system is fair in death penalty cases.

(continued)

Table 3.3 *(continued)*

In Massachusetts, Governor Mitt Romney testifies before a joint-stated House and Senate judiciary committee about his proposal to institute a "foolproof" death penalty statute. Romney admits that the proposed law would not prevent the potential for human error, saying, "A 100 percent guarantee? I don't think there's such a thing in life. Except perhaps death – for all of us." Aside from the governor's statement, almost all of the testimony presented at the hearing opposed the governor's bill.

In Missouri, the 1995 execution of Larry Griffin for the murder of Quintin Moss is called into question when the National Association for the Advancement of Colored People (NAACP) Legal Defense and Educational Fund releases the results of its year-long investigation into the case, presenting evidence of Griffin's innocence. Jennifer Joyce, the state's prosecuting attorney, says she has reopened the investigation and will conduct a comprehensive review of the case.

The New Mexico House of Representatives passes a bill to abolish the state's death penalty, marking the first time that either chamber of the state's legislature has passed such a measure.

In Oklahoma, the state court of criminal appeals reverses the conviction and death sentence of Curtis Edward McCarty. The court concludes that the conviction and sentence were based largely on forensic testimony by former Oklahoma City policy chemist Joyce Gilchrist, who had been with the police department for 21 years before being fired in 2001 for reckless and unethical lab work, and that Gilchrist either lost or destroyed critical evidence in McCarty's case at the time of the trial.

In Pennsylvania, Harold Wilson is exonerated after new DNA evidence clears him of murder charges. Wilson was prosecuted in 1989 by former Philadelphia assistant district attorney Jack McMahon, who gained notoriety for participating in a training video instructing new Philadelphia prosecutors about how to use race in selecting death penalty juries. Before new DNA testing was available to clear Wilson of all charges, the Pennsylvania Supreme Court granted Wilson a new hearing based on evidence that McMahon used racially discriminatory practices in jury selection during the capital trial, improperly exercising his peremptory strikes to eliminate potential black jurors from the case.

In the first action of its kind by a Texas governor in decades, Texas governor Rick Perry issues an executive order appointing a nine-member special council charged with reviewing an array of legal issues ranging from police investigations to court appeals.

In Virginia, an audit of the state's central crime laboratory commissioned by Governor Mark Warner and conducted by an independent research agency finds that the lab had botched DNA tests in the death penalty case of Earl Washington. After hearing these results, Governor Warner orders a review of 150 other criminal cases and the institution of procedures to insulate the lab from outside political pressures.

In Texas, the results of an investigation into evidence testing at the Houston Police Department crime lab are released, showing that analysts at the lab fabricated findings in at least four drug cases. At least one case involved the illegal practice of "dry labbing," in which the lab scientist fails to conduct testing before issuing conclusions to support police suspicions. Although the DNA division of the Houston crime lab came under such scrutiny in 2002 that it was forced to close, and additional errors have subsequently been exposed in three other lab divisions – toxicology, ballistics, and blood-typing – this report is the first to criticize the lab's largest division, controlled substances. This division, which is responsible for testing suspected drug substances, performs approximately 75 percent of the Houston Police Department's forensics work.

In Texas, the *Houston Chronicle* publishes a two-part investigative series about the case of Ruben Cantu, a San Antonio man executed in 1993 despite consistent claims of innocence. Cantu was 17 when he was charged with capital murder, and now his guilt has been called into question by statements by a key eyewitness and Cantu's codefendant, who both say Cantu was innocent. Sam Millsap, the former San Antonio district attorney who once described himself as a "lifelong supporter of the death penalty," states that he is now opposed to the death penalty, saying his doubts were recently affirmed by evidence that Ruben Cantu was innocent. Cantu was sentenced to die under Millsap's watch as district attorney, and Millsap now says that he never should have sought the death penalty in a case that rested so heavily on suspect identification that an eyewitness made only after being showed Cantu's photograph three separate times. Millsap, in private practice as an attorney, speaks regularly about the issue and urges abolition of the death penalty because of the inevitable errors that will occur.

In Virginia, an audit of the state's division of forensic science finds multiple flaws in the crime laboratory's procedures for testing DNA evidence. The review was prompted by an earlier audit of the lab, which raised criticisms over the lab's handling of DNA evidence in the case of Earl Washington, Jr., a man who spent 17 years on death row before being exonerated in 2000 after DNA evidence confirmed his innocence, replacing the crime lab's earlier flawed DNA findings. State officials launch an investigation into the lab's findings in 160 cases that hinged on DNA evidence, including approximately 24 death penalty cases. Governor Mark Warner orders 660 boxes containing thousands of files from 1973 through 1988 to be tested using updated DNA technology in an effort to uncover any additional wrongful convictions that might exist. Virginia has executed more people since the death penalty was reinstated in 1976 than any other state except Texas, but recent high-profile exonerations in the state, including that of Earl Washington, have called the accuracy of its death penalty system into question. Peter Neufeld, co-director of the Innocence Project in New York, estimates

(continued)

Table 3.3 *(continued)*

the innocence rate in Virginia as "a 7 percent innocence rate – among people who never even asked for testing – that should give pause to people who think mistakes in our criminal justice system are flukes."

Jed Horne publishes a book entitled *Desire Street*, which explores the exoneration of Louisiana death row inmate Curtis Kyles, looking in particular to understand how Kyles's case has affected the New Orleans criminal justice system, plagued with problems of racism, questionable eyewitness identification procedures, and a troubling relationship between elected attorneys and judges and death penalty policy.

The documentary *After Innocence* opens in cities around the country after garnering awards at Sundance and other film festivals. The film, by Jessica Sanders and Marc Simon, profiles several wrongfully convicted defendants who, after being exonerated through DNA evidence, try to rebuild their lives.

Thomas Frisbie and Randy Garrett publish a book entitled *Victims of Justice Revisited* about Rolando Cruz, who was one of three men wrongly convicted in Illinois for the 1983 murder of 10-year-old Jeanine Nicarico and then exonerated of the crime by then-governor George Ryan. The authors use Cruz's case as a backdrop for a detailed investigation of the death penalty in the United States.

The NAACP Legal Defense and Educational Fund releases the findings from its year-long investigation into the case of Larry Griffin, who was executed by the state of Missouri in 1995 after being convicted of a drive-by shooting murder. Investigators say Griffin's case is the strongest demonstration yet of an innocent man being executed.

2006   In Arizona, several members of the state legislature offer their apologies to Ray Krone, the Arizona man exonerated from death row in 2002 through DNA testing.

In Arizona, Kenneth Phillips, Jr., is convicted and sentenced to life in prison for the murder of Kim Ancona, the same crime for which Ray Krone was convicted and sentenced to death in 1992. Krone was exonerated in 2002, the 100th person to be exonerated from death row since 1972. Phillips pleaded guilty to the crime and DNA evidence has implicated him. The Maricopa County Attorney's Office initially intended to seek the death penalty against Phillips, but dropped the request in light of mitigating evidence presented by defense attorneys.

In California, the state Commission on the Fair Administration of Justice unanimously recommends that state lawmakers require that all jailhouse interrogations be recorded electronically to avoid the false confessions that often lead to wrongful convictions.

In Florida, John Robert Ballard becomes the 123rd individual to be exonerated from death row in the United States since 1972 and the 22nd exoneree in Florida, the state that leads the nation in exonerations. The Florida Supreme Court, which overturned Ballard's conviction unanimously, concluded that the evidence against Ballard was so weak that the trial judge should have dismissed the case immediately.

In Michigan, Detroit joins a growing list of jurisdictions now requiring that suspect interrogations be videotaped. The procedural change is prompted, in part, by the 2002 exoneration of Detroit man Eddie Joe Lloyd, a mentally ill man who spent 17 years in prison for a rape and murder he did not commit.

In Missouri, a federal district court places a stay on state executions and releases the findings from its review of the state death penalty system, citing many problems in the way executions are carried out. Specifically, the court finds that the state's lethal injection procedure subjects the inmate to an unnecessary risk of pain and suffering and suggests adopting the use of anesthesiologists during lethal injections.

In New Jersey, the state Death Penalty Study Commission convenes, a commission created by the state legislature at the same time that it voted to halt executions in the state so that investigations could be made into the death penalty system. The commission hears testimony from legal experts, religious leaders, murder victims' families, and exonerees such as Larry Peterson, who was wrongfully convicted of rape and murder and who spent 18 years in prison before being exonerated.

In North Carolina, former Union County prosecutor Scott Brewer comes under fire for withholding crucial evidence in the death penalty trial of John Gregory Hoffman. The North Carolina State Bar accuses Brewer and another attorney of committing felony obstruction of justice and subornation of perjury. Hoffman, having been removed from death row, has also been granted a new trial.

North Carolina becomes the first state to institute an Innocence Inquiry Commission, a permanent body charged with reviewing defendants' claims of innocence. The eight-member panel, composed of judges, prosecutors, and defense lawyers, will review all requests from defendants who have not pleaded guilty. In a case in which the commission finds a case of possible innocence, it will refer the decision to a three-judge panel, the members of which will be chosen by the chief justice of North Carolina. For the defendant to be exonerated, all three judges on the panel must agree that the defendant has presented "clear and convincing evidence" of factual innocence.

In Pennsylvania, state senator Stewart J. Greenleaf, chairman of the Senate Judiciary Committee, announces the formation of an advisory committee to be composed of state prosecutors, defense attorneys, judges, corrections officials, police, and victim advocates, charged with examining cases of wrongful conviction in the state. The formation of the committee is prompted in part by the case of Nicholas Yarris, who in 2004 became the first person to be exonerated from Pennsylvania's death row by means of DNA testing. Yarris had spent 22 years in prison on a wrongful conviction of rape and murder.

(continued)

Table 3.3 (continued)

In Pennsylvania, Dennis Counterman is released from the state's prison after serving more than 15 years behind bars. Counterman was convicted and sentenced to death in 1990 for the deaths of his three children in a fire, which prosecutors contended that Counterman had set. Counterman's conviction was overturned in 2001, in part because it was revealed that prosecutors had withheld evidence indicating that Counterman's oldest child had a history of setting fires. A fire expert hired by the prosecution also testified that the prosecution's theory of how Counterman started the fire "is not properly supported by today's standards." Counterman was released after entering an *Alford* plea, meaning that the defendant does not admit guilt but agrees that the prosecution might have been able to convince a jury of his guilt. Counterman decided to enter the *Alford* plea, which carried a maximum of 18 years in prison, because he had already served that many years so would be released and would not have to face the uncertainty of another trial in an attempt to prove his innocence.

In Texas, an independent analysis of the DNA division of the Houston Police Department crime lab (closed in 2002 in the midst of heavy criticism about flawed lab procedures) reveals that of 1,100 samples reviewed, 40 percent of DNA samples and 23 percent of blood evidence samples had serious problems. It is also revealed that among the 43 DNA cases and 50 serology (blood) cases that were processed at the lab since 1980 and have since been identified as having "major issues," at least one case is a capital case, that of death row inmate Derrick Lee Jackson. As of 2006, the DNA section of the Houston crime lab remains closed.

In Texas, the *Houston Chronicle* and the *Dallas Morning News* call for an independent investigation into the case of Ruben Cantu, who was executed in 1993. Evidence gathered in a *Chronicle* investigative report the year before suggests that Cantu was innocent.

In Virginia, new DNA tests are performed on evidence from the case of Roger Keith Coleman, a man executed in Virginia in 1992 for the brutal rape and murder of his sister-in-law, Wanda McCoy. The tests provide nearly conclusive evidence of Coleman's guilt. Innocence Project co-director Peter Neufeld applauds Governor Mark Warner's action to have the evidence retested. "The real issue," Neufeld says, "is not whether one man was in fact guilty or innocent, it's rather that he set the example of what the other 49 governors should do" in cases of executions in other states where DNA evidence is still available.

The town of Monroeville, Alabama, is featured in the January 2006 edition of *National Geographic* magazine as the home of *To Kill a Mockingbird* author Harper Lee and exonerated death row inmate Walter McMillian. The article points out how McMillian's case is "an eerie echo" of the book's storyline. McMillian, wrongly convicted in 1987 despite a lack of reliable evidence of murdering a white woman, spent seven years on Alabama's death row before being exonerated, in part because his story was featured on *60 Minutes*.

John Grisham publishes his first nonfiction book, entitled *The Innocent Man*, about Ron Williamson, a man who was sentenced to death in the early 1980s for the murder of a young woman from Ada, Oklahoma. Williamson was exonerated in 1999 (the 80th death row exoneration in the nation) after new DNA testing proved his innocence.

Robert Mayer publishes a book entitled *The Dreams of Ada*, which tells the story of two other defendants, Tommy Ward and Karl Fontenot, in the same Ada, Oklahoma, case featured in John Grisham's book. Mayer, like Grisham, suggests that the defendants in this case were victims of a terrible miscarriage of justice.

The Federal Government: The Innocence Protection Act

As one would expect, given the limited federal role in death penalty issues, Table 3.4 shows that the federal government has responded to the innocence frame more slowly, and with less activity, than the states. But the Innocence Protection Act, signed in both houses of a Republican-controlled Congress and signed into law by President Bush in 2004, is proof enough that the innocence frame has taken hold. (It was not smooth sailing to get even this reform through Congress; the act had previously been introduced several times unsuccessfully starting in 2000, but by 2004 pressure was sufficient that it was indeed enacted as part of the larger Justice for All Act.) This law allows federal and state inmates to submit potentially exculpatory DNA evidence for consideration in support of their appeals and also establishes a commission charged with developing a set of minimum standards for death penalty defense counsels. The DNA evidence element of the law was named after Kirk Bloodsworth.

The Supreme Court: Two Key Decisions in a New Direction

Table 3.5 summarizes recent Supreme Court decisions culminating in the 2002 *Atkins v. Virginia* (536 U.S. 304) decision outlawing the death penalty in the case of mentally handicapped defendants and the 2005 *Roper v. Simmons* (543 U.S. 551) decision outlawing the death penalty for minors. Although these decisions do not invoke the innocence frame directly, they are powerful signals that the Court is softening to constitutional and procedural criticisms against the death penalty. Clearly, however, the Court has not been shaken in its overall views on the matter. As the ultimate overseer of the U.S. criminal justice system, the Court cannot be expected to move quickly to a conclusion that errors are inevitable. It may, however, reach a conclusion that executions have become so rare as to be constitutionally "unusual." This logic was an important element in

Table 3.4. *Innocence developments in the federal government, 1990 to 2006*

1990	The U.S. House of Representatives passes the Racial Justice Act, allowing individuals facing execution to challenge their sentence on the basis of patterns of racial disparities, just as such data are used in housing or employment discrimination suits. The bill is defeated in the Senate.
1993	The U.S. House of Representatives again passes the Racial Justice Act, which is again defeated in the Senate.
1994	The House Judiciary Subcommittee on Civil and Constitutional Rights releases an updated version of the 1993 report.
1996	Congress passes the Antiterrorism and Effective Death Penalty Act, in part as a response to the Oklahoma City bombing, making it more difficult for defendants on death row to secure federal review.
2000	The Innocence Protection Act is introduced in both houses of Congress. This bill allows federal and state inmates to have DNA considered in support of their appeals if the testing has the potential for revealing evidence of innocence. The bill also creates a commission charged with developing standards for death penalty defense counsels.
	The U.S. Department of Justice releases its own capital punishment investigation report, detailing numerous racial and geographic disparities in the application of the death penalty.
2001	The Innocence Protection Act is reintroduced in Congress.
2002	The U.S. House Committee on Government Reform releases a report criticizing the FBI for allowing at least two innocent men to be sent to death row decades earlier. According to the report, the FBI was so intent on protecting Boston informants that it did not prosecute those informants who had committed murder and, on at least one occasion, instead allowed four men that the bureau knew were not responsible for a murder to be tried and convicted of the crime. Two of these four men were sentenced to death, and the other two were put on death row; of the four, two died in jail and the other two were released after their sentences were commuted, 30 years after they were first imprisoned.
2003	The House votes 357 to 67 to pass the Advancing Justice through DNA Technology Act (H.R. 3214), of which the Innocence Protection Act is a part. This legislation would designate $25 million over five years for state DNA testing that could help exonerate some death row inmates, plus funding for state-level improvements in the quality of legal representation for those facing capital charges, and a funding package of more than $1 billion over the next five years to assist federal and state authorities in solving crimes and, thus, protecting innocent individuals.
2004	The Innocence Protection Act is folded into the larger Justice for All Act, which Congress approves. In addition to several other provisions, the law establishes rules and procedures for allowing federal inmates to apply for DNA testing, creates the Kirk Bloodsworth Post-Conviction DNA Testing Grant Program and authorizes $25 million over five years

to help states pay for post-conviction DNA testing, and authorizes state grants to improve the quality of death penalty trials and assist families of murder victims. President Bush signs the Justice for All Act into law on October 20, 2004 – the Saturday preceding the presidential election.

2005   During his State of the Union Address before Congress, President George W. Bush raises concerns about race, wrongful convictions, and adequate representation for those facing the death penalty: "Because one of the main sources of our national unity is our belief in equal justice, we need to make sure Americans of all races and backgrounds have confidence in the system that provides justice. In America we must make doubly sure no person is held to account for a crime he or she did not commit – so we are dramatically expanding the use of DNA evidence to prevent wrongful conviction. Soon I will send to Congress a proposal to fund special training for defense counsel in capital cases, because people on trial for their lives must have competent lawyers by their side."

2006   As part of President Bush's new DNA initiative, the *Advancing Justice through DNA Technology* Web site (www.dna.gov) is launched as an educational resource on DNA testing, training, and funding, and the history of forensic use of DNA. In one section of the Web site, entitled "Exonerated by Science," viewers can read case overviews of individuals, some formerly on death row, who were wrongly convicted and then exonerated by means of DNA evidence.

the *Atkins* and *Roper* decisions; the fact that so many states had moved to eliminate executions for juveniles and the mentally handicapped was seen as a sign of "evolving norms of decency." The Court clearly remains split on the issue, however, and there is significant support on the bench for two contrary views: 1) acceptance that errors are inevitable and acceptable even in this area of life and death; and 2) support for the view that the best solution to problems of imperfections in trials is to give greater resources to defendants, thereby "perfecting the mechanism" of capital punishment. Clearly, the Court is not entirely convinced of the innocence frame, but its actions in *Atkins* and *Roper* have contributed to the movement and its concern with changing social mores as reflected in state activities with regard to the use of the death penalty show that these actions may have constitutional import.

Media Attention to Exonerations

It is clear from the items chronicled above that dozens of events were happening in the late 1990s and afterward around the country reinforcing the idea that errors of justice are a serious problem in the death penalty debate. One remarkable aspect of this social cascade is that individual exonerees are more newsworthy now than they used to be. In this section, we trace

Table 3.5. *Innocence developments in the Supreme Court, 1968 to 2006*

1968	In *United States v. Jackson* (390 U.S. 570), the Supreme Court begins restricting the death penalty, marking a new interpretation of the Eighth Amendment as containing "an evolving standard of decency that marked the progress of a maturing society."
	In *Witherspoon v. Illinois* (391 U.S. 510), the Supreme Court rules that an individual's reservations about the death penalty are insufficient grounds on which to exclude the individual from jury service in a death penalty case.
1971	In *Crampton v. Ohio* and *McGautha v. California* (collectively under 402 U.S. 183), the Supreme Court rejects the claim that a jury's unrestricted discretion in death penalty sentencing violates defendants' Fourteenth Amendment right to due process, saying that giving guidance to capital sentencing discretion is "beyond present human ability."
1972	In *Furman v. Georgia, Jackson v. Georgia,* and *Branch v. Texas* (collectively under 408 U.S. 238), the Supreme Court holds that the death penalty is applied in an arbitrary and capricious manner in violation of both the Eighth and Fourteenth Amendments. The Court's five to four ruling, set out in nine distinct opinions, serves to void 40 death penalty statutes and commute the sentences of 629 people on death rows nationwide.
1976	In *Gregg v. Georgia, Woodson v. North Carolina, Jurek v. Texas, Proffitt v. Florida,* and *Roberts v. Louisiana* (collectively under 428 U.S. 153), the Supreme Court upholds the new death penalty statutes that Georgia, Texas, and Florida, respectively, have instituted in response to the Court's concerns expressed in *Furman,* effectively reinstating the death penalty in those states. The Court also specifies its position on jury discretion in capital sentences, ruling that it is unconstitutional to mandate capital punishment for all individuals convicted of capital crimes.
1989	In *Penry v. Lynaugh* (492 U.S. 302), the Supreme Court rules unanimously that executing the mentally retarded does not constitute cruel and unusual punishment under the Eighth Amendment.
1993	In *Herrera v. Collins* (506 U.S. 390), the Supreme Court rules that in the absence of other constitutional violations, new evidence of innocence is not sufficient reason for federal courts to award a new trial to a defendant. The ruling points to the clemency process through which an innocent inmate should seek to prevent execution, saying clemency is historically "the 'fail safe' in our justice system."
2001	In a speech to the Minnesota Women Lawyer's Group, Supreme Court justice Sandra Day O'Connor, who was previously a staunch supporter of the death penalty, voices her concerns about the fairness of the system. "If statistics are any indication," she says, "the system may well be allowing some innocent defendants to be executed."
2002	In *Atkins v. Virginia* (536 U.S. 304), the Supreme Court rules that it is unconstitutional to execute mentally retarded individuals.

2005   In *Roper v. Simmons* (543 U.S. 551), the Supreme Court rules that the
execution of minors violates the Eighth Amendment prohibition of cruel
and unusual punishment.

On July 11, the Supreme Court grants a last-minute stay of execution to
Robin Lovitt, scheduled to be killed at 9 P.M. The Court does not offer a
reason for the stay, but Lovitt says that he would have been able to
prove his innocence had Virginia state officials not destroyed DNA
evidence from his case after his trial. In 2001, the Arlington County
Court ordered that all evidence in Lovitt's case be destroyed, despite
Virginia legislators passing a bill three weeks earlier ordering that all
biological evidence in capital cases be housed in the state forensics lab in
case future testing (DNA or otherwise) was needed.

In an address to the American Bar Association in Chicago, Supreme
Court justice John Paul Stevens offers harsh criticism of capital
punishment, saying he is disturbed by "serious flaws" in the system.

2006   In *Kansas v. Marsh* (548 U.S. 1037), the Supreme Court upholds
Kansas's death penalty statute and process of requiring juries to sentence
a defendant to death when faced with an equal weight of mitigating and
aggravating evidence. In the five-to-four decision, the Court overturns a
Kansas Supreme Court decision that found the practice unconstitutional
because it violated the cruel and unusual clause of the Eighth Amendment.

In *Oregon v. Guzek* (546 U.S. 517), the Supreme Court rules that the
Eighth Amendment to the U.S. Constitution does not grant defendants
in capital sentencing trials the right to introduce new evidence of their
innocence during the sentencing trial if the evidence was not introduced
in the original trial and, thus, states wanting to exclude such evidence
from the sentencing phase of a capital trial would be able to do so legally.

In *Holmes v. South Carolina* (547 U.S. 319), the Supreme Court vacates
the rape and murder conviction of Bobby Lee Holmes, who had been
denied the right in trial court to present evidence of a third party's guilt
because of the trial court judge's belief that the prosecutor's forensic
evidence was so strong that the defendant's evidence of a third party's
guilt would be insufficient to imply Holmes's innocence. The Supreme
Court's unanimous ruling holds that by excluding the evidence of a
third party's guilt, the trial court had violated Holmes's right to have a
meaningful opportunity to mount a complete defense.

In *House v. Bell* (126 S. Ct. 2064), the Supreme Court provides a
narrow but important precedent for defendants to use new DNA
forensic evidence that becomes available post-conviction to appeal their
capital convictions, even when claims of appeal have defaulted pursuant
to state law. Although the Court does not find that Paul Gregory House,
convicted of the 1985 rape and murder of Carolyn Muncey, is
conclusively exonerated, it concludes that any reasonable juror would
not be convinced of House's guilt beyond a reasonable doubt if provided
with all the conflicting testimony in the trial. Accordingly, the Court
rules that House meets the threshold standard set forth in the 1995 *Schlup
v. Delo* (513 U.S. 298) ruling and thus remands his case for consideration
of the constitutional claims that had defaulted due to state law.

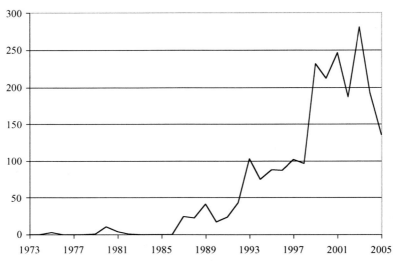

Figure 3.1. Annual number of exoneration stories as archived in Lexis-Nexis, 1973 to 2005.

attention to each of the 123 individuals who have been exonerated from death row between 1973 and 2006. Our data come from counts of all newspaper articles from major papers referring to issues of innocence in the case of an individual exoneree, as archived by Lexis-Nexis Academic Universe. These are not counts of news articles about the criminal cases themselves, but only of articles focused specifically on questions of innocence and possible exoneration. (That is, the article has to both mention the name of an individual exoneree and be related to his exoneration rather than his earlier trial and conviction or some other aspect of his case.)

In Chapter 2, we showed that the rate of exonerations has increased over time. We have argued that this increase is not alone responsible for the rise of the innocence frame; in fact, the causal arrows point in both directions. Here, we provide evidence for our main argument, showing that while the number of exonerations has increased, the amount of overall attention and the amount of attention per exoneree have increased much more dramatically.

We searched electronically for the names (including nicknames and spelling variants) of each of the individuals exonerated from death row since 1973, eliminating duplicate articles (because many mentioned more than one exoneree, therefore coming up twice in our search) and retaining only those related to the exoneration, not the original trial or crime. Figure 3.1 shows the total number of articles aggregated by year. Numbers were very low in the 1970s and 1980s (for the earlier years in the series,

Table 3.6. *Changes in exonerations, exoneration coverage, and coverage per exoneree, 1973 to 2005*

Time period	Average number of exonerations	Average number of stories per exoneree	Average number of exoneration stories
1973–1991	3	3	9
1992–1998	4	33	85
1999–2005	7	40	212

this may partly be the result of the lower numbers of newspapers indexed electronically in Lexis-Nexis; however, by the mid-1980s this is no longer a significant issue). From 1987 to 1992, the average number of stories about exonerations is below 30, but the numbers shoot up dramatically in two spurts. From 1993 to 1998 they average close to 100 stories per year, and from 1999 to 2004 more than double that number. The series reaches a peak in 2003 with 281 stories on exonerations; in 1990, before the innocence movement made the issue so prominent, there were just 17 stories. It is useful to look back at Figure 2.10; this graph shows the number of exonerations per year. There were five exonerations in 1990, and an average of six per year from 1998 to 2004. There is remarkably little relation between the steady but erratic numbers of exonerations documented in Figure 2.10 and the tremendous explosion of media attention to the issue we see in Figure 3.1.

Table 3.6 shows the real difference between the rise in exonerations and the rise in attention to these exonerations. Here, we have divided our data into three major time periods: 1973 to 1991 (the time before the emergence of the innocence frame), 1992 to 1998 (during the first swells of the innocence cascade), and 1999 to 2005 (with the innocence frame firmly established). For each time period, we have taken the average, by year, of each of three series: the number of exonerations, the number of stories per individual exoneree, and the total resulting number of Lexis-Nexis stories about these exonerations.

We see in Figure 2.10 that the number of exonerations increased over this time from an average of three per year in the early years to seven per year in the more recent period. This is an important increase, to be sure. But, because each individual exoneree has become more newsworthy, the yearly average of stories has multiplied almost twenty-four times. The average number of stories that an individual exonerated from death row today is likely to get is more than thirteen times the number that someone exonerated in the pre–innocence frame era could expect. Something changed, and it was not the facts. Exonerees are simply more newsworthy today than before the innocence movement began.

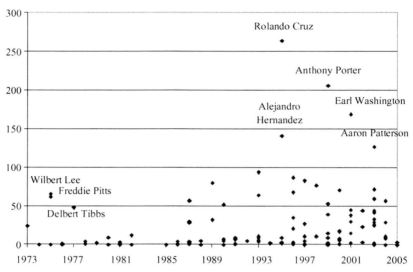

Figure 3.2. The number of stories about death row exonerees, plotted by date of exoneration, 1973 to 2005.

In Figure 3.2, we plot the total number of stories that each exoneree received across the entire time period, by the year in which he or she was exonerated. With a few outliers, we see a clear upward trend. Today's exonerated simply get more attention. The figure is remarkable in many ways, however. First of all, there are some "superstars." These are individuals whose exoneration received much more news coverage than average. Many of these became national symbols for flaws in the system, putting a human face on the issue. Second, there is a trend upward, more attention in general. However, perhaps most striking is the small amount of attention that most exonerees receive. As we mentioned, some of this could be because Lexis-Nexis was less complete in its coverage in the 1970s as most newspapers were not available electronically until the 1980s. Or it could be because some exonerees came from towns where the local papers are not included in the electronic database we used and larger papers did not cover the cases. But the analysis shows that almost half of the exonerees, fifty-two individuals, garnered fewer than five newspaper stories each. Almost half that number, twenty-two individuals, were the subject of not a single story whatsoever. In spite of increasing trends of coverage over time, glancing across the bottom part of the figure shows that there remain even today many cases in which exonerations occur without significant journalistic attention. This figure becomes especially interesting when we consider that each dot on the figure represents an individual who was released from death row; no person in this group is "more"

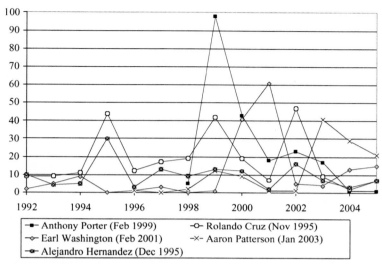

Figure 3.3. Yearly attention to the five exonerees with the most stories, plotted by date of exoneration, 1992 to 2005.

innocent than another. Some are much more newsworthy than others (usually a product of the circumstances of the crime), but the important point here is that as a group they are collectively much more newsworthy these days than they were in the period before the innocence movement took off.

Finally, in Figure 3.3, we map the over-time news attention paid to the five exonerees who netted the most overall attention: Rolando Cruz, Alejandro Hernandez, Anthony Porter, Earl Washington, and Aaron Patterson. The date of exoneration is in parentheses. Our purpose here is simply to get a sense of how news coverage for each person evolves over time. In each case, we see a spike in coverage when the individual is exonerated. In the case of Rolando Cruz, we see two additional spikes: the first in 1999 after the publication of a book about the Cruz–Hernandez case (*Victims of Justice* by Thomas Frisbie and Randy Garrett, published by Avon Books in 1998), and the second in 2002 when Cruz received a full pardon from Illinois governor George Ryan. Some of the superstar exonerees remain newsworthy for years after their exoneration. Others, as we see in Figure 3.2, never generate any media interest whatsoever. In any case, our analysis here shows a dramatic increase in total attention to exonerations across the nation's newspapers, a surge in attention to the issue that cannot be explained by any changes in the number of exonerations. On average, exonerations became newsworthy because of the innocence movement.

A SOCIAL MOVEMENT, A PUBLIC RELATIONS CAMPAIGN, OR WHAT?

How did the innocence frame take off? Some would point to individual factors, such as the actions of Governor George Ryan; the publication of Scheck, Neufeld, and Dwyer's book *Actual Innocence* in 2000; the presidential campaign between Al Gore and George W. Bush in 2000, which brought many national journalists to Texas and led to significant scrutiny of the candidates' views on the death penalty; the decline in violent crime starting in the 1990s; or other factors. In our view, it is impossible to pinpoint any single cause of these events; indeed it is unimportant to do so. Rather, in a positive-feedback system such as the one we have described, each event makes the next event more likely. No single event can be said to be the one that caused the others; they all reciprocally have influenced one another, each reinforcing the trend toward greater attention to questions of innocence.

Certainly the university-based innocence projects we have described here played an important role, especially in laying the groundwork for later increases in attention. Yet the factors behind the innocence frame are many and varied. In addition to the continued work of university-based innocence projects, the last two decades have witnessed Governor Ryan's moratorium, federal lobbying efforts to pass the Innocence Protection Act, the release of the study by the Liebman group and Columbia University on the rate of errors in capital cases (published and cited in Chapter 2 as Liebman et al. 2002, but initially released in 2000 to considerable media attention), and significant efforts by public relations professionals to take advantage of these factors and to keep them in the public eye.

In her book on the media framing of police violence, Regina Lawrence argues that high-profile media coverage of unplanned or "accidental" events – such as sex scandals, government corruption, and police brutality – provides a special opportunity for reframing (2000). In particular, Lawrence says, event-driven shifts in problem definition often may lead to a new dominant frame that favors the minority or nonofficial voices, such as victims of police brutality or, for that matter, a broken death penalty system. From this perspective, the unexpected and scandalous nature of so many of the events in and around the death penalty debate in the last two decades (police brutality, dry labbing and false evidence testimony, prosecutorial misconduct, and of course the wrongful convictions themselves) may have served to propel the innocence frame to the forefront of public attention. So not only has the death penalty debate experienced a surge of reciprocally influential events, but most of these events are of the particular variety that lend themselves toward heightened media attention and a redefinition of the problem at hand.

And, as we will see in Chapter 4, heightened media attention and the redefinition of the death penalty debate are exactly what have occurred; the innocence frame has proven highly successful. On the wave of events described above, the year 2000 saw unprecedented levels of media coverage of the death penalty debate, and as of 2005, media attention remains high. But this was no mere public relations campaign. Rather, it was the confluence of numerous interacting and self-reinforcing events and trends. We can say with some confidence that the conditions that made this surge of attention to innocence possible in the late 1990s and early 2000s began at least fifteen years before, with little initial success, on college campuses and in law firms around the country. In later years, with the help of professionals in New York and Washington and the combined reinforcing influence of high-profile events – including the advance of DNA technology, police and crime lab scandals, and a growing tally of exonerations – national attention has been focused on this issue as never before.

CONCLUSION

What began as a set of isolated hands-on journalism and law school projects with some support from legal foundations and individual activists blossomed in the 1990s to be a national movement generating more and more examples of errors of justice. This was a most unlikely social movement and indeed was more focused within a certain community of activists and student legal clinics than within a broad community of activists, as in the civil rights movement for example. There were no national protests, no mass demonstrations (though there were a few small ones in individual states). What began in the 1980s with these campus-based projects blossomed after some initial successes into a national movement in the 1990s. Each successful project led to its duplication elsewhere. Successful demonstration of innocence by students led lawmakers and governors to take the issue seriously. Official investigations into errors of justice led to further news coverage. News coverage affected public thinking. Investigations continued, often with more funding and from a greater number of sources. Individual exonerees got more newspaper coverage. In the end, we see the innocence movement as a self-reinforcing process that transformed the debate. In Chapter 4, we move on to assess how it affected the terms of the debate.

4 THE SHIFTING TERMS OF DEBATE

S INCE THE MID-1990S, dramatic shifts have occurred in how Americans discuss the death penalty. Public debate on this topic has never been completely monolithic, of course. Like any complex issue, the death penalty involves multiple dimensions of evaluation – constitutional ramifications, how the penalty is administered, how equal application of the law may be ensured, what crimes merit the death penalty, and what kinds of mitigating circumstances point against it – debate around the death penalty involves all these questions and more. In this and the following chapter, we review in detail the nature of media coverage of the death penalty since 1960. Our evidence demonstrates that the new "innocence" frame is the single most powerful frame and the one with the greatest potential impact ever to enter the debate. We focus in this chapter on explaining our data collection and coding processes and on describing the shifting nature of the debate as reflected in the *New York Times*. The chapter demonstrates huge changes in how the debate has been constructed and how the topics of attention have shifted over time. We also show that these characteristics are not peculiar to the one newspaper that is our main focus by comparing the *Times* with ten other news outlets. In the Chapter 5, we assess the strength and power of the innocence frame, comparing it statistically to other powerful frames that have existed and pointing out how many of the individual component arguments that together create the innocence frame are not themselves new to the debate. Rather than being constructed de novo, the arguments that together constitute the innocence frame have long been present but never have they had the resonance or power that they have today, because in the past they were not used together in the same way as they have been since the rise of the innocence frame.

DOCUMENTING THE SHIFTING FOCI OF DEBATE

We seek to trace the evolution of public debate surrounding the death penalty as systematically and as completely as possible. To do this, we analyze all coverage of the issue in the nation's leading newspaper, and we construct a list of every distinct argument made for or against the death penalty over time. In this way, we trace the shifting foci of attention: Does media coverage at some points focus exclusively on discussions of morality, later to focus on complex constitutional or legal questions? Is there a constant mix, with no particular theme dominating the others? Exactly what is the nature of public discussion of the issue at any point in time, as indicated by media coverage? Is discussion predominantly in favor, against, or neutral with regard to the death penalty? Do any trends in the critical or approving tone of coverage relate to shifts in attention from one aspect of the issue to another? If there are no clear trends here, then we cannot speak of the rise of the innocence frame, and we could not expect any significant impact on either the legal system, public debate generally, or public opinion. It is important to get these measurement issues right so that we can be sure that a shift in the public debate really has occurred.

We analyzed every article listed in the *New York Times Index* under the heading *capital punishment* between 1960 and 2005 (3,939 abstracts in all). We chose the *Times* not because we believe it has a direct impact on public opinion or courtroom behavior, but simply because it is the single best source of information available. As a national newspaper, it has a wider range of coverage than most others (though of course it has significant coverage of "hometown" issues relating to events in New York City as well as in New York and neighboring states). Several scholars have looked at the relationship between the *Times* and other sources, and there are substantial links; that is, in terms of amount of coverage, when one major newspaper covers a story, so do many other papers (see Althaus et al. 2001; Soroka 2002; Woolley 2000). Our interest is not so much exactly what the paper is reporting, however, but in how this reporting changes over time. Are there themes today that were once absent? Have previously important elements of capital punishment reporting fallen away over time? Even if the *Times* may differ from any other particular newspaper we might have chosen, we have no reason to expect that the trends we observe would be substantially different over time if we had looked at different papers (and we will verify this later). It stands to reason, for example, that the *Times* might differ from other papers in terms of levels of coverage and editorial tone. Even without considering different editorial stances or journalistic biases, the *Miami Herald* or the *Houston Chronicle* might be expected to show more pro–death penalty coverage simply because there are so many executions in those states compared with New York and its surrounding states. By itself, state sanctioning of the death penalty might lead to different levels of coverage and, most likely, to a higher percentage of stories that we would code as pro–death penalty in tone. Contrary to these expectations, however, we find well-matched coverage of the anti–death penalty innocence frame across major national papers, even the *Houston Chronicle*. In any case, we are less interested in absolute levels of coverage than in changes over time in the level of coverage and the topics of discussion. If social discussion, legal debate, constitutional arguments, and political responses to the death penalty have changed over time, this should be reflected in the *Times* as in any other news outlet. As we will discuss at the end of this chapter, we have also compared the amount of *Times* death penalty attention to attention by other major newspapers and found remarkable correspondence. This finding holds true, first, when comparing the *Times* to the *Readers' Guide to Periodical Literature*. And second, we have compared the *Times* coverage of the innocence frame with coverage of the innocence frame in other major papers. Again in this case, we have found the *Times* to track closely with alternate papers, including the *Houston Chronicle*, thus validating the *Times* as a representative source for our purposes.

Rather than perform a full-text search of *Times* articles using a computer-based search engine, we used the printed annual volumes of the index to the newspaper. Trained indexers at the *Times* assign each published article to one of several hundred distinct subject categories, one of which is "capital punishment." Not all articles dealing with the issue are included here – there are certainly individual court cases in which there is some possibility of capital punishment discussed; legislative debates that cover many issues, including capital punishment; and speeches by politicians or political leaders that mention the topic among others – none of those would necessarily be included here. By using the subject categorizations in the *New York Times Index* as opposed to an electronic search based on key words, we were actually able to retrieve a more appropriate set of articles. Electronic key word searches on *capital punishment, death penalty*, and word variants do not retrieve the entire set of abstracts that appear in the *Index*; such searches also yield high numbers of irrelevant or only marginally relevant hits. What is included in our database is every article in which the *primary focus* is capital punishment. This is exactly what we want.

Finally, we coded the abstracts appearing in the *Index*, not the full text of the articles themselves. Abstracts are typically just a few sentences long and summarize the main points of the article. Of course, much information is lost in this process; analysis of the full text would undoubtedly yield a richer knowledge of what was discussed. On the other hand, the shorter abstract included in the *Index* creates a high threshold of importance; only the most essential ideas of the article are included. This means that our analysis is automatically limited only to the most important themes. A full text search would have required that we distinguish somehow between those elements of the article that were most central compared with those that were mentioned in passing, for example. By using the *Index*, then, we limit our focus only to those articles whose central focus is capital punishment, and by using only the abstracts we know that we are analyzing only those themes that were the most important elements of each story. (Of course, limiting our work in this way made the project much more feasible as well, allowing us to cover more than forty-five years of history without sampling.)

With copies of the *Index* abstracts in hand, we designed a database to record systematically what was included in each story. Two coders worked in parallel to read each abstract and code it according to the coding procedures described briefly in this chapter and more fully in Appendix A.[1] These coders met regularly together and with the senior author to ensure they were in agreement on any marginal cases, and both coders coded a number of cases to test reliability. Most of the variables included were purely factual (e.g., the date of the story), and for those that required substantial judgment, we tested reliability by having each coder code a sample of cases without seeing how the other had coded them. Agreement was always over 90 percent.

Much of the information we gathered was purely descriptive: the date of the story, the article type (i.e., news, editorial, op-ed, or letter to the editor), and whether the article mentioned any of the following things – characteristics of the victim (e.g., victim is police officer, child, woman, or elderly), characteristics of the defendant (e.g., defendant is terrorist, racial minority, juvenile, mentally handicapped, or suffered abuse as child), mode of execution (e.g., electric chair, lethal injection, or firing squad), type of crime committed, violent or gruesome nature of crime committed, and legislative action. These variables were straightforward, as the coders' instructions were simply to indicate whether the item was mentioned. We designed a data entry form so that the coders merely checked a box for each item if it was mentioned. A single abstract could be coded in many ways depending on how many relevant elements were mentioned.

We were interested as well in the overall tone of the article, of course. For each article, the coders noted whether it had an overall pro– or anti– death penalty orientation. This tone measure did not necessarily refer to any editorial stance by the journalist or the *Times*, but rather to whether the story focused on actions or opinions that would tend toward or against the application of the penalty. So a story about a defendant or an inmate losing an appeal of habeas corpus would be coded pro–death penalty; a story about a legislative debate to enact a moratorium on death sentences would be coded anti–death penalty. Stories including mentions of both anti– and pro–death penalty arguments were coded neutral if they were perfectly balanced or pro– or anti–death penalty if the majority of the arguments or actions reported tended in one way. This coding allowed us to summarize the overall tone of each article. Thirty-five percent of the stories were coded pro–; 44 percent anti–, and 21 percent neutral/not codeable.

The most important element of our coding was in constructing an exhaustive list of sixty-five possible arguments about the death penalty, divided for their own part into pro–, anti–, and neutral arguments.[2] These sixty-five arguments constitute the building blocks of framing as we understand it. In the political science literature on framing, scholars have used various techniques to study how an issue, or a particular text addressing that issue, is framed. Generally, scholars agree on more or less the same definition of framing: the presentation or discussion of an issue from a particular viewpoint to the exclusion of alternate viewpoints. Most scholars also agree that framing falls into the "you know it when you see it" category of phenomena. But the process of identifying and recording frames for the sake of research is more difficult, and over time researchers have developed a number of different methods to accomplish this task. Some have used qualitative analyses, focusing on informal narratives to describe how framing of an issue has changed over time (Carroll and Ratner 1999; Elder and Cobb 1983; Hancock 2004; Kingdon 1984; Pollock 1994; Riker 1982; Sparks 2003). Others have used quantitative approaches, typically devising a coding system to count attention to the arguments and dimensions of a given debate (Baumgartner 1989; Kellstedt 2000; Terkildsen and Damore 1999; Terkildsen and Schnell 1997) to a reference category – a "framework" – from which to view an issue. So, for example, Baumgartner and Jones (1993) counted articles on issues such as nuclear power, pesticides, and drug abuse. They either coded the articles by their tone (e.g., positive or negative toward the industry in question) or focused on a small number of predefined underlying dimensions (e.g., education and treatment versus enforcement and punishment in the area of drug abuse). In general, these dimensions are small in number and are based around commonly understood core concepts such as morality, economic issues, and so forth. This method allows researchers to trace which frames are dominant at various periods and, thus, to show how overall attention is distributed differently among dimensions at different times. We build on these approaches here. And although our primary purpose is to describe the methods used in our analysis of the *New York Times* death penalty coverage, we encourage the reader to consider our approach to the study of framing as a more generic method that could be employed in the study of any other issue debate.

We understand framing to be a complex process, but one that nonetheless may be identified, broken down into component parts, and analyzed. We treat specific arguments that may be made about an issue – for, against, or in neutral reference to a particular policy stance – as the smallest units of framing. And we hold that these arguments fall naturally into broader dimensions of debate, such as cost or morality. "Framing" may occur through use of a single argument, a cluster of arguments within a single dimension, or even a cluster of arguments across different dimensions (we discuss this last option in detail in Chapter 5). This is why we coded each story at such a detailed level, with sixty-five specific arguments, and why we allowed each story to be coded for as many arguments as were mentioned.

The sixty-five exhaustive arguments we developed were clustered within seven dimensions: efficacy, morality, cost, constitutionality, fairness, mode of execution, and international issues. We based these predefined dimensions and component arguments on our understanding of the issue gained from reading books, scholarly articles, and newspaper stories on the topic and also from conversations with activists in the area. We attempted to be systematic and complete. Within a single dimension, such as efficacy, numerous more specific arguments may coexist, and these may be either complementary (the death penalty deters potential criminals; the death penalty incapacitates criminals from striking again), or contradictory (deterrence effects are strong; deterrence effects are weak). Each general dimension may consist of many individual arguments, and each may contain arguments both in favor of and in opposition to the death penalty. For example, in the case of deterrence, there may be arguments or assertions that it deters crime, that it does not, or that there is no agreement or not enough evidence to reach a conclusion. Table 4.1 provides a list of all sixty-five arguments we identified across the seven major dimensions of debate. The table also indicates the number of times we recorded the use of each argument. Recall that each story could be coded multiple times if it mentioned multiple arguments.

Table 4.1 is long, but easy to read. Listed first are arguments about efficacy; 217 stories. Of these, 26 are general efficacy discussions that are neither pro– nor anti–death penalty in tone; we coded these as argument 100: general efficacy. Argument numbers 101 to 109 are particular pro–death penalty arguments, as shown: the death penalty deters crime (argument 101, made 39 times), it incapacitates criminals, alternative sentences are not effective, and other pro–death penalty arguments. Argument numbers 110 to 119 are anti–death penalty arguments along the same theme of efficacy, as shown. For each of the seven major dimensions (efficacy, morality, fairness, constitutionality, cost, mode, international, and other), we show the individual arguments in support of and in opposition to the death penalty and how many times each argument is made. Reading the table with attention to the frequencies reported gives a sense of what are the most common arguments in the debate; for those familiar with the issue, there should be few surprises. Each dimension

Table 4.1. *An exhaustive list of arguments used across all 3,939 abstracts of New York Times stories on capital punishment, 1960 to 2005*

Pro–death penalty arguments	Anti–death penalty arguments
Efficacy (217 total stories) 100. *General* (26)	
101. Deters crime (39)	110. Does not deter crime (68)
102. Incapacitates criminals (3)	111. Alternate systems (e.g., life without parole) more effective (62)
103. Alternative systems, e.g., life without parole, less effective (8)	119. Other anti–death penalty efficacy arguments (14)
109. Other pro–death penalty efficacy arguments (12)	
Morality (622 total stories) 200. *General* (38)	
201. Retribution; "eye for an eye" (10)	210. Killing/vengeance is wrong, even when performed by the state (68)
202. Victim's family deserves justice/vengeance (8)	211. Victim's family is opposed to death penalty (8)
203. Some crimes are so heinous, they warrant the death penalty (300)	219. Other anti–death penalty moral arguments (198)
209. Other pro–death penalty moral arguments (36)	
Fairness (1,099 total stories) 300. *General* (61)	
301. Death penalty proceedings are fair (22)	310. Defendants receive inadequate legal representation (106)
302. Proceedings are in fact too lenient; appeals should be abbreviated (60)	311. Death penalty is applied in arbitrary/capricious nature (37)
303. Wrongful conviction concerns are overstated (5)	312a. Proceedings are racist (143)
304. Vulnerable populations, e.g., juveniles, mentally handicapped, should not receive blanket immunity from death penalty (23)	312b. Proceedings are classist (32)
309. Other pro–death penalty fairness arguments (115)	312c. Capital punishment unfair to other demographic groups, e.g., defendants in Texas (23)
	313a. Unfair to execute vulnerable populations, e.g., juveniles, mentally handicapped (152)

313b. Mitigating factors, e.g., defendant's childhood abuse, are not given proper consideration in capital cases (28)

314. Unfair for system to sentence an individual to death automatically without taking particular circumstances into account (23)

315. Many juries would not impose death penalty if alternate system, e.g., life without parole, was available (3)

316. Defendants denied sufficient access to evidence, e.g., DNA (89)

317. Innocence/wrongful conviction; human-run system cannot avoid making some mistakes (219)

318. System is broken; moratorium should be established, at least until errors are reduced or eliminated (170)

319. Other anti–death penalty fairness arguments (250)

410. Death penalty constitutes cruel and unusual punishment (66)

411. Proceedings violate rights of due process and equal protection (27)

412. Popular support/sovereignty; the death penalty goes against the will of the people (75)

413. States should maintain jurisdiction over capital punishment decisions; states should not be forced to use death penalty (5)

Constitutionality/popular control (1,467 total stories) 400. *General* (213)

401. Death penalty does not constitute cruel and unusual punishment (31)

402. Proceedings do not violate rights of due process and equal protection (29)

403. Popular support/sovereignty; the death penalty is the will of the people (82)

404. States should maintain jurisdiction over capital punishment decisions; states should be allowed to enforce death penalty (16)

(continued)

Table 4.1 *(continued)*

Pro–death penalty arguments	Anti–death penalty arguments
405. Federal government should maintain jurisdiction over capital punishment decisions; government should be allowed to impose federal death penalty even in non–death penalty states (6)	414. Federal government should maintain jurisdiction over capital punishment decisions; government should be allowed to overrule state-level death sentences (3)
409. Other pro–death penalty constitutionality and popular control arguments (461)	419. Other anti–death penalty constitutionality and popular control arguments (671)
500. General (5)	
Cost (20 total stories)	
502. Life imprisonment is more expensive than capital punishment (2)	510. The capital punishment system is not worth the high costs (8)
509. Other pro–death penalty cost arguments (1)	519. Other anti–death penalty cost arguments (4)
600. General (124)	
Mode of Execution (241 total stories)	
601. Particular mode of execution, e.g., lethal injection, electric chair, gas chamber, is acceptable/humane/just (26)	610. Particular mode of execution, e.g., lethal injection, electric chair, gas chamber, is unacceptable/inhumane/unjust (90)
609. Other pro–death penalty mode of execution arguments (4)	619. Other anti–death penalty mode of execution arguments (7)
700. General (15)	
International (116 total stories)	
709. Other pro–death penalty international arguments (5)	710. Other countries denounce death penalty; call on U.S. to establish moratorium (64)
	711. Complications with extradition due to death penalty (3)
	712. U.S. should not execute foreign nationals (29)
	719. Other anti–death penalty international arguments (23)
900. General (4)	
Other (4)	

Note: The table shows each of the 65 arguments grouped by topic and tone. Numbers in parentheses indicate the number of *New York Times* stories in which the code in question was used from 1960 to 2005. We coded a total of 3,939 stories, and each story could include multiple arguments; thus the individual argument story counts usually sum to more than the total story count for each overarching dimension. In all, we identified a total of 4,543 arguments, as listed above.

includes a −oo code (for neutral discussions) and a −9 code (for "other" and miscellaneous arguments). The reader can see that some of the dimensions have more individual arguments than others, and they are not all completely balanced. For example, in the general area of fairness, we identified five pro–death penalty arguments (the system is fair, the system is too lenient, appeals should be abbreviated, etc.), but we identified thirteen different arguments in opposition to the death penalty. For each of these arguments, there could theoretically have been a directly opposed argument, but these were never made (and we do not list any arguments here that were never observed, though our initial coding scheme allowed for them). So the imbalance is a finding, not something imposed on the data by our coding procedures. International comparisons also are quite unbalanced, with few pro–death penalty arguments in this area. On the other hand, there are directly contradicting and parallel arguments within the areas of efficacy, constitutionality, cost, and mode of execution, and in these areas we have roughly similar if not exactly identical numbers of arguments pro– and anti–. The note at the bottom of the table indicates that we identified 4,543 arguments in total across all the stories we read; an average of about 1.25 arguments per story. Most stories have just one.

The painstaking and detailed approach we have taken has many advantages. Each of the arguments laid out in Table 4.1 is defined in a consistent manner over time. That is, no arguments are defined in historically or contextually specific terms. For example, there is no argument for "Timothy McVeigh" or any other single defendant. No codes are created for any items that are unique historically or limited to only a single historic period. Rather, they are all listed in terms of the underlying question that they raise, and a different code is listed for each distinct argument made. In this way, we can compare the relative prevalence of different arguments over time. If we see the use of certain arguments rising or falling over time, we know that these are real trends, not artifacts forced on the data by our own coding processes. Each argument, at least in theory, could have been made at any point during the period from 1960 onward.

The second and most important benefit of our detailed approach is that it allows us to observe, rather than assert, the degree to which any given argument tends to be used in concert with others and the degree to which the topics of attention are associated with either pro– or anti–death penalty conclusions. The literature on framing and strategic advocacy suggests that proponents and opponents may well prefer to focus attention on different topics, justifying their conclusions not through direct refutation of a given argument, but by changing the subject to a topic that is more to their benefit. In other work, we have suggested that the innocence frame is more effective in influencing individual's opinions than frames that reinforce the moral dimension (Dardis et al. 2007). We can directly assess the hypothesis that proponents and opponents work to focus attention on different dimensions of the debate, and we do so in this chapter.

We described above the reasons for our decision to use the *New York Times Index* rather than the full text of the stories for our study. Is there sufficient information in these abstracts to allow the types of inferences we seek to make? Here are four sample abstracts:

1. In the death penalty cases decided a few days ago, the Supreme Court was asked whether, at the levels of civilization America had achieved by 1976, the taking of a human life was not so harsh and cruel as to be an impermissible punishment for the state to inflict. After reflecting on the judgments of a number of state legislatures, the Court decided that under the right circumstances, the death penalty does not violate the Constitution. (July 15, 1976)
2. For those who believe in capital punishment, Lemuel Smith seemed the perfect person for whom to reactivate New York's electric chair. Already serving long prison sentences for murder, he was convicted of savagely killing Donna Payant, a guard at Green Haven, and dumping her mutilated body in the prison trash. Could some mitigating circumstance possibly argue against his execution? (July 5, 1984)
3. When Governor George Ryan of Illinois called last month for a moratorium on executions in his state, he focused on the fact that 12 men on death row had recently been proven innocent. Sentencing an innocent person to death was, the governor said, "shameful," but he said little about how the legal representation these inmates had received at trial may have contributed to justice gone wrong. (February 13, 2000)
4. State of Missouri will execute 26-year-old Antonio Richardson, a mentally retarded man, despite pleas for clemency from the mother of his two victims; he was 16 years old in 1991, when he murdered 20-year-old Julie Kerry and her 19-year-old sister Robin. (March 6, 2001)

Table 4.2 shows how we coded information from the four stories.

As these examples show, the abstracts contain enough information to gauge the main thrust of the story. Most of the coding is completely straightforward, noting simply whether certain factors, such as characteristics of the victim or defendant, are mentioned or not. The tone of the story is a subjective evaluation, but as these examples show, it is usually very clear. In the case of abstracts that report a specific action, such as a court ruling or a state's impending execution, the tone is based on the directionality of that action, not on any effort to ascertain irony or the viewpoint of the journalist or writer. Any story reporting on actions favorable to a defendant is coded anti–death penalty. Any story about an

Table 4.2. *Example of coding for four* New York Times *abstracts*

Codes received	Story 1	Story 2	Story 3	Story 4
Type of story	News	News	News	News
Victim characteristic(s)	–	Female	–	Female
		Police officer/guard		Multiple
				Victim's family
Defendant characteristic(s)	–	–	–	Mentally handicapped
	–	–	–	Juvenile
Mode of execution specified?	No	Yes	No	No
Crime specified?	No	Yes	No	No
Heinousness specified?	No	Yes	No	No
Legislative action?	Yes	No	No	No
Tone	Pro–death penalty	Neutral	Anti–death penalty	Pro–death penalty
Argument(s)	401: not cruel & unusual	313b: mitigating circumstances	317: innocence	211: victim's family opposed
	–	–	310: inadequate representation	–

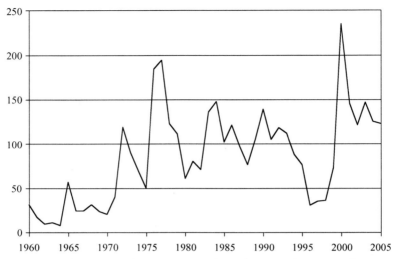

Figure 4.1. The number of stories on capital punishment in the *New York Times Index*, 1960 to 2005.

action making the death penalty more likely to be applied, or an opinion supporting this, is coded pro–death penalty. So the third abstract example is coded as anti–death penalty, not only because the person being quoted is critical of the death penalty but because of the moratorium decision that was decidedly anti–death penalty in nature. The fourth example, however, is coded as pro–death penalty because, despite the report of pleas for clemency from the victims' mother, the final action in this case is pro–death penalty in nature, namely, Missouri will indeed execute Antonio Richardson. Our list of sixty-five arguments is of course more complicated, but as we noted, we achieved over 90 percent agreement when we had two coders code the same stories without seeing each other's work.

In sum, we have systematically coded almost 4,000 abstracts covering forty-six years of history. If there are important trends in how capital punishment issues have been discussed or debated in American society over this time, our analysis should reveal it. If not, our data should reflect this null finding as well. In fact, we find that there have been important shifts in the nature of news coverage of the issue, and we describe these shifts in the next section.

THE AMOUNT AND TONE OF ATTENTION

We begin with a simple presentation of how overall attention to the death penalty has changed over time. Figure 4.1 shows the number of *New York Times Index* abstracts relating to capital punishment from 1960 to 2005.

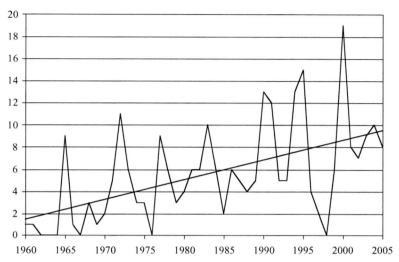

Figure 4.2. Front-page stories on capital punishment in the *New York Times Index*, 1960 to 2005.

A total of 3,939 stories appeared during this time, with substantial peaks of coverage in 1976 to 1977, just after the Supreme Court reinstated the death penalty after the 1972 decision invalidating state capital punishment laws, and then again in 2000. During these two periods, the newspaper carried more than 150 articles per year: more than one story every other day. As the figure makes clear, the issue emerged onto the media agenda in the 1970s; there was little coverage, less than one article per week, before 1972. Coverage has grown substantially in recent years, even though there has been no monumental Supreme Court decision such as those of 1972 and 1976. Rather, more recent coverage, especially that peaking in the unprecedented levels of coverage in 2000, related to the size of the death row population and various challenges to the system based on juvenile offenders, the mentally handicapped, and the concept of "innocence" as we have already discussed.

Not only has the total amount of attention to the death penalty grown over time, but the issue has become more important as well. Figure 4.2 shows the number of stories about the death penalty that appeared on the front page, with a linear trend line imposed on the figure. Remember that although the overall size of the paper may have changed over time (in fact, it was much bigger in the mid-1970s than in earlier or later years; see Baumgartner and Jones 1993, 265), the front page of today's *New York Times* is precisely as big as it was in 1960 and in every year in between. So when we see that there was just one front-page story in 1960, two in 1970, four in 1980, eight in 1990, and nineteen in 2000, this means something. Although these numbers fluctuate considerably around the trend line,

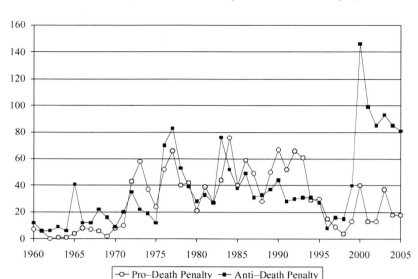

Figure 4.3. Pro– and anti–death penalty stories in the *New York Times Index*, 1960 to 2005.

this figure leaves no doubt that the death penalty has become increasingly prominent on the public agenda, and attention has been especially strong since the late 1990s.

The tone of coverage of the death penalty has also changed dramatically over time. There are many ways to assess this, but we start in Figure 4.3 by showing the simple counts of how many pro– and anti–death penalty articles appeared each year, according to our coding of each abstract's tone.

The figure shows separate lines for pro– and anti–death penalty stories; typically these rise and fall together. Periods of increased attention typically feature increases in both pro– and anti–death penalty stories. One story might mention trial events that led to a successful appeal of a sentence, whereas another may mention an execution taking place or being scheduled. If media attention is to have a strong impact on public response to the issue, then we would want to know the relative mix of stories. Many stories, but an even balance between pro– and anti–death penalty tone, would indicate a broad mix of coverage with no substantial bias or overall net expected effect on public opinion. On the other hand, many stories focusing on one side of the debate without corresponding stories on the other side would reflect processes that are heavily biased toward one direction or the other. Such periods would reflect important social changes.

Although the two series presented in Figure 4.3 are generally similar, there are some important differences between them. The overall balance

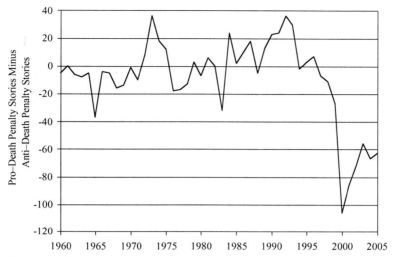

Figure 4.4. The net tone of *New York Times Index* coverage, 1960 to 2005.

of stories can most simply be assessed by taking the difference of the two series from Figure 4.3. Positive values, then, represent a surplus of pro–death penalty stories, just as negative values indicate a surplus of anti–death penalty stories. Figure 4.4 shows the "net tone" of *New York Times* coverage: the number of pro–minus the number of anti–death penalty stories.

Figure 4.4 makes several things clear. First, coverage tends to be relatively balanced. That is, as we see in Figure 4.3, positive articles tend to be counterbalanced by negative articles, so the net tone variable typically fluctuates within a relatively narrow range centering around zero. It is rare, in fact, for the values to exceed twenty in either direction. Second, there nonetheless are important trends. And third, the period around 2000 was the most unbalanced in history, by a large margin. This imbalance, unprecedented by historical standards, continues to the end of the series.

A net anti–death penalty tendency was apparent in news coverage of capital punishment leading up to the ban on executions in 1972. During the period of the constitutional moratorium (1972 to 1976), a substantial increase in pro–death penalty coverage followed; much of this was reporting of state legislative efforts to craft new capital laws that would pass constitutional muster. In the ensuing period, from approximately 1978 to 1993, a steady if erratic trend is apparent toward increased pro–death penalty reporting, reflecting increased use of capital punishment and greater numbers of death sentences. By 1993, the imbalance toward pro–death penalty abstracts appearing in the paper was as high as it had ever been, slightly higher even than in 1973, when states were just revising their laws to reinstate the penalty after they were overturned in 1972. This trend reverses again, and very dramatically, after the 1993 peak. From 1993 onward, a dramatic shift began to take place so that by 1997 there was a net predominance of negative abstracts. By 2000, after this trend had continued, a barrage of anti–death penalty news was consistently in the press. Coverage was the most unbalanced in history. In fewer then 10 years, we had moved from one historic imbalance in public discussion to its exact opposite. The second one, in 2000, was by far the larger and was the result of the rise of the innocence frame.

Again, our use of the overall tone of the stories is based not on journalistic preference or editorial stance of the newspaper. Any article reporting on activities that would lead toward the application of a death sentence is coded pro–death penalty; any story reporting activities that would tend against an execution is coded anti–death penalty. We were able to code the vast majority of the articles present in the paper in one direction or another (some were coded neutral/uncodeable). So the trends we observe in Figure 4.4 are not solely the result of journalistic traditions of "balance" or covering both sides of any issue. Such a tendency would make each individual story balanced, but what we observe in Figures 4.3 and 4.4 are not individual stories, rather their sum over twelve months. Even though the editorial stance of the *Times* was anti–capital punishment throughout this period, and it can safely be assumed that most of its writers shared this perspective on the issue, a great many stories appeared that were pro–death penalty, and in some periods of history, notably in the 1970s and again in the 1990s, a substantial preponderance of the stories appearing each year were coded pro–death penalty. Clearly, these things do not necessarily reflect any individual preference by the journalists, but are reflections of the activities relating to the issue "out there" in the legal community, in political circles, and in society. Note also that our measure of net tone relates not to any percentages, but to the absolute numbers of stories appearing. Where the coverage is balanced, reflecting equal numbers of pro– and anti–death penalty stories, this reflects a range of activities and should not be expected to have a substantial effect on public opinion or policy outcomes. Where coverage is substantially off balance, this reflects larger numbers of reports of activities in one direction or the other. We can use the net tone of coverage, then, as a useful indicator of the state of public discussion. Where it is substantially off balance, we expect that it will indeed have an impact on policy outcomes and public opinion.

There are many reasons for the shifts in tone that we have documented here, and these shifts have many impacts. We explore the impacts of changing tone in later chapters; in the next sections, we assess how the shifting tone of coverage came about. It was not simply a matter of shifting

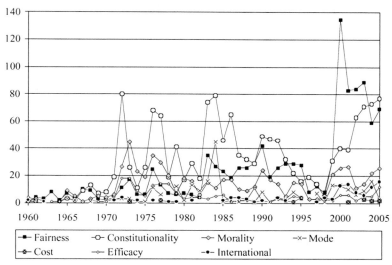

Figure 4.5. Topics of attention in the *New York Times Index*, 1960 to 2005.

tone; rather, the topics of attention – the seven main dimensions and their component arguments – determine the tone.

THE TOPICS OF ATTENTION

Shifting attention from one topic to another explains the variation in the net tone of attention that we have just documented. Some topics are relatively neutral or balanced, but most carry with them an almost automatic bias. When attention focuses on the idea of flaws in the system, for example, this is almost always bad news for supporters of the death penalty. Similarly, when attention focuses on the vicious nature of some horrible crime, the stories are overwhelmingly pro–death penalty. Here we explore the linkage between topic and tone.

As described earlier in this chapter, we coded each abstract for the presence of the comprehensive list we developed of sixty-five different arguments, clustered into seven major dimensions. Figure 4.5 shows the number of abstracts falling into each of these major topics over time.

Issues of constitutionality are the single most common theme in *New York Times* coverage over most of this period; 1,467 articles mentioned discussions of this type, with peaks coming in 1972, 1976 and the years following that, in the mid- to late 1980s, and finally in the early twenty-first century as the constitutionality of capital punishment for juveniles

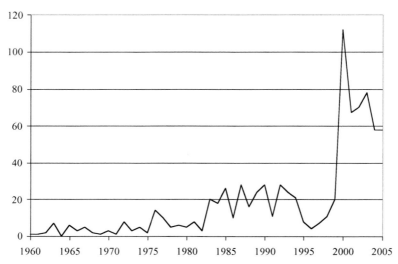

Figure 4.6. The number of stories mentioning innocence, evidence, flaws in the system, or defendant characteristics, 1960 to 2005.

and the mentally handicapped became important controversies. Morality issues have also been prominent over time, with a total of 622 abstracts focusing on these. Discussion of morality has been prominent since 1972, especially from 1972 to 1978, when the constitutionality of the entire death penalty was hotly debated. Since then, moral issues have never completely disappeared from the media agenda, but they have been significantly less prevalent. The fairness dimension (including arguments of innocence, evidence, and flaws in the system) was not prominent before the 1980s but began growing in 1983. It reached a peak in 2000, with 135 abstracts in that year alone; over the entire period, there were 1,099 abstracts with innocence/fairness arguments. Many abstracts fit into other categories focusing on international comparisons, efficacy (whether the penalty serves as a deterrent or not, for example), cost, mode of execution, or "other" topics (miscellaneous mentions of various particularities of the cases or those that otherwise do not fit into any particular theme).

In general, we can see from Figure 4.5 that constitutionality is a perennial theme, that morality has been an important theme as well, and that innocence/fairness has shown a dramatic increase from virtually no coverage before the 1980s to constituting more than half of the entire amount of coverage annually in many recent years. We can see this trend in greater detail in Figure 4.6, which delves deeper into the dramatic rise of the innocence question.

Figure 4.6 shows the number of abstracts each year presenting any of the following: 1) claims of innocence, 2) problems relating to evidence used in the trial, 3) problems or imperfections in the justice system, or 4) characteristics of the defendant. This cluster of issues, ranging from simple humanization of the defendant to demonstrations of actual innocence through exonerations, has always been present, as the figure shows. However, none of these issues was a prominent aspect of media coverage of the death penalty until they collectively surged to unprecedented levels of coverage in 2000. From 1960 to the mid-1980s, there was trivial coverage of these questions, typically fewer than ten articles even mentioning them (note that this includes even any mention of the characteristics of the defendant in the trial; abstracts at that time were much more likely to discuss the victim than the defendant). Coverage grew from the 1980s to the 1990s but rocketed to new levels in 2000.

Figure 4.6 demonstrates how media attention to the question of innocence has been tremendously punctuated, but in Chapter 2 we show that the underlying process (i.e., the rate of exonerations) has been more incremental (see Figure 2.10). Further, the surge in media attention occurred in 2000, when there was no particular threshold or event relating to the absolute numbers of exonerations, though there was certainly increased discussion of flaws, especially beginning in 1995. The combined impact of clemency and exoneration is clearly important. However, the surge in media attention to "innocence" comes in 2000 whereas the clemency and exoneration numbers rise later. These data relate much more strongly to the findings we show in Chapter 3 about the rise of the innocence movement and increased media attention to individual exonerees than they do to the underlying trends discussed in Chapter 2. But how would the public know about the underlying trends unless they were discussed in the media?

THE TOPIC DETERMINES THE TONE

The increase in attention to fairness occurring in parallel with the increase in net anti–death penalty tone over the last decade exemplifies a more general finding: Knowing the topic of the abstract allows us to predict the tone. Some topics, such as the heinousness of a crime, are almost always associated with pro–death penalty coverage. Others, such as international comparisons and issues of innocence, are almost always featured in an anti–death penalty abstract. Figure 4.7 shows these relationships.

Abstracts mentioning morality issues may mention arguments on either side of the death penalty debate, of course. These abstracts in fact are quite evenly split between pro– and anti–death penalty tones. Similarly, abstracts mentioning constitutionality questions may focus on issues favoring the defendant or those favoring the state; here, too, the tone is quite split (though with an average tendency of sixty/forty anti–death

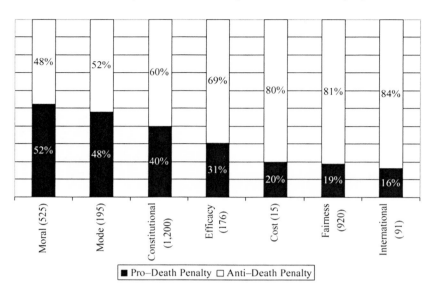

Figure 4.7. The topic determines the tone. The figure shows the percentage of stories on each topic that were coded pro– or anti–death penalty from 1960 to 2005. The number of stories (with pro– or anti– tone) is given in parentheses. Stories that were neutral or uncodeable by tone are not included.

penalty). When the topic shifts to fairness, however, the vast majority (81 percent) of the coded articles are anti–death penalty. International comparisons, although less common, similarly have a powerful anti–death penalty bias. The various tendencies present in Figure 4.7 make clear that the shifting attention to various topics that we demonstrate in Figure 4.5 can be expected to relate to powerful changes in the overall tone over time, just like those shown in Figure 4.4.

FROM VICTIM TO DEFENDANT

Just as the topic of attention matters, whether an abstract mentions anything about the victim(s) or the defendant goes far in determining the overall tone of the article. Figure 4.8 shows this.

Overall, among all the stories we coded that received a tone, about 57 percent were anti–death penalty and 43 percent were pro–death penalty. This tone varies substantially, however, by mention of the victim or the defendant. Most articles mention neither a particular victim nor an individual defendant, discussing such things as the implications of Supreme Court decisions in general or state legislative debates about revising capital punishment laws and procedures. In fact, more than two thirds of

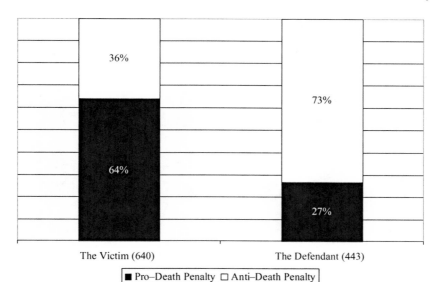

Figure 4.8. Tone and mention of victim and defendant. The figure shows the percentage of stories mentioning either the victim or the defendant that were coded pro– or anti–death penalty from 1960 to 2005. The number of stories (with pro– or anti– tone) is in parentheses. Stories that were neutral or uncodeable by tone are not included.

the stories (2,817 abstracts) mentioned neither a victim nor a defendant, and of the 2,159 stories in this group that were given either a pro– or anti–death penalty tone, about 40 percent were coded pro–death penalty, very similar to the overall total. Figure 4.8 shows, however, that stories mentioning anything about the victim are 64 percent pro–death penalty. Similarly, those mentioning anything about the defendant have only a 27 percent likelihood of being pro–death penalty.[3] Clearly, something about discussing the defendant can be said to humanize him or her, or is associated with discussions about imperfections or problems in the trial. Similarly, a focus on the victims of crime typically is related to pro–death penalty abstracts, focusing, for example, on the heinous nature of the crime itself.

Contrary to what one might expect, *what* the article mentions about the victims, including whether they were police officers, women, or children, or if there were multiple victims has no significant impact on the tone of the article overall; *any* discussion of the victim is related to a pro–death penalty tone overall, as can be seen in Figure 4.9.

Figure 4.10 shows that, just as for victims, there are few differences across types of defendants: Be they female, of various racial categories, or whatever, any focus on the defendant tends to be associated with an anti–death penalty tone. The one exception here is where the defendant

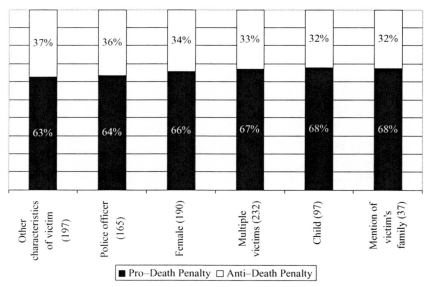

Figure 4.9. Tone of coverage by characteristics of the victim. For every story mentioning any characteristics of the victim, the figure shows the percent that were coded pro– or anti–death penalty from 1960 to 2005. The number of stories (with pro– or anti– tone) is in parentheses. Stories that were neutral or uncodeable by tone are not included.

is characterized as a terrorist, in which case the tone is more likely to be pro–death penalty. There are few such cases, however, as a proportion of the total.

Certainly, in the post-9/11 era, there has been a rise in discussion of terrorism, so it may be remarkable that the anti–death penalty trends we have shown so far have persisted. It is, after all, an extremely hostile environment at the international level, and the nation has been at war since 2002. The vast bulk of death penalty cases in the United States, however, remain of the mundane domestic criminal variety, not related to international terrorism. The focus on flaws in the justice system has not been overwhelmed by the war on terror. Yet one could easily imagine a scenario in which this would not have been the case. Shortly after the 9/11 attacks, in fact, the Washington, D.C., sniper shootings drew attention to crime in a powerful way, and there was considerable pro–death penalty discussion at the time. The states of Virginia and Maryland actually waged a short-lived dispute to decide who would be allowed to try, and potentially execute, John Muhammad. Clearly, the turn away from the death penalty we document here is related to the topic of discussion; if the topic turns to terrorism or particularly heinous crimes, the tone could

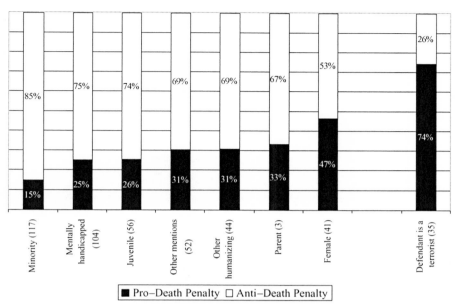

Figure 4.10. Tone of coverage by characteristics of the defendant. For every story mentioning anything about the defendant, the figure shows the percent that were coded pro– or anti–death penalty from 1960 to 2005. The number of stories (with pro– or anti– tone) is in parentheses. Stories that were neutral or uncodeable by tone are not included.

shift again. However, there are many reasons to suspect that this turn will not happen soon or easily.

Figures 4.8 through 4.10 clearly show that whether we are paying attention to the victim or to the defendant helps explain the tone of the coverage. One of the most remarkable shifts in newspaper coverage and public discussion about the death penalty over the past few decades may be simply that we pay less attention to the victims and more attention to the defendants now. Figure 4.11 shows the number of mentions of the victim and the defendant.

Many stories mention neither the victim nor the defendant, of course. But attention to victims regularly outpaced attention to defendants throughout the period from 1960 to the early 1990s. There is some tendency for attention to both victims and defendants to increase and decrease in tandem, associated with fluctuations in overall levels of coverage. Figure 4.12 shows the number of mentions of the victim minus the number of mentions of the defendant, allowing a simple comparison of net attention to victims, just as we constructed in Figure 4.4 a measure of the net tone of coverage.

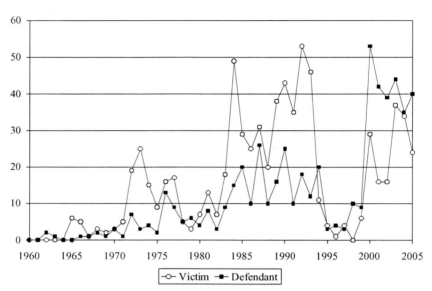

Figure 4.11. The number of stories mentioning the victim and the defendant, 1960 to 2005.

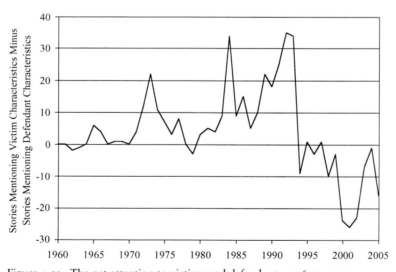

Figure 4.12. The net attention to victims and defendants, 1960 to 2005.

Figure 4.12 makes clear that attention has shifted dramatically from a traditional focus on the victim to a new emphasis on the defendant. Net coverage is consistently focused on the victim rather than the defendant throughout the series from 1960 through the early 1990s. We see the increased discussion of the victims of capital crimes during the 1970s (associated with significantly more pro–death penalty discussion in general during that time), some decline in these numbers after the reinstatement of the death penalty in 1976, a steady rise in attention to the victims of crime in discussions of death penalty issues until 1993, and then a dramatic and sustained reversal after that date. Since 1993, attention has increasingly focused on questions relating to the defendants in criminal trials rather than to victims.

Combined, the data in Figure 4.8 and 4.11 offer a clear example of why proponents and opponents of the death penalty have different foci. Although certainly not all of those close to the victims of violent crime support the death penalty, attention to victims is clearly associated with more abstracts favorable to the application of the death penalty. Similarly, many stories focusing on the defendant are pro–death penalty. On average, however, increased attention to the defendant rather than the victim is correlated with stories more critical of the death penalty. Again, we see that topic of discussion determines the tone.

COMPARING THE *NEW YORK TIMES* WITH OTHER MEDIA OUTLETS

We validated our use of the *New York Times* as a proxy for national media coverage in two ways: first, by comparing the *Times* to the *Readers' Guide to Periodical Literature*, second, by comparing the *Times* to available data from nine other major U.S. newspapers archived by Lexis-Nexis. We began by taking a count of the death penalty articles listed in the *Readers' Guide*, which catalogues all articles published in nearly 400 general interest magazines. The results of our count of articles listed in the *Readers' Guide*, shown in Figure 4.13, support the conclusions we have drawn from the *New York Times Index*.

In parallel to the *Times* coverage presented in Figure 4.1, Figure 4.13 shows an unprecedented rise in *Readers' Guide* attention to the death penalty in 2000. The *Times* shows much greater sensitivity to constitutional developments surrounding the issue in the 1970s, issues that did not register in the more general periodical coverage indexed in the *Readers' Guide*. Yet both sources show the surge in attention associated with the rise of the innocence argument. These findings illustrate the innocence movement as a major social phenomenon, not the creation of just one newspaper.

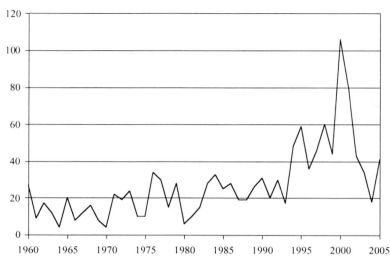

Figure 4.13. The number of stories on capital punishment in the *Readers' Guide*, 1960 to 2005.

We also coded the tone (pro–, anti–, neutral/uncodeable) of the title of each article, and our findings relating to the tone of coverage in the *Times* can be tested against the *Readers' Guide*. Figure 4.14 shows the net tone of the stories appearing in the magazines and periodicals indexed there.

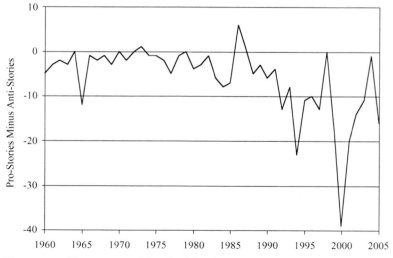

Figure 4.14. The net tone of *Readers' Guide* coverage, 1960 to 2005.

Like the *Times*, the *Readers' Guide* shows relatively even balance throughout most of the period. Coverage is consistently biased against the death penalty, remarkably more so, in fact, than in the *Times*. Coverage in the *Times* may have been more pro–death penalty at some times than that in the *Readers' Guide* because the *Times*, as a newspaper of record, reports on many factual activities related to state legislative debates, Supreme Court activities, or individual trials that reflect the efforts of prosecutors to obtain a death sentence, revise capital sentencing guidelines to make them more clearly acceptable, and other pro–death penalty actions. Significantly fewer of these appear in the *Readers' Guide*. For example, the *Readers' Guide* does not show the same increase in net tone during the 1980s and 1990s. However, like the *Times*, the *Readers' Guide* shows a dramatic decline in net tone of coverage around 2000. And both the *Times* and the *Readers' Guide* show that, although net tone has risen slightly since its dramatic drop in 2000, by 2005 the amount of anti–death penalty coverage in both venues significantly outweighs the amount of pro–death penalty coverage.

Our comparison of the *Times* to nine other major U.S. papers offers additional validation of the use of the *Times* as a proxy of national news coverage. We employed Lexis-Nexis Academic Universe to count the number of death penalty articles[4] appearing in each of the following sources: *Boston Globe, Chicago Sun-Times, Denver Post, Houston Chronicle, Los Angeles Times, Miami Herald, New York Times, Pittsburgh Post-Gazette, Seattle Times,* and *Washington Post.*[5] The *Times* corresponds closely with these other news sources. Comparing the number of death penalty articles in the *Times* each year with the average number across the other papers yielded a correlation of about 0.7. Figure 4.15 shows this comparison.

In both the *Times* and across the other papers, we see a steady increase in attention to the death penalty over the last two decades.[6] Coverage peaks in 2001 but remains high from 2002 through 2005. The *Times* consistently devotes more attention to the death penalty than do other papers, a fact that does not concern us. What matters is that the *dynamics* of the attention run parallel between the sources. When the *Times* increases its coverage of the death penalty, so too do other major papers. When death penalty stories lag in other papers, so too do they lag in the *Times*. Factor analysis provides yet another view of how well the *Times* coverage tracks with these other papers; the *Times* loads strongly (0.69) on the first factor based on the annual counts of stories across all ten papers.[7] This means that it moves statistically in tandem with the bulk of the other papers, not separately or independently from the others.

Finally, within the death penalty articles we located in Lexis-Nexis, we took a count of the number of articles employing the innocence frame – specifically, stories including reference to wrongful conviction, exoneration, or DNA evidence. As with the general death penalty coverage, the

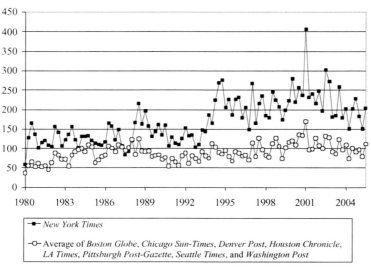

Figure 4.15. *New York Times* attention to the death penalty as compared with other papers, monthly, 1980 to 2005.

New York Times proved to be highly indicative of national coverage. The number of *Times* stories giving attention to the innocence frame correlates at about 0.9 with the average number of such stories across the other major papers. Again, a scatter plot offers confirmation that this correlation is accurate. And in factor analysis, the *Times* loaded very highly at 0.92 with the nine other series.

Figure 4.16 shows the comparison of innocence frame coverage in the *Times* and the other papers. Again, we see that the *Times* consistently pays more attention to issues of innocence than do the other papers, but the dynamics of this coverage – the ups and downs – track one another in parallel. In fact, this figure gives perhaps the strongest indication we can provide about the dramatic rise of the innocence frame. Across ten different newspapers in many areas of the country, it is clearly apparent. The coverage of the *Times*, on which we have focused, is largely replicated in the other papers.

As a final illustration of the validity of the *Times* as a proxy for national coverage, we offer Figure 4.17, which compares attention to the innocence frame between the *New York Times* and the *Houston Chronicle*. If any major U.S. paper could be suspected to buck the trend of giving credence to the innocence frame, the *Houston Chronicle* would be it. The death chamber in Texas is more active than any other in the nation, and Houston's Harris County is at the epicenter of many of these events. Instead, we see that attention to the innocence frame in the *Houston Chronicle* runs

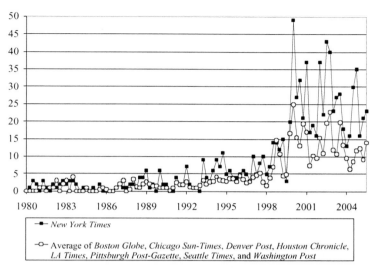

Figure 4.16. *New York Times* attention to the innocence frame as compared with other papers, monthly, 1980 to 2005.

directly in line with the *Times* coverage. The *Times*, of course, pays more attention, but the *Houston Chronicle* pays its fair share – in 2003, it even surpasses the *Times*. In fact, the *Houston Chronicle* ranks fourth among the ten newspapers we studied in terms of total number of stories with

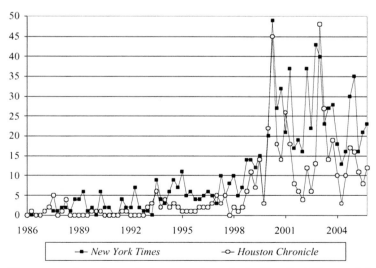

Figure 4.17. Attention to the innocence frame in the *New York Times* and the *Houston Chronicle*, monthly, 1986 to 2005.

reference to the innocence frame, following (in order) the *Washington Post*, the *New York Times*, and the *Chicago Sun-Times*.

In short, no matter which source we consult, we see an increase in attention to the death penalty over the last few decades, and most importantly, a dramatic rise in use of the innocence frame. This changing definition of the death penalty debate was not a construct of a single, liberal-biased news source, and it was not limited to a particular city or geographic area; the redefinition of the death penalty from an issue of morality to an issue of system fallibility has been a national phenomenon of great consequence, as we demonstrate in later chapters.

WHAT CAUSED THE SURGE IN ATTENTION IN 2000?

We see in Figure 4.1 that *New York Times* coverage of capital punishment skyrocketed to its highest level in 2000, with 235 articles on the death penalty, surpassing the previous peak of 194 articles in 1977, the year following the reinstatement of the death penalty in the United States. Figure 4.6 shows that 2000 also saw attention to innocence surge to the highest level on record, and in Figures 4.13, 4.15, and 4.16 we see that these trends were not peculiar to the *Times* but were reflected as well in the *Readers' Guide* and in a selection of other major newspapers searched electronically since 1980. We have described this surge in attention to the death penalty as one manifestation of a larger social cascade surrounding the new innocence frame. Here we briefly consider whether the spike in media attention to the death penalty in 2000 could have been the product of a "perfect storm" of conditions focused on then–Texas governor George W. Bush's presidential campaign and election. This alternate hypothesis posits that a handful of reporters, perhaps bored with the standard campaign beat or looking for a new angle on an old story, became interested in Texas's death penalty policies and high execution rate. The spike in attention to the death penalty that we have observed, then, was not about innocence at all, this argument goes. It was about the fact that the Republican nominee was a man who had sanctioned more executions than any other person in the nation's history. After all, during 2000, while occupied with campaigning for the presidency, George W. Bush authorized forty executions in Texas. As Center for Media and Public Affairs president Dr. Robert Lichter stated, "They say that if it bleeds it leads, but it took a presidential election to make capital punishment newsworthy. The only certainties in life may be death and taxes, but the certainties in the campaign news this year are death and Texas."[8]

To test this "perfect storm" hypothesis, we analyzed the full text of all 235 *New York Times* death penalty articles in the year 2000 (remember that our larger data set was collected by reading article abstracts from the *New York Times Index*). We coded each article for certain issues, including: mention of the presidential campaign/election; mention of George W. Bush, Jeb Bush, Bill Clinton, or Al Gore; mention of a specific capital punishment case (e.g., Gary Graham, David Earl Gibbs, John Raul Garza); mention of individual states; and the author of the story. If the surge in attention to the death penalty in 2000 was actually the work of a few dogged journalists and not related to the rise of the innocence frame, then surely we would see prominent mention either of the campaign in general, of individual politicians, or of particular death penalty cases over which George W. Bush had presided.

Our results, however, show that none of these factors alone constitutes a sufficient explanation of the rise in articles. Our analysis suggests that it was not the politics surrounding the presidential elections that led to increased death penalty coverage but rather many different dimensions of the death penalty debate. As we expected, the 2000 coverage in fact centers around the concept of innocence: DNA testing, the possibility of executing the wrongly accused, and the death penalty moratorium declared by pro–death penalty Illinois governor George Ryan. Further, we can see that arguments about innocence and evidence became linked with arguments about the execution of juvenile defenders and the mentally disabled, arguments about race, and arguments about class. (The increased "resonance" of the innocence issue, how it came to be related to other, previously existing criticisms of the death penalty, is a theme we explore in greater detail in Chapter 5.) The result of all this analysis is the conclusion that the surge in attention to the death penalty that we have observed had everything to do with intersecting questions of fairness and surprisingly little to do with the 2000 presidential election.

Our review of all the articles published in 2000 shows that Texas did, in fact, receive substantial death penalty media coverage in 2000, with close to 50 percent of articles mentioning Texas. However, many articles in fact made reference to more than one state, with references to Texas constituting only about 30 percent of the total references to all states. (This amount is approximately the same percentage as Texas contributes to the national rate of death sentences.) Although Governor George W. Bush was mentioned in approximately 36 percent of the articles in 2000, only 12 percent of the articles made reference to the electoral contest. In contrast, then–Illinois governor George Ryan was mentioned in approximately 16 percent of the articles, and the state of Illinois was referenced in about 20 percent of them. These findings suggest that coverage of the death penalty in Texas was framed around particular fairness, humanistic, and legal issues that emerged in particular cases rather than Bush and his bid for the presidency. Indeed, about 50 percent of all death penalty articles in 2000 made reference to one or more specific death penalty cases.

Another speculation regarding the increased media coverage of 2000 has been that a small number of journalists, stuck in Austin while covering George W. Bush's presidential campaign, were responsible for the majority of articles. In fact, the eight journalists with the greatest number of stories published together combined for fifty-seven, or about 20 percent, of the articles that year. Besides 57 articles written by the eight journalists with the most common bylines, there were 21 Associated Press stories, 14 editorials, 6 Reuters stories, and 137 stories written by 125 different authors/sources (this includes op-eds). In sum, the articles that appeared in the paper were written by a variety of sources, not a single journalist or small group of them on a campaign to publicize this issue. It was a large and collective event.

These findings reaffirm the Death Penalty Information Center (DPIC) conclusion that the year 2000 served as "perhaps the most significant single year affecting death penalty opinion in United States history" due to the "broad change" in popular American views of capital punishment (Dieter 2000). This change, as we have shown, was not triggered only by Texas death penalty politics, then-governor George W. Bush, and the electoral contest. Rather, the rise in attention constitutes "a steady sequence of eye-opening events," such as a number of death row exonerations, increased commentary on the unfairness and inaccuracies of the death penalty system, government action to "limit or halt" the death penalty, and the apparentness of a "broken system" as attested by Governor Ryan's actions to end the death penalty in his state (Dieter 2000).

CONCLUSION

Results of this data analysis show that the death penalty has long been understood and discussed in the media in terms of constitutionality and morality. Since the mid-1990s, however, a new issue-definition has arisen, and dramatically. The idea of flaws in the system, of innocent people being on death row, of the wrong people possibly being executed, has transformed the debate. In 1996, thirty articles appeared in the *New York Times* concerning capital punishment; the bulk of these reported opinions, news, or events leading toward the application of the death penalty. In 2000, 235 articles appeared, and the overwhelming majority of them were critical. In just a few short years, the issue was reframed to focus on errors, mistakes, and the possibility of executing the wrong person.

This chapter presents our highly detailed approach to studying the content of capital punishment stories in the media. We not only document the historic shifts in the tone of coverage, from a preponderance of pro–death penalty stories to a surge in attention critical of capital punishment, but we also take some initial steps in explaining why this occurred. The tone of coverage is strongly associated with the topic of coverage. The topic of coverage has not only shifted from morality and constitutionality to the new questions associated with the innocence frame, but has also shifted from victims to defendants. The mid-1990s were a period during which a powerful shift occurred. This was all the more remarkable because this shift reversed a trend that had been steady since the modern era of capital punishment began in 1976: Increased use of the death penalty led to increasingly routine newspaper coverage of its application, a cycle that corresponded with consistent and growing public support for the penalty. But these powerful trends came to a halt, reversing so dramatically that we can truly identify the mid-1990s as a tipping point. Attention swelled to a new set of questions that previously had gotten very little traction in the public discussion about the death penalty. Some of these arguments were not in fact new, but they took on new power when they were combined into the innocence frame.

Here we show that these huge shifts can be measured with some simple content analytic techniques and that they were indeed very powerful changes. In later chapters, we show the impact of these changes on both public opinion and policy outcomes. Before moving on to those questions, we explore the questions of framing in greater detail in the following chapter. We demonstrate the unique power of the innocence frame by comparing it to previous frames that were most important during earlier historical periods. We show that the frame's component arguments were not all new by any means. However, they were brought together in a single coherent set of related arguments that had a much greater resonance and power than the individual arguments could possibly have had alone or indeed than they did have when considered in earlier periods, when they were not seen as part of a single coherent critique of the process. We can also assess empirically the strength and resonance of the new innocence frame as compared with previous frames that dominated attention at other times.

Chapter 5 develops some new methodological techniques to assess the evolving nature of public debate over the death penalty. The methods we develop there build on the detailed content analysis we present in this chapter and should allow scholars to do similar studies in other issue-areas. However, the most important element of these new techniques is to allow us to assess the reasons for what we have observed in this chapter. The innocence frame is the most powerful new set of arguments ever to enter this debate. How did that happen?

5 INNOCENCE, RESONANCE, AND OLD ARGUMENTS MADE NEW AGAIN

W E HAVE ARGUED, in previous chapters, that the innocence frame is one of unparalleled potency. In Figure 4.5, we showed that the fairness dimension, fueled by arguments 316 (evidence), 317 (innocence), and 318 (system is broken), has come to dominate the death penalty debate at unprecedented levels of attention. But just how different is it? In this chapter, we subject the innocence frame to more rigorous scrutiny. We begin by offering a theoretical account of the components of the issue-framing process in general, and we present an accompanying methodology called evolutionary factor analysis (EFA). We use this new method to assess statistically the muscle power of the innocence frame. As suspected, it packs a wallop.

Our theory of framing centers on the premise that defining an issue debate involves more than just the frequency of attention. How often arguments like evidence or innocence are used matters, of course, but also important is the extent to which these arguments are used in conjunction with one another to form a larger cohesive frame, as well as how long the frame persists. Following our theoretical understanding of how framing works, the EFA method allows researchers to trace how frames evolve over time in an issue debate. We apply this method here to our study of capital punishment, and we are rewarded for our efforts in two important ways. First, our results here confirm results presented in previous chapters based on the more basic technique of "frequency analysis" (i.e., counting the number of stories using each argument at each point in time). Second, these EFA results offer new insights into the evolving nature of the debate – we can see, for example, how individual frames become associated with new component arguments, sometimes old arguments that become newly associated with each other. This new method, therefore, not only confirms what we have done already but deepens our understanding of *how* the arguments that we counted in previous chapters have worked together to define the death penalty debate. We knew at the end of Chapter 4 that the innocence frame is powerful, and by the end of this chapter, we will be an important step closer to understanding how and why. The result is a more solid grasp on the mechanics of the issue-framing process than that afforded by any previous research and a technique that, having successfully enriched our study of the death penalty debate, may be applied to future framing studies in other topic areas.

The EFA results we present here confirm several ideas from previous chapters. First, in Chapter 1 we develop the idea that shifts in attention may be surprisingly rapid, not incremental, as new ways of thinking about an old issue surge onto the public's consciousness. We also noted that attention in public debates tends to be incomplete; people focus on one set of issues at one time, but on another set of questions later. We illustrate these elements below with a more sophisticated analysis of the rise of the innocence frame than the one we offered in the last chapter, showing with richer detail how the innocence frame came on powerfully in such a short period of time. Further, we reiterate how the innocence frame has displaced previous topics of discussion, even topics that once dominated the debate.

Second, in Chapter 3 we develop the idea that the "innocence movement" provided exactly the type of social cascade that could generate an explosive rise in attention. Through the processes we describe there, where one development leading to more attention to the innocence argument made the next development more likely, we see the slow beginnings of the innocence argument in the 1980s leading, step by step, to more rapid growth in the late 1990s. These actions are clearly reflected in the data we show below. Arguments associated with innocence have always been around, but they were only a small part of the overall discussion in the early years of our study. They began to grow in tandem with the growth of the innocence movement in the 1980s, and they exploded in the late 1990s, when the movement flourished. Today they dominate the debate.

Third, our new techniques allow us to confirm our more general understandings from Chapter 4 about the evolving nature of the debate. We show that the death penalty has been associated with eight major frames since 1964. During the 1960s and 1970s, the debate centered principally on questions of morality and constitutionality, but in later years shifted to other topics, including innocence. We can compare the strength of the different frames that have been used, and we show that the constitutionality and morality frames that once dominated discussion were never as strong as the innocence frame is now.

Finally, we show that the measure of net tone of media coverage that we develop in Chapter 4 is a strong indicator of the overall tenor of the debate and therefore a useful summary of the direction of the media stimuli to which the public and political leaders are exposed. As the various frames we identify have emerged and receded from public debate, the overall tone of the discussion has shifted correspondingly from a more pro–death penalty focus to one that is more critical. Although different arguments may be more or less convincing, and different frames may be more or less powerful over time, one constant over time is the fact that the public is regularly exposed to news stories emphasizing arguments that point in one direction or another. The directionality of the debate, or net tone, has great consequences for public and policy response. We demonstrate these consequences in Chapters 6 and 7; in this chapter, we focus on our detailed analysis of the evolution of the debate.

WHAT IS DIFFERENT ABOUT THE INNOCENCE FRAME?

Using a new set of statistical techniques and basing our work on the comprehensive review of sixty-five distinct arguments we identified in the *New York Times*, as described in Chapter 4, here we can address some basic questions: Is the innocence frame really different from those that have come before it? What is different about it? Why does it seem to have been so effective? What distinguishes it from the arguments that have been made in previous decades? Is it really new?

We begin by identifying three key components of a successful frame. First is *salience*, or how often a related set of arguments is used. Second is *resonance*, or how many individual arguments cluster together to constitute the frame. Third is *persistence*, or how long the frame lasts. The new statistical approach we have developed, EFA, takes each of these components into account. Our analysis in this chapter reveals eight powerful frames that have defined the death penalty debate in different periods of time from 1960 to the present. The earliest frames focused on morality and constitutionality, but more recent frames have incorporated a different set of arguments altogether. The greater the salience, resonance, and persistence of a frame, the more powerful it can be said to be. Compared with all previous frames in the death penalty debate on these grounds, EFA confirms that the innocence frame surpasses all other frames during the period of our study. Yet as powerful as the innocence frame is, the component parts of this frame are not themselves new to the debate. In fact, some of them – most interestingly, the argument that racial disparities pervade the system – have been around for decades. By linking many different arguments into a single, more coherent critique of the system, the innocence frame gives greater resonance to each of them. We explain our complicated statistical procedures that lead to these conclusions in the appendix at the end of this chapter.

In brief, the EFA method involves factor analyzing our set of sixty-five root arguments within moving five-year time windows to isolate clusters of arguments that dominate the debate in each historical period. Factor analysis is a statistical tool for uncovering any links that might exist between individual series moving, in this case, over time. It tells us which arguments are working independently from one another and which, if any, are working in harmony. If the frequencies with which distinct arguments are used rise and fall in tandem over time, these arguments may all be reflecting the same underlying factor; and in any case, they may come to serve as a cohesive framework, a cluster of arguments that revolve around similar themes. When there are no patterns of arguments being used in conjunction with other arguments, the debate is diffuse, cacophonous. When, on the other hand, use of one argument tends systematically to be accompanied by use of specific other arguments, then we can identify statistical patterns of resonant themes in the debate. These themes are theoretically and statistically equivalent to frames. Thus, we can operationalize statistically the concept of a frame and compare the strength of one frame with that of another. So this is exactly what we want.

In what may be surprising, we also demonstrate that although the innocence frame is driven by a few core arguments regarding wrongful conviction, calls for a moratorium, and the availability of DNA evidence, this frame is also fueled by several other arguments that are anything but new. These other arguments have been raised – unsuccessfully – at other points in time but are now finding unprecedented traction in the death penalty debate by "piggybacking" on the innocence frame. This concept of piggybacking goes a long way in explaining the remarkable power of the innocence frame. The frame offers a compelling story that helps make sense of arguments, such as racial bias, that were raised previously outside the context of such an overarching critique of the system and which, therefore, had less impact. When a new argument is raised in the context of no similar or cognate arguments, or where the dominant theme of discussion is morality, those citizens initially predisposed to resist the new argument find it easy to do so; this argument and its overarching frame, then, will have difficulty finding traction in the issue debate. If the argument is linked to morality or religious views in particular, and an individual exposed to the argument has religious views that support the death penalty, then psychologically that individual is primed to interpret the new information as being related to the religious or moral dimension. In this way, priming may lead to powerful psychological rebutting mechanisms, called cognitive resistance.[1] But when a new argument is raised in the context of complementary arguments being made in tandem, and those other arguments relate not to morality but rather to logistics or errors of fact in trials, the arguments may be interpreted in a different way that leads to less cognitive resistance. This combined influence is especially potent in the case of the innocence frame, in which the arguments serve to displace the dimension of debate from questions of morality to questions of fairness.

One of the most interesting findings we show in this chapter is that in the case of the innocence frame, some old arguments have apparently gained much greater credibility. For example, the argument that the system has a racial bias can be seen as a moral failing, and indeed it has often been seen in that light. But if it is seen as part of a broader pattern of imperfections, and if these imperfections are brought to light not by criminal defendants and defense attorneys themselves but by university-based innocence projects staffed by people who are volunteering their time, and if the claims of imperfection are backed up by substantial proof, such as DNA evidence, and if public officials such as governors and official commissions appointed by state legislative bodies take them seriously, then the arguments coalesce into a different kind of story. The story in this case becomes not one of an individual inmate attempting to defend him- or herself in a criminal trial (potentially "playing the race card" if it suits his or her interest) but of outside observers attempting to evaluate the quality of the justice system. The resulting overarching story makes it easier for individuals to understand and to make sense of previously existing attacks on the system; the innocence frame, in effect, has given new purchase power to old arguments. The story is no longer about a suspected criminal trying to avoid a rap or about the justice system being weak on crime, but about bureaucratic incompetence, mistakes, errors, or possibly official malfeasance and corruption. People naturally respond differently when considering the same facts in these dramatically different lights.

In this way, our EFA technique allows us to see the reemergence of perennial debates such as the argument that the system has a significant racial or class bias or that the system harbors tremendous geographical arbitrariness and perverts the equal protection of the laws by making criminals in some jurisdictions liable to a death sentence while not holding those guilty of the same crimes in other areas of the country to the same standards. Our analysis of resonance shows that these arguments, made unsuccessfully in isolation, have grown to constitute a more coherent cluster with the rise of the innocence frame. We can replicate statistically the substance of the debate, and these patterns help explain why the new innocence frame is so powerful. It is powerful, in part, because it is not entirely new. Rather, it gives a coherent overall structure to a number of arguments that have, in fact, been around for decades.

We find that the innocence frame really *is* different from those arguments that were more common in previous periods. However, the unique character of the innocence frame stems not from any individual component argument. The novel elements of the innocence frame are how many different arguments have come together to form a single coherent story, one quite critical of the application of the death penalty but different from previous critiques because it is not based on a moral condemnation of capital punishment in theory. The message here is that the combination of many arguments into a single comprehensive critique of the system has been more effective than the individual arguments taken separately could ever be. Further, as the innocence frame raises practical questions about the functioning of the justice system rather than theoretical questions about what is right and wrong, this new set of arguments is easier for opponents to accept than the more controversial morality argument.

EVOLUTIONARY FACTOR ANALYSIS

Evolutionary factor analysis is quite simple in concept, although some of the technical details of its calculation are more subtle. Recall from Chapter 4 that we know from our analysis of the *New York Times* how many times each of the sixty-five specific arguments for or against the death penalty was made, across any given time period. Some arguments, such as the statement that certain crimes are so heinous that they deserve the death penalty (argument 203), were made hundreds of times over the forty-five years of our study. Others, such as the statement that life imprisonment costs taxpayers more money than does capital punishment (argument 502), were made fewer than a dozen times.[2] Each individual argument, if plotted over time, shows periods of greater or lesser use. Our technique identifies statistically which arguments rise and fall together. If a set of arguments has nothing in common, then an increase in the use of one argument should be unrelated to the use of the other – they reflect different themes. If a number of arguments all rise and fall in tandem, however, then attention to them likely reflects attention to some underlying theme or frame, a statistical "factor" that is manifested in the stories we observe. We cannot directly observe the underlying factor, but we measure it indirectly by noting that a series of related arguments move in concert with each other. Factor analysis, then, allows us to identify the frames that structure the debate. As these frames may change over time, we move our analysis over time as well, performing standard factor analysis on overlapping five-year windows; this process is dynamic factor analysis, on which our EFA method is based. Using this technique we can assess 1) whether there are any coherent frames at each point in history, 2) what those frames are, 3) how many arguments make up the frames (resonance), 4) how much attention there is to each frame over time (salience), and 5) how long the individual clusters of arguments that create a frame continue to cluster together (persistence).

Our technique allows arguments and their rebuttals to emerge as a single theme. That is, if every time media attention increases to argument 401 (the death penalty is neither cruel nor unusual), attention also increases to argument 410 (the death penalty is indeed cruel and unusual), then we would see that these parallel arguments, directly contradicting each other, would constitute a single factor. The morality of the death penalty can be discussed by directly competing arguments, for example, going head to head in a clear confrontation. If so, then in searching for shared variation over time, our technique would be able to identify this morality dimension and the accompanying polarization of the debate.

Actually, what we observe is that the themes that emerge from our analysis tend to have clusters of similar arguments, not contradictory ones. During periods when we see many occurrences of the argument that the death penalty is neither cruel nor unusual (argument 401), in fact we are more likely to see greater attention paid to additional pro–death penalty arguments within this same dimension, such as the argument that public opinion supports the death penalty (argument 403) or other pro–death penalty constitutionality arguments (argument 409). The clusters of arguments that emerge from our analysis are not the same as our coding of the arguments themselves, as we sometimes observe that what appear to be quite different arguments often go together (e.g., a moral argument coupled with a constitutionality argument, an efficacy argument, and perhaps a cost argument). The clusters dominated by pro–death penalty stories often include one or two anti–death penalty arguments, and vice versa. However, clusters are often heavily weighted toward one side or the other. That is, attention emerges to an entire cluster of associated and similar arguments during certain periods of time. These clusters may sometimes be relatively balanced, representing both pro– and anti–death penalty arguments, or they may be heavily biased toward one side or the other. In the case of the innocence frame, for example, attention is quite unbalanced, but this aspect by itself is not new – similar imbalance occurred in some previous decades as well. The content of the debate shifts over time as attention moves from topic to topic, where each topic is really a cluster of individual arguments. So in fact, the clusters we observe are often quite unbalanced. Confrontation (some might say balanced argumentation, pro and con) is the exception rather than the norm.

The noncontradictory nature of most of the factors we identify is itself significant. It means that as new arguments rise to prominence in the public debate, they do not typically generate an equal and opposite reaction by protectors of the status quo. Such a process would generate a homeostatic equilibrium, a policy status quo from which any deviation would be only marginal and temporary. For example, if every time attention rose to the concept that defendants have inadequate legal representation (argument 310), attention also rose to the argument claiming that inadequate representation is not a problem in the first place (301), then we would see a factor emerge that would contain an argument and its direct opposite. We do see some of this. But much more common is a spillover effect – a cascade of attention – to similar cognate arguments rather than contradictory ones. These findings confirm the notion of the sudden emergence of new themes in an old debate, as Jones and Baumgartner (2005) developed, as well as the notion of "noncontradictory argumentation" (Baumgartner and Jones 1993). These authors noted that when faced with a compelling argument by a rival, political leaders often do not directly address the argument. Rather, given the multidimensional nature of most public debates, they raise a completely different argument, countering an apple with an orange, so to speak. If environmentalists raise the issue of threats to endangered species, business interests are more likely to counter by talking about jobs and supporting communities than they are by denying the environmental threat – and they will have more success in doing so. Complex public debates are made in a multidimensional space, so if one side raises one set of questions, there is no reason to assume that the other side will respond along the same dimension, especially because often specific dimensions "favor" one side of the debate over the other. In the analysis below, we see some evidence of all these things and strong evidence that the innocence argument simply has not been countered at all. It is tremendously unbalanced, more so than any other frame in history.

A NEW LOOK AT THE EVOLUTION OF THE DEATH PENALTY DEBATE

Using the procedures that are explained in detail in the appendix at the end of this chapter, we have identified eight major evolutionary frames at the core of the death penalty debate, each one prominent in a different time period. Table 5.1 shows the component arguments of each of the eight frames identified, as well as the "salience," "resonance," and "persistence" of each frame. The salience of each component argument (i.e., the number of stories using that argument during the period when it contributed to the frame) is indicated in parentheses. The value in parentheses next to the name of each frame indicates the sum of these counts across all component arguments. The resonance of each evolutionary frame can be measured by taking a simple count of the number of component arguments. The persistence of the frame is how long it lasts, as shown in the date ranges listed. We have more to say on each of these points later, but Table 5.1 offers a useful first summary of the relative salience, resonance, and persistence of the evolutionary frames that have shaped the death penalty debate.

The first major evolutionary frame, we see, lasted from 1964 to 1976 and had just three arguments: The moral argument that certain crimes are so heinous that they justify the death penalty contributed 130 stories to this frame, the argument that the death penalty is an effective deterrent contributed 27 stories, and the "other" pro–death penalty fairness argument

Table 5.1. *Major evolutionary frames and their salience, 1964 to 2005*

1: "Eye for an eye," 1964–1976 (158)
    203: pro moral – crime deserves death penalty (130)
    101: pro efficacy – deterrence (27)
    309: pro fairness – other (1)

2: Constitutionality – pro, 1969–1974 (116)
    400: neutral constitutional – general (35)
    409: pro constitutional – other (24)
    410: anti constitutional – cruel and unusual (16)
    403: pro constitutional – popular support up (14)
    401: pro constitutional – not cruel and unusual (11)
    100: neutral efficacy – general (6)
    210: anti moral – killing/vengeance wrong (5)
    419: anti constitutional – other (5)

3: Constitutionality – anti, 1973–1978 (129)
    419: anti constitutional – other (73)
    319: anti fairness – other (18)
    600: neutral mode (15)
    210: anti moral – killing/vengeance wrong (12)
    300: neutral fairness (6)
    200: neutral moral (5)

4: Humanizing the defendant I, 1979–1986 (213)
    409: pro constitutional – other (70)
    419: anti constitutional – other (47)
    600: neutral mode (44)
    400: neutral constitutional – general (12)
    319: anti fairness – other (11)
    210: anti moral – killing/vengeance wrong (8)
    312a: anti fairness – racist (8)
    110: anti efficacy – not a deterrent (5)
    314: anti fairness – mandatory sentencing wrong (5)
    309: pro fairness – other (3)

5: Humanizing the defendant II, 1985–1988 (89)
    419: anti constitutional – other (60)
    312a: anti fairness – racist (14)
    710: anti international – international complaints (8)
    309: pro fairness – other (7)

6: "Eye for an eye" redux, 1988–1992 (97)
    203: pro moral – crime deserves death penalty (31)
    400: neutral constitutional – general (27)
    317: anti fairness – innocence (19)
    312a: anti fairness – racist (13)
    411: anti constitutional – violation of due process (4)
    110: anti efficacy – not a deterrent (3)

7: Innocence, 1992–2005 (542)
    317: anti fairness – innocence (100)
    419: anti constitutional – other (94)
    319: anti fairness – other (92)
    310: anti fairness – inadequate representation (57)
    312a: anti fairness – racist (37)
    318: anti fairness – system is broken (34)
    409: pro constitutional – other (31)
    316: anti fairness – evidence (25)
    302: pro fairness – system is "too" fair, should be abbreviated (22)
    710: anti international – international complaints (14)
    312b: anti fairness – classist (12)
    312c: anti fairness – other demographic inequity (12)
    411: anti constitutional – violation of due process (7)
    301: pro fairness – system is fair (6)
    712: anti international – foreign nationals should be exempt (5)
    719: anti international – other (1)

8: Popular support down, 1999–2002 (101)
    419: anti constitutional – other (79)
    412: anti constitutional – popular support down (20)
    203: pro moral – crime deserves death penalty (2)
    309: pro fairness – other (1)

Note: Numbers in parentheses represent salience: the total number of stories using that argument during the time of that argument's contribution to the evolutionary frame. Component arguments are listed in descending order of salience. There are two instances (argument 719 in the "innocence" evolutionary frame and argument 309 in the "popular support down" evolutionary frame) in which we report a 1 in parentheses when in fact there were no articles containing those arguments during their years of contribution to their respective frames. We report 1s instead of 0s in these two cases to avoid confusion. As we explain in more detail in endnote 3, although the component arguments of each evolutionary frame are identified in a process involving the sum of each argument's story counts across each five-year window, the parenthetical values in the table list only the number of stories containing that argument in the central year of the five-year window.

contributed a single story.[3] We call this the "eye-for-an-eye" frame. No other arguments were part of this frame, and all three arguments were pro–death penalty in nature. The frame was amazingly persistent, lasting more than a decade and coming to an end just after the death penalty was reinstated with the Supreme Court's *Gregg* ruling. Clearly, the substance of this frame was to argue that the death penalty has a place in the justice system. Note the predominance of the morality argument; more than three quarters of the stories associated with this frame were on the moral or just-deserts theme.

In the 1970s, two additional frames emerged, both with a constitutionality focus, but these were statistically independent from each other. The "constitutionality – pro" frame lasted from 1969 to 1974 and consisted of three main pro–death penalty constitutional arguments, including argument 401 that the death penalty is not cruel and unusual and argument 403 that the death penalty should be allowed because popular sentiment supports it. Although we label this frame as being primarily pro–death penalty in nature, it also contained a number of counterarguments, including the arguments that the death penalty is cruel and unusual punishment (410) and that killing/vengeance is wrong (210). This period of time was clearly one in which substantial and relatively direct arguments were taking place about the constitutionality of the procedures surrounding the death penalty. If nothing else, the identification of this frame shows that our technique picks up on the most important elements of the debate; this frame is exactly what we would expect to find given the constitutional arguments and Supreme Court decisions of the time. But this finding also provides a baseline by which to compare future frames, as we will do below. This "constitutionality – pro" frame was quite resonant, with eight different component arguments. The saliency values in the parentheses of Table 5.1 make clear that attention focused here for the most part on constitutional issues and that the bulk of the articles were pro–death penalty, hence the name.

The "constitutionality – anti" frame, lasting from 1973 to 1978, included a number of different arguments, including some on both sides of the debate. However, as the table shows, the driving force behind this evolutionary frame was argument 419 (anti constitutional – other), and we name this frame accordingly. This frame was much weaker than its "constitutionality – pro" counterpart, an accurate reflection of the death penalty debate in that era. Together, these frames capture what we know to be true about public debate during the 1970s – that it focused strongly on questions of constitutionality and morality. The death penalty debate at the time, especially during the period surrounding the constitutional moratorium of 1972 to 1976, was dominated by these issues. The frames that dominated debate in the 1970s are of particular interest because the 1970s was a period during which executions were extremely rare and the Supreme Court issued its most important decisions to date on the issue. (Recall from Chapter 2 that there were no executions in the United States from 1968 to 1977.)

The 1980s saw the beginning of a different set of arguments rising to prominence. From 1979 to 1986 we see a fourth frame focusing on what at first glance may appear to be a smorgasbord of questions spanning five of the seven major dimensions of debate. Together, however, these arguments signal a fundamental shift in attention from the plight of the victim to the plight of the defendant. At the heart of this evolutionary frame are resilient arguments about constitutionality put to new use alongside discussion of modes of execution, as questions were raised about malfunctioning electric chairs during this period. The two most salient component arguments (pro constitutional – other and anti constitutional – other) signal the increased attention to specific defendant trials (in our coding system, codes 409 and 419 were used to track attention to the outcomes of capital sentencing trials). Additionally, this is the first evolutionary frame to include specific fairness arguments (the fairness arguments in both constitutional frames were general or "other" in nature) to the virtual exclusion of moral and efficacy issues. Clearly, the debate had begun to move away from constitutionality toward new grounds. Although the two constitutionality frames of the 1970s had considerable combined influence, this first "humanizing the defendant" frame was the most salient, resonant, and persistent individual evolutionary frame to appear yet. This frame was the beginning of a trend. An attention-shift was beginning.

From 1985 through 1988, we see a cousin frame to the one just discussed; we call it "humanizing the defendant II." As mentioned above, the main component argument of this frame, 419, traces discussion of specific court cases in favor of the defendant. The next most salient component argument, 312a, contends that the death penalty system is racist. This second humanizing evolutionary frame is much weaker than the first, but together these twin humanizing evolutionary frames represent an enormous shift in attention to the perspective of the defendant. We see in Chapter 4 that a focus on defendants rather than on victims was one of the biggest changes in the nature of media coverage in the 1980s and 1990s, strongly related to the shift in the overall tone of media coverage that we documented there as well. Figure 4.11 shows that 1985 was the first year in which there were as many as twenty mentions of defendant characteristics. It took some additional years for the relative focus to shift from victims to defendants in general, but the two "humanizing" frames suggest that attention was beginning to shift to new topics at this time and that the focus on defendants was part of a broader theme. Together, these frames were the first steps in what would become a much larger process by which new topics came to gain prominence over old arguments of constitutionality and morality.

From 1988 to 1992, we see the recurrence of a frame driven by the same argument 203 (crime deserves the death penalty) that was at the heart of the earlier eye-for-an-eye frame. This "redux" evolutionary frame is a short-lived and relatively small frame, but it represents the last occurrence of a pro–death penalty frame in our analysis; an unsuccessful but noteworthy counterpunch to the new defendant-centered epoch.

The evolutionary frame at the center of our focus, the "innocence" frame, began in 1992, followed by the accordant "popular support" evolutionary frame in 1999. Both very strong; these frames together capture the rise of the innocence movement that we trace throughout this book. At the fore of this frame are eight distinct anti–death penalty arguments that we had originally coded as part of the "fairness" dimension in Chapter 4 (317, innocence; 319, anti fairness – other; 310, inadequate representation;

312a, racist; 318, system is broken; 316, evidence; 312b, classist; and 312c, other demographic inequity). Also present are the oft-present 419 (anti constitutional – other) argument again signaling attention to capital judicial outcomes in favor of the defendant and the opposing but much weaker 409 argument (pro constitutional – other); a single anti–death penalty constitutional argument (411) about the violation of due process; two fairness arguments in direct opposition to the anti-fairness arguments at the heart of the frame (302, system should be abbreviated, and 301, system is fair); and three anti–death penalty international arguments (710, international complaints; 712, foreign nationals should be exempt; and 719, anti international – other). In total, the innocence frame comprises thirteen anti– and three pro–death penalty arguments, illustrating once again our lesson from Chapter 4, that "the topic determines the tone." Looking at the number of stories mentioning each argument, the imbalance is overwhelming; only 59 of the 542 stories comprising this frame were made in support of the death penalty.

Finally, the "popular support" frame we observe from 1999 through 2002 is much weaker than the "innocence" frame, but it too contributes to the major shift in tone, with 99 of its 101 stories being anti–death penalty. Most notably, second to the familiar 419 (anti constitutional – other) argument, the 412 argument about popular support opposing the death penalty reflects the rising public discomfort with capital punishment that we document in Chapter 6.

MEASURING THE POWER OF THE INNOCENCE FRAME

We turn now to investigating the strength of these eight major evolutionary frames in greater detail, reiterating their differences in terms of salience, resonance, and persistence. Our main aim, of course, is to examine the empirical evidence by which to gauge the weight of the innocence frame, comparing it with previous frames, such as the constitutionality ones of the 1970s and 1980s.

Looking at salience, or story counts, presented in parentheses in Table 5.1, we see that the innocence frame (542 stories) is by far the most salient of the eight frames we identified. The evolutionary frame with the next most salience, "humanizing the defendant I," shows less than half as much attention (213 stories). In fact, Table 5.1 makes clear that the 1990s differed from earlier periods in that the innocence frame completely dominated media discussion, with no alternative frame existing. In contrast, during the 1970s and 1980s, several distinct frames were simultaneously present. The innocence frame is thus unparalleled in that it has come to have a monopoly on media attention; none of the previous frames so dominated the debate in its time as the innocence frame does today. A single coherent story has been told through the media since the mid 1990s, and that story has reinforced the idea that fairness – not constitutionality, not morality, and not efficacy – is the appropriate lens through which to view questions about the death penalty in America.

We can also use Table 5.1 to assess resonance; this is simply the number of component arguments that comprise each frame. As with salience, we see that in terms of resonance the innocence frame, with sixteen component arguments, is unsurpassed. The second most resonant evolutionary frame, "humanizing the defendant I," has only ten arguments.

Persistence, of course, is how long the frame lasts. So far, the innocence frame has lasted fourteen years, from 1992 through 2005, when our data come to an end. The only other evolutionary frame to come close to this level of persistence, the eye-for-an-eye frame, lasted thirteen years.

Although Table 5.1 portrays all the information relevant to our examination, we can get a better sense of all these elements together in Figure 5.1, which shows the chronological evolution of the eight frames over time. The thick black lines show the historical coverage of each frame; the striped lines show the periods during which each individual argument was part of the associated frame. Note that unlike the numbers in parentheses in Table 5.1, which indicate the raw number of stories, the numbers in parentheses in Figure 5.1 show the summed "weighted attention" to each component argument and to the evolutionary frames themselves across the time period for which they lasted; weighted attention is the number of stories in a given time period in which an argument received attention multiplied by the factor loading of that argument in that time period. Given our theoretical understanding of the framing process as dependent on resonance as well as salience, these "weighted attention" scores are a valuable way of measuring each frame's potency. Figure 5.1 thus allows us to see the changing composition of each frame (by noting how long each individual argument remains statistically associated with the frame) as well as the overall persistence and the resonance of the frame (by noting how long the frame lasts, and how many arguments comprise it at different periods). Some evolutionary frames are short-lived, whereas other, more fluid frames persist across several years.

Glancing from top to bottom of the figure, we see a visual depiction of the progression from one evolutionary frame to another that we have already documented. As this picture makes clear, there is rarely a clean break between an old frame and a new one. Rather, we see periods when an old frame remained in place while a new one arose, with neither frame dominant. Some periods see several evolutionary frames present at the same time, and others show only one or associated frames. The most recent period is, of course, unprecedented in the degree to which only anti–death penalty frames dominate the debate. Looking across the figure from left to right, it also becomes clear that certain arguments were core

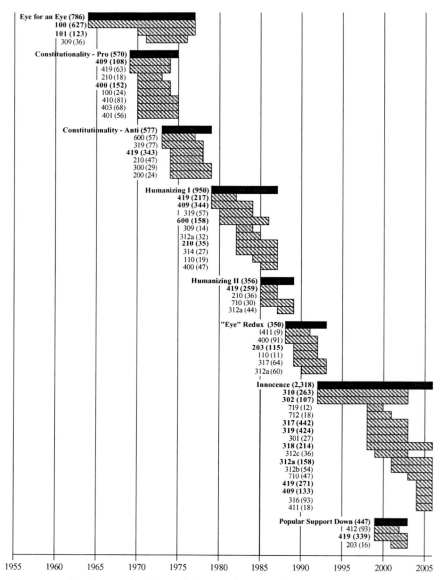

Figure 5.1. Persistence of major evolutionary frames and component arguments, 1964 to 2005. Numbers outside of parentheses refer to the argument numbers; see Table 5.1 for their short titles. Numbers in parentheses represent weighted attention, calculated for each argument by multiplying the number of stories using that argument in a given time window by the factor loading for that argument in that time window, then summing across the duration of the argument's contribution to that evolutionary frame.

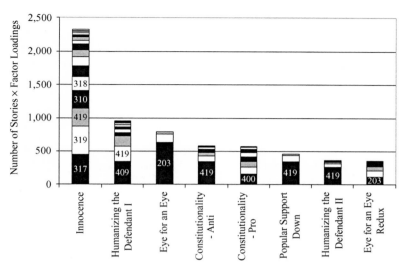

Figure 5.2. Weighted attention to major evolutionary frames and their component arguments, 1964 to 2005.

elements of their associated frames for many years, that some frames have many stable arguments, and that others have evolved over time. The constitutionality frames of the 1970s had various numbers of component arguments over time, generally fewer as the years went on. The argument composition of the humanizing I frame, on the other hand, seems to have evolved gradually over the frame's duration. The innocence frame, by contrast, has gained new arguments over time. The length of the innocence frame's black line gives visual representation to what we already know, that the innocence frame is the longest in the modern history of the death penalty debate. What is more, it is still going.

We can visualize the resonance of the evolutionary frames by looking at their composition in Figure 5.2. The figure shows the total weighted attention for each frame, with the contribution of each individual component argument identified separately. Where room allows, the figure gives a label to the individual sections of each bar.

By looking simply at the height of each bar in this figure, we can get a better sense of the relative weighted attention of each evolutionary frame than the numbers alone in Figure 5.1 allow. At a value of 2,318, the innocence frame is more than twice as powerful as the next strongest frame ("humanizing the defendant I" at 950). In terms of resonance, Figure 5.2 shows the broad base of the innocence frame; a number of related arguments almost equally contribute to the frame, not just one or two. By contrast, the constitutionality and morality frames from previous time periods were generally much more focused on just a few predominant arguments.

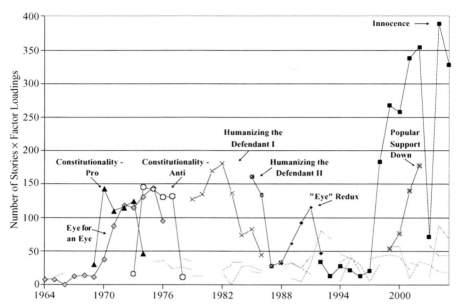

Figure 5.3. Weighted attention to evolutionary frames over time, 1964 to 2005.

We see that both the "constitutionality – pro" and the "humanizing the defendant I" frames are highly resonant, but neither as much as the innocence frame.

We complete our comparison of the eight evolutionary frames by showing the weighted attention of each frame over time. Figure 5.3 presents these results. The figure lists all eight frames discussed previously and also shows, in thin gray lines toward the bottom of the figure, all other evolutionary frames that were statistically identified but not prominent enough to merit discussion. (These much smaller evolutionary frames were, in effect, statistical artifacts, frames that were statistically identified but that did not make strong substantive sense – noise, in other words. We show them here for completeness and to demonstrate that our method clearly identified eight frames that stand completely apart from all the rest.)

The data presented in Figure 5.3 allow us to distinguish clearly the current period, completely dominated by the innocence (and associated "popular support down") frame, from previous periods, when there were often three or more frames competing for attention. The y-axis in this figure again represents the "weighted attention" of each evolutionary frame in each time window. Of key importance, the progression of the frames over time and the weighted attention of each frame corresponds with a more qualitative assessment of what one might expect, providing a sense that our complicated statistical methodology unearthed theoretically sensible and logical patterns in the newspaper coverage on which it is all based. In fact, Figure 5.3 is reassuringly similar in terms of substantive implications to Figure 4.5, in which we trace the changing attention over time to each of the seven dimensions used in our more basic frequency analysis in Chapter 4. The 1970s really were dominated by morality and constitutionality issues, and many frames competed for attention. Since then, the issue has evolved, but at no point before the 1990s was the debate as dominated by a single rhetorical frame as in the current period, when the innocence frame has risen to unprecedented levels of salience.

Looking just at the 1960s through the early 1980s, the period during which most of the fundamental constitutionality arguments about the death penalty in America took place, the figure clearly reflects these developments. These arguments come to an end in the early 1980s, and no single argument or set of arguments achieves much salience for almost fifteen years. However, those arguments that are manifest during the 1980s and early 1990s reflect the beginning of the innocence movement. Slowly, the debate shifts away from constitutionality and morality and to issues of fairness, concerns about the mode of execution, humanization of defendants, and then finally, in the late 1990s, to the tremendous surge that we see toward the innocence frame.

Methodologically speaking, Figure 5.3 is most important in the confirmation it provides for our findings from Chapter 4. It demonstrates that our EFA method produces the same overall substantive story as we obtained through frequency analysis, but with richer detail. These results suggest that, under the right circumstances, EFA may be employed as an equally reliable but more rigorous and fine-grained method of framing analysis.

OLD ARGUMENTS MADE NEW AGAIN

Through our assessment of salience, resonance, persistence, and weighted attention, we have measured the innocence frame against all other evolutionary frames and found it to be by all accounts the most powerful frame in the modern history of the death penalty debate. Here, we look at the component arguments of the innocence frame individually to understand just what gives this frame its remarkable strength. As stated above, the innocence frame is a combination of thirteen complementary (anti) and three contradictory (pro) arguments that together constitute the cascade of media coverage apparent in Figure 5.3. Figure 5.4 shows the raw number of stories per year for each of these sixteen component arguments.

Figure 5.4 makes clear that there has always been some attention to the arguments that today constitute the innocence evolutionary frame. Except for a surge in 1976 (the year the death penalty was reinstated,

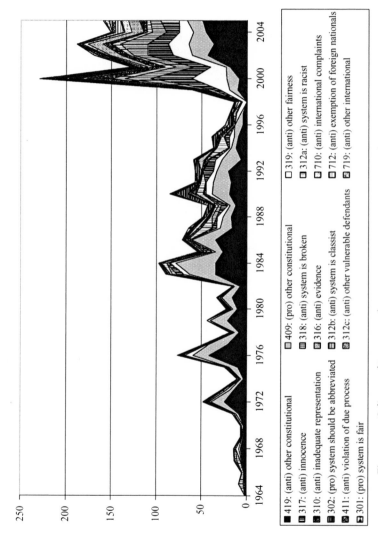

Figure 5.4. Salience of innocence frame component arguments over time, 1964 to 2005.

Legend:
- 419: (anti) other constitutional
- 317: (anti) innocence
- 310: (anti) inadequate representation
- 302: (pro) system should be abbreviated
- 411: (anti) violation of due process
- 301: (pro) system is fair
- 409: (pro) other constitutional
- 318: (anti) system is broken
- 316: (anti) evidence
- 312b: (anti) system is classist
- 312c: (anti) other vulnerable defendants
- 319: (anti) other fairness
- 312a: (anti) system is racist
- 710: (anti) international complaints
- 712: (anti) exemption of foreign nationals
- 719: (anti) other international

when the overall number of death penalty stories surged), attention to the component arguments of the innocence frame was limited to fewer than fifty stories per year from the beginning of the series until the early 1980s, when it began to grow substantially. During the 1980s when the innocence projects were getting off the ground, attention increased dramatically, hitting nearly 100 stories by 1984. In the late 1990s, of course, attention surged to unprecedented levels. Figure 5.4 offers a clear illustration of a social cascade as reflected in media coverage.

This figure also allows us to look at the individual arguments separately. The three most prominent arguments are at the top of the figure: "(anti) other constitutional," "(pro) other constitutional," and "(anti) other fairness." All three of these arguments had found some play in media coverage of the death penalty before the rise of the innocence frame; as we have said, the two constitutional "other" arguments, in particular, trace attention to individual capital trials and so naturally have been staple elements of the evolving debate. Looking at the next level of arguments, however, we see that neither argument 317 (innocence) nor 318 (system is broken) received more than eleven stories in a single year before 2000, after which attention to these arguments exploded. In the last five years, between thirty and ninety *New York Times* stories used one or both of these arguments each year. Three more arguments – "system is racist" (312a), "inadequate representation" (310), and "evidence" (316) – also contributed substantial shares to the innocence frame. Again, these arguments had received some coverage before the rise of the innocence frame, but – with the exception of a slight surge in attention to the racist argument in 1994 – nowhere close to the levels manifest since 1998. The final eight component arguments contribute significantly fewer stories to the overall salience of the innocence frame, but with all these arguments except 302 ("system should be abbreviated"), we see a bump in attention during the last five years of our series from the previous three and a half decades.

The argument that the death penalty is driven by deep racial disparities is of course a substantial element of the debate, and always has been. From 1964 to 1984, there were twenty-eight mentions of this argument, slightly more than one per year. From 1985 to 1998, this number rose to fifty-eight, or four times as many per year. From 1999 to 2005, there were fifty-six stories, or eight per year. Even more important than this surge in attention to an old issue is the fact that the racial argument became associated with a different set of critiques, not moral or constitutional ones, but ones associated with the rise of the new theme. Old evidence of flaws and imperfections gained new meaning with the rise of the new frame.

Finally, the imbalance of the innocence frame is remarkable. Argument 302 that the system should be abbreviated (i.e., the system already has too many safeguards for defendants and should be streamlined) is part of the innocence frame, but as Table 5.1 shows, it contributes only twenty-two stories to the total. In fact, this argument was quite common in the earlier periods. As attention to questions of innocence surged, attention to its most direct counterargument declined. These findings show that there has been very little push-back in the innocence debate. As Jones and Baumgartner (2005) suggested, a surge in attention to one new topic has not led to an equal and opposite reaction by those attempting to protect the status quo with direct counterarguments. Rather, the innocence and related arguments have overwhelmed the public attention and have caused more attention to cognate arguments rather than to contradictory arguments. The result of a shift in attention such as the one we observe here is not a counterargument but a cohesive social cascade, a new focus in an old debate.

ATTENTION-SHIFTS AND TENOR OF THE DEATH PENALTY DEBATE

In Chapter 4 we show how the shifting topics of discussion powerfully affect the overall tone of coverage. We can do the same with our review of the eight evolutionary frames we have identified. Each component argument within each frame is coded either pro– or anti–death penalty, and we can sum all the contributing elements to all the evolutionary frames and subtract the pro–death penalty arguments from the anti–death penalty arguments, just as we do in Figure 4.4. Figure 5.5 replicates the data from Figure 4.4 and shows the results of our new analysis.

The two series are not perfectly identical, but the common features are obvious (the correlation between the two series is r = 0.76). Both move in a positive direction in the late 1960s and early 1970s then decline around the period of the reinstatement of capital punishment in 1976. Whereas the raw series (from Figure 4.4) rises relatively steadily from 1976 to 1993, the measure based on the evolutionary frames is more erratic. This reflects the shifting frames that are counted; the new measure simply ignores all the "noise" in the debate – any articles that are not part of a statistically identified frame are excluded. Both series decline dramatically after the mid-1990s. Whether we look at the simple counts of how many pro– and anti–death penalty stories there were or look in a more complex fashion at the tenor of the arguments that are part of the evolutionary frames we have identified, we find a common story. The focus of attention has shifted quickly in recent years. And because the focus of attention determines the tenor of the debate, this tone can have a dramatic impact on subsequent policy outcomes. We explore these questions in Chapters 6 and 7.

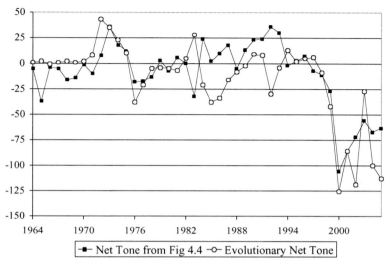

Figure 5.5. Comparing net tone from Figure 4.4 with evolutionary net tone, 1964 to 2005.

CONCLUSION

The innocence frame is the strongest in modern history. It is unique in terms of salience, resonance, and persistence; it is the strongest single frame we have observed, by far. Further, unlike frames from earlier periods of history, the innocence frame completely dominates current discussion. This dominance shows through when we consider the weighted attention of the innocence frame, as we do in Figure 5.4; it is far greater than that of any other frame in modern history. It includes a combination of arguments that together serve to criticize the practice of capital punishment without taking issue with the moral underpinnings of the death penalty in theory. There are both statistical and substantive reasons to expect that the frame should have a great impact.

In Chapter 3, we discuss the surprisingly rapid rise of the innocence movement from its beginnings in the 1980s to its explosion in the 1990s. In Chapter 1, we discuss theories of attention-shifting, suggesting that public discussion of complex policy issues is never complete, never comprehensive, never fully rational; rather, we collectively "discover" various dimensions of the debate that may have been hiding in plain sight all along. Further, attention to a new dimension is often not met with counterarguments, but rather may take on characteristics more commonly associated with momentum, self-reinforcement, and cascades. When we collectively discover a new element in an old debate, we may then pay more attention to similar arguments or even see connections between the new dimension and other arguments pointing in the same direction that we had previously discounted because we had considered them in a different light. Thus, attention-shifts can be self-perpetuating rather than self-limiting, at least for a time. Finally, in Chapter 4 we note how the topic of discussion can determine the tone. In this chapter, we illustrate all these things with our (admittedly complicated) approach to the history of media coverage of the debate over the past forty-six years.

The death penalty debate has been transformed by the rise of the innocence frame. Previously dominant morality and constitutionality frames have certainly not been forgotten, but they have been relegated to the background in media discussion over the past decade. These shifts in attention were tremendously rapid once the social cascade brought on by the innocence movement took hold in the late 1990s. They cannot be explained only by the rise in exonerations or by any other single factor; rather, they correspond with what one would expect from a cascade. And they contribute to the cascade. We look next at the effects that the new focus on innocence has had on public opinion (in Chapter 6) and on the direction of public policy (in Chapter 7).

APPENDIX: EVOLUTIONARY FACTOR ANALYSIS

We begin the EFA approach by employing "dynamic" factor analysis, or standard factor analysis techniques employed on successive moving windows of time. The dynamic factor analysis approach identifies the arguments and argument sets that hang together in the chosen time period to form coherent clusters (for more on the background of this technique, see Kim and Mueller 1978a and 1978b). We use five-year windows as the most appropriate time span for our particular dataset, and through factor analysis, we identify whatever sets of our sixty-five arguments move up and down in concert during these periods. Dynamic factor analysis produces a small number of "factors," each listing a set of individual arguments that cluster together in that time window. As the five-year period we use is very short, any single window will show some clusters that are purely the result of chance – arguments that had no coverage in four years but that each had a story in the fifth year, for example, may well emerge as a single factor for that window. (Statistically, it is fair to say that the first step in the EFA process is quite "noisy." It cleans up in subsequent steps, however.) The "dynamic" part of dynamic factor analysis means that we perform standard factor analysis in successive overlapping time windows, one per year. So each window consists of a five-year period, but we do this for each year, effectively taking the period of two years before through two years after the year of interest. For example, for 1990 we factor analyze data from 1988 through 1992, for 1991 we use 1989 through 1993, and so on.

The result is a wealth of raw factor analysis output files that, looked at separately, are of little help in painting the evolutionary picture we desire. We develop a set of rules by which to identify common argument clusters that move *across* the successive windows. Think of a series of photos taken of consecutive overlapping sections of a mountain range, and you get the idea. Our goal is to trace distinct bodies of frames as they rise and fall throughout successive snapshots, and so first and foremost our rules give us a consistent approach to identifying frames common to multiple windows of time. Yet because we know that in the real world a single frame may look a little different from one window to the next (as it picks up new arguments or discards old ones), our rules are constructed so as to allow frames to evolve over time. Our rubric dictates how to identify clusters of arguments that consistently load together on a single factor, again and again over many time periods, as well as how to trace the evolution of each cluster's argument set. We call clusters that persist over multiple windows "evolutionary" frames, because they continue to appear (and to evolve) over time. Individual arguments may drop in or out of the frame, but the frame itself continues, in the form of a predominant factor with roughly the same component set of arguments. In contrast to evolutionary frames, many frames are "nonadaptive" in that their component arguments appear in a factor for a single year but then disappear. These frames are the result of statistical flukes, the kind of thing one observes by pure random chance when analyzing just five points of data at a time. But the evolutionary frames consistently appear again and again over time, thereby precluding the possibility of being the result of chance. Rather, these are true clusters of arguments that constitute important issue-definitions, important components of the evolving debate.

As already mentioned and as the name implies, evolutionary frames may evolve over time as individual component arguments come in and out of use. For instance, an evolutionary frame labeled "fairness" may contain arguments relating to innocence of the defendant and fairness of the process during several years. Later, it may also include arguments about racism. At another time, it might drop the due process element. In this way, EFA may be performed on any dataset that measures attention over time to a sufficiently large array of arguments related to a single issue over time. It allows us to trace exactly how the entire debate evolves over time, as attention shifts from frame to frame. In addition, it allows us to understand the evolving nature of the frames themselves, as they sometimes include certain component arguments but other times do not.

In the next section, we give a step-by-step explanation of how we apply our EFA rules to identify evolutionary frames and the value of each frame's weighted attention in each time window. Because this chapter offers the first application of these techniques in the literature, it is important that we demonstrate the validity of the methodology, specifically by showing how the results we obtain are substantively interpretable and correspond to what a knowledgeable observer would expect to see.[4] The findings we present here correspond in large measure to those from the simpler content analysis approach presented in Chapter 4. That is reassuring. However, the EFA results go beyond those obtained using the simpler approach because they allow us to see the dynamic evolution of issue-definitions over time, a process that is fundamental to the theoretical expectations in the literature but impossible to assess with the older empirical approach. It is complicated, but worth it.

APPLICATION

In this section, we provide a detailed description of the steps involved in the EFA method, which allows a more sophisticated way of tracing – and measuring – shifting attention to evolving frames over time. As illustrated in this chapter, the EFA process delivers a descriptive understanding of which frames, composed of which arguments, are present in the debate at which points in time, as well as ways of measuring the size of each frame. As we have shown, we can measure a frame by looking at the raw number of stories that employ the frame's component arguments in each time period of its existence. We can also calculate the weighted attention of a frame in a given time window by multiplying the factor loading of each component argument by the number of stories using the argument in that window and then summing across all component arguments. Finally, we can calculate the "evolutionary net tone" of the debate by subtracting the number of stories toned in one direction from the number toned in the other direction (just as with the standard net tone measure we describe in Chapter 4), but this time using only the arguments contributing to an evolutionary frame in each time window. We have demonstrated each of these measurement options already. In this application section, our goal is to walk through the EFA process step by step. In doing so, our hope is that our explanation will confirm that the resulting data we present are accurate representations of the evolving nature of the real-world debate and that we can provide other researchers with a road map for applying this technique to the study of framing in other topic areas.

Step 1: Develop a Comprehensive Dataset

As is clear from Chapter 4, we begin with a comprehensive set of argument codes. Each of the 3,939 *New York Times* abstracts was coded for the occurrence of each of sixty-five distinct arguments. We aggregated these to annual counts.[5] So we start with a dataset containing sixty-five rows (one for each argument) and forty-six columns (one for each year, 1960 to 2005). Each cell contains the total number of *New York Times* abstracts mentioning that argument in that year.

Step 2: Perform Dynamic Factor Analysis (i.e., Standard Factor Analysis Performed on Moving Windows)

This dataset is used to estimate dynamic factor analysis across windows of time. Standard factor analysis refers to "a variety of statistical techniques whose common objective is to represent a set of variables in terms of a smaller number of hypothetical variables" (Kim and Mueller, 1978a). Factor analysis, then, is a statistical technique that seeks out shared movement among a number of variables, identifying those that share variation over time – in plain English, those that go up and down together. The idea is that beneath any system of observed variables (e.g., the frequency of media attention to specific arguments in an issue debate) is a system of underlying unobserved factors or common trends. Factor analysis may be "confirmatory," in which case it is used to check that theoretically related variables really do share common variation, or it can be "exploratory," in which case any number of variables may be included and unexpected relationships may possibly be revealed. This statistical method has been used in economics, sociology, and other fields, but never quite in the way that we lay out here.

As with any statistically intensive procedure, factor analysis works best where there are large numbers of observations. We begin by conducting a standard factor analysis on all sixty-five arguments present in our annual dataset in each five-year window, beginning in 1960 and ending in 2005.[6] Our decision to use five-year windows was based on the nature of the issue at hand (i.e., the average frequency of *New York Times* articles written on the death penalty each year) and the statistical demands of the factor analysis technique. Statistically, the technique is less stable when fewer observations are used. Applied to our *New York Times* dataset, a five-year window allows enough observations for reliable estimates as well as a precise enough temporal focus for identifying frames that may have existed only during certain historical periods.

We calculate our factors for each five-year window, "moving" the windows forward just one year at a time (e.g., 1970 to 1974, 1971 to 1975, 1972 to 1976). This process allows us to observe shifts in the composition of frames that occur over time. Because data from each year contribute to five different time window analyses (e.g., argument frequencies for 1974 contribute to all three example windows just listed as well as to the 1973–1977 and 1974–1978 windows), we are able to trace subtle patterns of movement. To avoid placing too much emphasis on unreliably small counts (e.g., where the pattern of number of articles mentioning a given argument within a certain window might be something like 0,0,0,1,0), we ignore all arguments that appeared fewer than five times within a five-year window.

The analyses produce some number of "factors" in each time window. Each factor is presented with a list of the arguments that contributed to that factor in that time period, and each contributing argument is given a factor "loading" (also called an eigenvalue) ranging from 0 to 1.0, which represents the extent to which that argument trended with that factor. The higher the factor loading, the more strongly tied the argument was to the other arguments in that cluster. In the death penalty dataset, every five-year time window produced between two and four factors, which together consistently explained 100 percent of the movement within that window.[7] Across windows, the different arguments can combine in any of a large number of ways to comprise the factors.

Step 3: Identify the Frames and Component Arguments within Each Time Window

The clusters of arguments that load heavily on each factor (whether the loadings are positive or negative) are "frames," pure and simple. As noted above, the loadings, or eigenvalues, listed for each argument indicate the level of contribution of the argument to the factor. Those with extremely high values (close to 1.0) are highly associated with the underlying factor, whereas those with lower loadings are unrelated or moderately related. In this step, we eliminate all arguments from a given frame whose eigenvalue is below 0.85, retaining only the arguments that are highly central to the identified frame.[8] In practice, then, we eliminate more of the identified factors in this way, leaving us with only one or two in each time period (because often the third and fourth factors have no individual arguments that load above our threshold). These omitted frames are highly diverse – argument clusters moderately associated with several different dimensions, but not strongly so with any single one. Because we are looking for frames that clearly represent the most dominant ways of discussing the issue, we ignore these frames. Thus, we are left with a series of frames and the associated arguments that load extremely highly on them, just one or two frames for each time period.

Step 4: Identify Evolutionary Frames

The next step is to trace the continuity of the frames over successive time periods. Because there are only five years in each time period, some of the factors we identify are statistical flukes, appearing once but then disappearing immediately. To capture the evolutionary nature of frames and their content, we want to identify sets of arguments that not only move together within single time windows but are stable over time as well. Across successive periods, sometimes the factors identified have no common arguments. A factor may be identified in one time period and in the next five periods never appear again; we call these "nonadaptive" frames. "Evolutionary" frames are frames that are statistically identified in several time periods in a row; these are the frames that persist. They may change in the component arguments according to the following procedures.

First, we look to see what arguments are used in tandem (i.e., in the same factor) across two or more time windows, labeling each tandem argument set as part of the same evolutionary frame. Thus, we ignore each argument that is the only one to load above our threshold in a given factor. An evolutionary frame lasts as long as its component arguments load together in the same factor across consecutive time windows, allowing for a single skipped window. For example, if argument number 110 – the death penalty does not deter crime – appears in the same factor of the same window with argument number 203 – crime deserves the death penalty – for two or more consecutive windows, these two arguments constitute an evolutionary frame. We allow a single skipped window, but no more.[9] So when arguments 110 and 203 load together in the 1988 window (i.e., 1986 to 1990) and again in the 1989 and 1991 windows, we forgive the fact that argument 203 appears without argument 110 during the 1990 window (in practice, however, there are only a handful of instances in which one or more component arguments of an evolutionary frame skip a window). Over time, individual arguments may be attached, then disappear, from an evolutionary frame. They are part of the frame as long as they continue to load above 0.85 on the associated factor. Sometimes individual arguments drop out or new arguments join an existing factor as it evolves over time. (Note that additional arguments may load highly on the factor once, but they are not counted as part of the frame unless they do so in two out of three consecutive periods.) Overall, this procedure allowed us to identify twenty-eight evolutionary frames, along with their component arguments, for the entire period. The frames lasted from as few as two years to as many as fifteen. Among these frames, eight stood out clearly as the major evolutionary frames of the death penalty debate over the last half-century; these are the eight frames presented in Table 5.1 and Figures 5.1, 5.2, and 5.3. The others, twenty frames in fact, were clearly less important, and we have shown those as the thin gray lines at the bottom of Figure 5.3.

Step 5: Define and Name the Frames

For each evolutionary frame identified, we know the component arguments. It would be possible, statistically, for the component arguments of each evolutionary frame to consist of a messy mix of unrelated ideas. In practice, however, by reading through the list of component arguments (e.g., Table 5.1), we can gain a strong sense of each frame's content. We name each of the eight major evolutionary frames with a name reflecting the primary substance of the component arguments and what we know of the history of the policy debate during that period in time.

Evolutionary frames typically consist of several types of component arguments. First are those logically consistent arguments corresponding to what the analyst may have expected based on general knowledge of the issue. For example, in the case of the death penalty, we would expect different particular arguments within the general area of morality or constitutionality to be accompanied by logically consistent arguments; when one of these is used, others may also be used. Second, arguments often correspond to counterarguments (or a neutral background discussion of the same dimension of debate). We see several instances of counterarguments in the eight major evolutionary frames we identify in the death penalty debate, such as the presence of the pro–death penalty arguments 301 – the system is fair – and 302 – the system should be abbreviated – in the "innocence" evolutionary frame that is dominated by anti–death penalty arguments from the same fairness dimension. Third, attention to one argument may spill over to other arguments from other dimensions – that is, it may *resonate*, leading to more attention to other kinds of arguments supporting the same conclusion. Attention to the racist element of the death penalty under the fairness dimension may lead to more attention to failures of due process within the constitutional framework, for example. Finally, of course, there may be some random elements, though our threshold of 0.85 loading and our requirement that the frames occur twice in succeeding time windows dramatically limits the resulting noise. We see all these occurrences in our data.

Step 6: Incorporate Salience

Shared movement up and down in the volume of attention to the component arguments is what creates a statistical factor. But we are also interested in the total amount of coverage a frame receives. In fact, we already measured the salience of each individual argument when we presented simple counts of the number of stories using each argument in Chapter 4. We can improve on these simple counts by taking a measure of salience weighted by factor loadings. This measure, which we will call "weighted attention," is simply the sum, across all the component arguments in a frame, of the number of articles using an argument in a given time period multiplied by the factor loading of that argument in that time period. Because each argument loads above 0.85 on the frame by definition, this is similar to a count of the number of stories, but it is weighted nonetheless.

The resulting weighted attention scores produce a single value for each frame in each time window of its existence.

In sum, the EFA approach allows us to do some new things and to corroborate some old ones. Although admittedly complex, the methodology allows us to see whether certain arguments are in fact dominating the debate at any given time or whether the debate is cacophonous, filled with unrelated and changing mixes of statements, developments, and arguments that add up to no consistent, shared pattern of movement over time. If consistent patterns emerge in the nature of which arguments are made in concert over time, and if these patterns are relatively stable, then it should be easier for members of the public to discern clear patterns from public discussion. Thus it should come as no surprise in Chapters 6 and 7 that the innocence frame we show here to be so powerful has had an effect on both public opinion and public policy. If there are no such consistent patterns in the data, then we could reasonably conclude that it would be harder for individuals to draw consistent lessons from what they are reading and hearing about in the media. Equally important, the new technique allows us to measure three things very precisely. Salience is the number of articles using a given argument. Resonance is the number of component arguments. Weighted attention is the salience of a frame's component arguments weighted by their factor loadings, and we advocate using this measure in place of salience or resonance alone. Finally, persistence is the number of years in which we continue to see the same frame appear.

6 PUBLIC OPINION

IN PREVIOUS CHAPTERS we documented shifts in how Americans discuss the death penalty. In particular, we showed the sharp rise of the innocence frame in the mid- to late 1990s and how this new focus of attention redefined the entire debate. The shift in focus prompted citizens to consider the issue in new ways, leading to the potential for significant changes both in aggregate public opinion and in public policy. Changes in opinion and policy do not come easily in a status quo–oriented system, especially in cases like the death penalty, in which beliefs are firmly rooted in moral and religious viewpoints and in which policy plays out these views (Alvarez and Brehm 2002; Baumgartner and Jones 1993; Kingdon 1984; Poole and Rosenthal 1984). As we show in this chapter, public opinion on the death penalty is remarkably stable. The practice of sentencing criminals to death is as entrenched a policy in American political history as one could imagine, in large part because Americans have long supported the practice. And yet with enough momentum, attention cascades can produce dramatic shifts in opinion and policy, even in the hard case of the death penalty.

In Chapter 7, we examine the effects of attention cascades on policy as measured by the number of death sentences each year from 1961 to 2005. Here, our focus is on aggregate public opinion, and our time orientation is more fine-grained. We work at the quarterly level of analysis to model net public support for the death penalty (i.e., the percentage of Americans supporting the death penalty minus the percentage opposing it) as a function of framing (net tone), homicides, and major events in the history of the death penalty debate. The analysis we offer here provides an important foundation for the work we do in the next chapter, but it is important on its own. To our knowledge, ours is the first presentation of public opinion on the death penalty that uses information across hundreds of national surveys; moreover, we do so at the quarterly level, rather than the annual level that is the standard for policy opinion research. Our understanding of the body politic tells us that although large changes are slow to occur in aggregate opinion on a topic like the death penalty, public attitudes rarely take a full year to react to stimuli such as homicides and media framing. A quarterly analysis, then, is appropriate. This more detailed analysis affords valuable insight into how aggregate views of the death penalty have functioned over time and the degree to which media framing has influenced these views. We show here important effects of media framing on public opinion, and in the next chapter we show that these opinion shifts have had additional effects on public policy.

First, we review what is known about who supports and who opposes capital punishment in general. Scholars have accumulated considerable knowledge about the individual-level correlates of support for the death penalty. Second, we consider how aggregate public opinion has changed over time. According to hundreds of polls conducted over many decades, most Americans support the death penalty, at least in the abstract. Opinion in this area changes only slowly, but it does change. We reconstruct the historical record of public support for and opposition to capital punishment based on hundreds of polls, showing periods when support has drifted up and when it has declined. The result is a single time series of aggregate net support for the death penalty. Then we analyze these trends systematically to determine the relative importance of innocence-related events, homicide rates, and the tone of media coverage. Results show that net support for the death penalty is strongly affected by homicide rates and the tone of media coverage. In fact, the overall impact of the net tone of media coverage, introduced in Chapter 4, appears to be equal to that of movements in homicide levels over the last forty years.

MOVING FROM THE INDIVIDUAL LEVEL
TO AGGREGATE ANALYSIS

The vast majority of studies of public opinion on the death penalty analyze the opinions held by individual Americans, analyzing the differences between who supports and who opposes it; most studies identify the correlates of individual-level support. From this research we learn that opinions on the death penalty tend to be grounded in moral values and related to social conditions and to demographics, both of which are mostly fixed. This analysis suggests that we need not study over-time change in death penalty opinions, yet we do exactly this. Our approach is quite different from typical studies of opinion change, not only because we examine the dynamics of changing attitudes over time but because we focus on the balance of opinion on the death penalty in the public as a whole. Here we see orderly change in opinion as it unfolds over time in response to changes in the nature of the debate and the facts surrounding it. How is it possible that when we study individuals, the overriding characteristic that we observe is constancy but when we study aggregates, orderly change appears?

Consider that when most people – call them group A – are constant in their opinions, public opinion follows a flat line over time. Opinions remain fixed, whether because opinions are grounded in fixed moral attitudes, because the public knows little, or because the public pays little attention to the flow of information on a topic. But when a small portion of the public – call it group B – moves systematically in response to the environment, group B's opinion moves up or down in response to new information. When a few citizens turn attention to the innocence frame or homicide levels and these pieces of information systematically affect their attitudes, these shifts produce predictable changes in aggregate opinion for this group. Merging together these two groups of citizens integrates the variance associated with a flat line with that associated with systematic change. The systematic change – the signal – is what we view over time, and in this case the signal is entirely the result of group B, those whose opinions are changing in response to changes in the environment. It is also possible that for some – group C – opinions are ambivalent. Group C's responses to survey questions about the death penalty are answered randomly in a pro– or anti–death penalty direction at any given point in time. This random response imparts noise in our aggregate time series of attitudes on the death penalty. Yet this noise does not interfere with the signal in the systematic movement of that second group of citizens, Group B. If the American public is made up of three groups, one with set attitudes that never change, one that is affected by factors in the environment, and one that is ambivalent or unsure about the issue, the result at the aggregate level is that public opinion as a whole will move in the same direction as that of the second group – even though all are not open to change, the net direction of movement of public opinion over time will be determined by the group that is affected by the systematic cues from the environment.

Focusing on public opinion in the aggregate takes us away from questions about what distinguishes one citizen's opinion from another's and instead leads us to the question at hand: What distinguishes how citizens, collectively, feel about the death penalty at one point in time from how they feel about the same issue at another time? The argument we lay out gives prominent roles to both media framing and homicides. It is important to note at the outset, however, the ways in which our analysis, at the aggregate level, differs from most studies of public opinion, which have an individual focus. Aggregates are made up of individuals, so we review these studies first.

INDIVIDUAL ATTITUDES TOWARD THE DEATH PENALTY

Public opinion always matters in a democracy, but it plays a particularly important role in the case of the death penalty. Compared with many areas of public policy, ordinary Americans have relatively firm opinions on the topic. What is more, the U.S. Supreme Court has recognized public opinion on the death penalty as a relevant consideration in determining whether the punishment is constitutional. In fact, the majority opinion in each major death penalty decision in the last century cited polling data by Gallup or other major survey houses in support of the ruling, whether for or against capital punishment. Dating back to *Weems v. United States* (217 U.S. 349) in 1910, the Court legitimized a dynamic interpretation of the Eighth Amendment to the Constitution, which forbids cruel and unusual punishment; an interpretation that "is not fastened to the absolute but may acquire meaning as public opinion becomes enlightened by a humane justice" (*Weems* 1910). This sentiment, indeed this exact quotation, was cited in the majority opinions of both *Furman v. Georgia* – the 1972 decision banning capital punishment – and *Gregg v. Georgia* – the 1976 decision reinstating the death penalty. In *Furman*, the justices specifically recognized the role of public opinion as one of the indicators of social values and, therefore, an indicator of "contemporary standards of decency." In *Gregg*, the Court again focused on the will of the people, but this time concluded that as long as the penalty is not cruel and unusual – which the Court majority in this opinion said it was not – the Court may not override criminal legislation made by elected officials. The justices in the *Gregg* decision noted that "a heavy burden rests on those who would attack the judgment of the representatives of the people." Later, in the *Roper v. Simmons* decision of 2005, the justices noted that a declining trend in state usage of the death penalty for juveniles was further indication of changing social values and, therefore, of constitutional interest. In sum, the importance of public opinion in determining the constitutionality of the death penalty means that public opinion survey data – reflecting how many people support the death penalty and why – are of intrinsic interest. Shifts in public opinion could affect the behavior of juries, of elected leaders, and, most likely, future decisions by the Supreme Court.

Another reason public opinion on the death penalty matters is that citizens cast votes on the basis of candidate positions on the issue. Surveys indicate that voters both know presidential candidates' positions on the death penalty and cite them as very important in their voting decisions.[1] Politicians, too, are acutely aware of public opinion; as levels of support for the death penalty have historically topped 50 percent, politicians of both parties have touted their support for the policy. There are several ironies related to public opinion on the death penalty. For one, the questions posed in public opinion surveys are highly abstract, but when juries are faced with the decision about whether to sentence a given individual to death, the question is anything but theoretical. In fact, as we argued in previous chapters, the movement away from a moral/constitutional frame in public discussion of the death penalty toward the innocence frame is related to this shift from thinking of the issue in the abstract to considering a concrete decision about a particular individual. (We note in Chapter 4, for example, the increasing number of newspaper stories mentioning the name of the defendant in the trial, and the linkage between this focus and an anti–death penalty tone; courtroom events and jury deliberations, of course, always relate to a particular individual sitting just feet away from the jurors.) Juries impose the death sentence only in a small fraction of cases in which it is considered, and only a tiny fraction of murderers are charged with a capital crime in the first place. Public support as measured in the polls, however, is much more sizable. If juries and prosecutors behaved in a manner consistent with what the polls seem to indicate, there might be thousands of executions each year; but of course we do not see that. The reason, probably, is that the polls typically ask about a distant hypothetical situation whereas actual cases as they are presented to the nation's juries are much more nuanced; an actual capital trial represents the polar opposite of the distant or the hypothetical. The second irony associated with mass attitudes here is that voters mention the death penalty with respect to their votes for president of the United States, but the president (and the federal government in general) has very little to do with decisions about the death penalty; these are typically made in state courts. In any case, despite these ironies, public opinion appears to matter.

Given its importance, it is not surprising that there is a large body of research examining both aggregate and individual-level opinion on the death penalty. Much of the work is descriptive, informing us about the character and depth of public support. We know, for example, that the public is largely misinformed about facts such as the frequency of the use of the death penalty, the manner in which it is decided, and the alternatives available to jurors (Bohm et al. 1991; Sarat and Vidmar 1976; Vidmar and Ellsworth 1974). We know, too, that proponents of the death penalty habitually allude to retribution and the cost of life imprisonment as reasons for supporting the death penalty whereas opponents tend to cite the potential miscarriage of justice (Bedau 1997; Bohm 1987; Ellsworth and Gross 1994, 1983; Gross 1998; Haddock and Zanna 1998; Radelet and Borg 2000; Tyler and Weber 1982). We also know that although abstract support for the death penalty for persons convicted of murder tops 50 percent, support for capital punishment falls when 1) respondents can select alternative punishments, especially when coupled with some form of restitution to the victim's family; 2) the crime committed is not murder; and 3) the defendants in question are juveniles or mentally retarded, or, in many cases, simply when a defendant is named (Bowers 1993; Cullen et al. 2000; Durham et al. 1996; Ellsworth and Gross 1994; Fox et al. 1991; Vidmar and Ellsworth 1974). This last set of findings, about the humanization of the defendant, reflects our discussion in Chapter 4 about the nature of media coverage of the death penalty as well. Newspaper stories mentioning characteristics of the defendant are significantly more likely to carry an anti–death penalty tone.

In addition to these descriptive accounts of public opinion, a great deal of attention has also been paid to the question of who supports the death penalty – the correlates of individual-level support. The answers focus on the role of race (Halim and Stiles 2001; Young 1991 and 1992), religion (Grasmick and McGill 1994; Grasmick et al. 1992), and other demographic and political factors. Men, those with higher income, whites, Republicans, conservatives, members of the middle class, and those with lower levels of education tend to be more supportive than others of the death penalty (Ellsworth and Gross 1994). However, some research has found that after controlling for a range of attitudes, many of these socio-demographic differences disappear (Halim and Stiles 2001). Individual-level analysis has also examined the effect of the local environment in which people live, with the weight of evidence finding that murder rates in the community where a family lives predict death penalty support. That is to say, people living in areas with greater numbers of murders may be more supportive of the death penalty, controlling for race and other factors (Soss et al. 2003 and Taylor et al. 1979; but see Tyler and Weber 1982 for competing evidence).

A small number of state-level analyses consider the influence of political context in determining support for the death penalty. Crime rates (or the perception of crime) are at the center of these analyses. More crime, the argument goes, leads to the fear of victimization and the desire for "law and order" policies with tougher punishments for crimes. States with higher crime rates are more likely to have death penalty statutes, to execute those on death row, and to see strong public support for the death penalty (Jacobs and Carmichael 2002; Nice 1992; Stack 2000).[2] Additionally, Republican Party strength and conservative opinion climate are correlated with higher levels of support for and use of the death penalty. Percentage of minorities and percentage of urban population also explain state-to-state differences in the existence and use of the death penalty as well as the level of public support (Jacobs and Carmichael 2002; Nice 1992; Stack 2000). So we know a lot about state- and regional-level variations in popular support.

The first over-time analyses of death penalty opinion were conducted in response to the increased levels of support that followed the end of the moratorium. Although analysis was largely anecdotal or limited to sets of individual surveys at different points in time, one finding emerged: Growth in the violent crime rate – and later, when crime rates leveled off and then dropped, change in perceptions of crime and its importance – precipitated higher levels of support for the death penalty (Cullen et al. 2000; Gross 1998; Warr 1995). A few analyses also considered trends in conservative and Republican strength, which were associated with harsher modes of punishment more generally and with greater support for the death penalty in particular (Grasmick and McGill 1994; Page and Shapiro 1992; Rankin 1979; Taylor et al. 1979; Tyler and Weber 1982).

Noticeably absent from studies of opinion is the role of media frames. Although scholars have identified historical periods in which particular types of arguments have been made (Bohm 1987; Radelet and Borg 2000), no one has systematically tracked attention to the arguments used in the death penalty debate and analyzed their relationship with public opinion over time.[3] Of course, with the analyses we show in Chapters 4 and 5, we are in a position to do this here.

The absence of a single indicator of death penalty attitudes asked regularly over time has limited the ability of scholars to do more than talk of general trends in opinion or focus on geographical variation in public opinion as these relate to crime rates or other characteristics. But, as we will see, a great deal of information about Americans' attitudes toward the death penalty over time is available, and this information can be used systematically to identify the correlates of aggregate-level death penalty support. It also allows us to assess the role of media framing on public sentiment. In the next section, we introduce our time series of death penalty sentiment. From there we test our hypothesis that media framing influences opinion and we explore the causal dynamics of opinion more generally.

THE DYNAMICS OF AMERICAN ATTITUDES TOWARD THE DEATH PENALTY

Accumulated research has taught us a lot about the individual correlates of public opinion toward the death penalty. State and regional variations are clear, as are the individual-level characteristics that make some Americans more likely than others to support capital punishment. We know a great deal about who, at any given time, is more likely to support the death penalty, as well as the crimes or circumstances for which more Americans support it. By contrast, there is only scant literature addressing trends over time in levels of support. We know that, in response to general questions, support tends to be widespread. Also, it appears that this support fluctuates over time roughly in response either to crime/homicide rates or to fear of crime, although these trends have not been systematically addressed. A number of difficult methodological issues, mostly related to changes in survey question wording, make it hard to assess public opinion clearly and precisely in this area over long periods of time. In this section, we attempt to solve these problems and to provide a more complete analysis of public opinion over time than has been done before. This analysis allows us to 1) know when opinion has moved up or down with regard to the death penalty and 2) assess the relative importance of media framing, controlling for homicides and other factors.

In the abstract, we know a great deal about Americans' opinions on the death penalty over time. Survey data are plentiful, but sporadic. Three survey questions have been asked of random samples of Americans more than a dozen times each, and we can chart general support for the death penalty beginning as far back as December 1936, when 61 percent of Americans "believed in the death penalty for persons convicted of murder" (Gallup). From November 1953 to May 2006, Gallup asked, "Are you in favor of the death penalty for persons convicted of murder?" 42 times, making this the longest-running single measure of public opinion available (in the figures that follow, we refer to this question as "Gallup Murder"). In addition, Gallup asked, "If you could choose between the following two approaches, which do you think is the better penalty for murder – the death penalty or life imprisonment, with absolutely no possibility of parole?" 18 times from 1985 to 2006 (we call this the "Gallup Life" series). Naturally, responses vary when the alternative punishment is made available as it is in this question, a point we explore below. Finally, as part of the General Social Survey (GSS), the National Opinion Research Center (NORC) asked, "Do you favor or oppose the death penalty for persons convicted of murder?" 25 times from 1972 to 2004 (NORC-GSS Murder). Because of its regular timing and identical administration, the NORC-GSS Murder question has been extensively analyzed, producing the closest thing to a time series on death penalty attitudes that exists to date. Together, the Gallup Murder, Gallup Life, and NORC-GSS Murder series represent the three most frequently asked questions tapping death penalty attitudes by any survey house, providing a great deal of information about death penalty support in the modern era. Figure 6.1 shows public responses to these three repeated questions.[4]

The Gallup Murder measure shows that nearly three quarters of Americans supported the death penalty for persons convicted of murder in 1953, the earliest year this question was asked.[5] Support hovers around 55 percent – sometimes closer to 50 percent, other times to 60 percent – until 1974, when we see a gradual but steady increase in support, leading to a peak of 86 percent in 1995. After this date, support falls, ending at a low of 70 percent in 2006. The NORC-GSS Murder measure maps nicely onto this Gallup measure. During the period when both measures are available, they show substantial overlap, each moving upward in the 1970s and 1980s, and dropping markedly in the late 1990s, holding

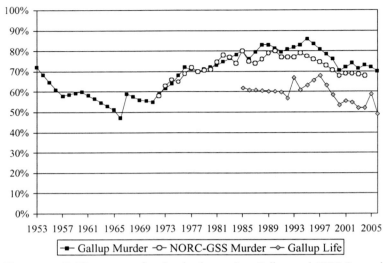

Figure 6.1. Public support for the death penalty: Gallup and NORC, yearly from 1953 to 2006. In years in which multiple surveys were conducted, simple averages are used.

steady at these lower levels during the most recent years. The correlation between the Gallup Murder and NORC-GSS Murder series is substantial: $r = 0.90$. The Gallup Life question consistently produces lower responses than do the other two questions, but the dynamics are strikingly similar. As we noted earlier, when given alternative and severe punishment options, Americans' opinions are not so staunchly supportive of the death penalty (Bowers 1993; Cullen et al. 2000; Durham et al. 1996; Fox et al. 1991; Vidmar and Ellsworth 1974). In fact, Figure 6.1 shows that answers to this question are much more evenly split, with just about half, rather than a majority, of respondents voicing support. Forty-eight of the fifty states do, in fact, offer the alternative punishment of life without parole, so the responses to this question may be more relevant to the actual situation, rather than the more general questions. We return to this question later. For now, there are two points: The Gallup Life question is available only for a short time period (much less than the other two questions), and responses to this question vary over time in strong parallel to those of the other two. It correlates highly both with its sister Gallup measure and with the NORC-GSS Murder measure, $r = 0.79$ and $r = 0.67$, respectively. Combined, these three surveys give us a good idea about the general level of support for the death penalty in America (high, though the precise level depends on the exact question) and how this support has changed over time. Clearly, different questions lead to different responses. However, there is substantial shared movement in the series no matter which particular question is posed.

Although these three data series tell us much about Americans' attitudes toward the death penalty, much of political time is left uncovered, and a systematic analysis of attitudes over time is not possible with any of these. Each survey item is missing data for too many time periods. It would be far preferable to have a single series with many more observations. Unfortunately, no single survey question has been asked more frequently than the three questions just reviewed. To build a single time series, we need to draw on information in additional survey questions that tap attitudes toward the death penalty and devise a method to compare trends in the responses to all these questions asked repeatedly over time, combining the responses not just from the three questions reviewed above, but from a much larger number. This process will allow us to recreate the history of public opinion toward the death penalty with much greater confidence.

For this task, we turn to the Roper archive, which has catalogued a wealth of publicly available survey data on the death penalty. From Roper we located sixty-seven survey houses asking some 350 different questions related to the death penalty between 1953 and 2006: a total of 763 surveys. Some of these questions were asked in such a way as to make them unfit for our analysis – for example, "As far as you know, do Catholic bishops in the United States favor or oppose the death penalty for persons convicted of murder?" and "In general, how would you rate the job the press has done in covering...the Supreme Court ruling that bans the death penalty for the mentally retarded...excellent, good, only fair, or poor?" Often questions were of state samples or other limited samples. These unusable surveys were excluded, leaving us with 292 separate times when the public was surveyed regarding their attitudes on the death penalty. Data come from not only Gallup and NORC but from a total of nineteen different survey organizations. Our final set of 292 surveys includes sixty-six different question wordings/survey house combinations. We exclude any question wordings that were used only once, as explained below.

We use a mathematical formula first developed by Professor Jim Stimson in his analysis of the "public mood" to create a single indicator from so many different series (see Stimson 1991, Appendix 1, for details on how he originally developed this method). Stimson was interested in a broad measure of the public's sense of liberalism or conservatism. He noted that in response to many questions, such as whether the United States was spending too much or not enough on education, health care, the environment, or other issues, different individuals would of course have different opinions at any given time. But when the average response of all Americans moved upward over time – indicating a more liberal position on government spending toward education, for example – the other series tended to move in the same direction as well. When one moved down, the other ones tended to move down as well. Each individual series was separate from the others, but they all shared some degree of common variation over time. Stimson called this shared variation the "public mood" and developed a method of combining results from hundreds of different polls asking many different questions on similar but not exactly identical topics to measure the public mood very accurately over long periods of time. The great advantage of his method is that it makes use of so much information, literally hundreds of polls over time. His findings fit well with the accepted understanding of movements in the public mood or general ideological trends among the public over time – a knowledgeable observer seeing Stimson's results would recognize that they reflect a qualitative assessment of historical periods when American public opinion was more liberal or conservative. The method works well, so for our particular situation, we adopt the techniques Stimson developed.

Each survey of the public regarding its death penalty attitudes provides important information, but how can we compare answers to one question with answers to a different question? The key is to look at shared trends over time. From 1973 to 1993, public opinion in the United States grew more supportive of the death penalty. This would be reflected in almost any question asked repeatedly in any national opinion poll. Each question, asked just once, may elicit different responses. When a question is repeated multiple times over many years, however, we can see how public opinion moves – up or down. For any given question wording, the series may have some particularistic variation (e.g., the Gallup Life question from Figure 6.1 is always quite a bit lower than the Gallup Murder question; this difference is clear from the figure). However, the series may have some shared variation with all the other series as well; we see precisely this commonality between the Gallup Life series and the other two we examined. The idea here is that if underlying public sentiments toward the death penalty are changing over time, this will be reflected, at different levels, in each survey question, no matter what exact question wording is used. Thus, we use the information from each data series to build a single measure of Americans' support for the death penalty (see Appendix B for a full list of survey houses and questions used in our measure).

At the heart of the measure is the assumption that, regardless of its own peculiarities, each question asked by each survey house taps some aspects of the public's latent, underlying attitudes toward the death penalty.[6] Responses to each question should thus move in parallel over time, exhibiting common patterns of movement. This result is apparent in Figure 6.1. Although each series has its own average level and shows some seemingly random fluctuations associated with the sampling error related to any single poll, overall the three series also show considerable shared movement over time. Each shares in the overall story about Americans' changing attitudes. Covariation in movement across the various series is the key to creating a single measure of public support for the death penalty over time. Two problems prevent us from simply averaging the percentage of people who support the death penalty: First, differences in question wording and methodologies across survey houses result in differences in measured levels of support. Second, there is a large amount of missing data; in many early years there are no survey questions at all. So the method must reasonably aggregate across the different series, and it must generate expected values for time periods during which no questions were asked, based on what we know about opinion in adjacent time periods as well as on the trends of opinion over time. This is a tall order, but we proceed!

Here is how we do it. Essentially, if the same question was asked more than once, we can see whether support went up or down. Of course, as Figure 6.1 shows, different question wordings will produce different responses at any given time, even if underlying attitudes are the same. So we cannot compare the answers from question A with those from question B. But we can construct a full set of comparable time series in the *degree of change* in the responses over time, in response to the *same question* when posed by the *same survey house*. If we rescale each series to some baseline, then for each year for which data are available, we can see whether, compared with the baseline, support was higher or lower, and by how much. Although the procedure is complicated, it allows us to make use of 292 surveys, producing vastly better estimates of the state of public opinion at any given moment than those derived from the simpler but much less complete series presented in Figure 6.1.[7]

With change ratios in opinions in hand, we can compute a simple weighted average of the change ratios in each time period. The resulting series may be thought of roughly as a weighted average of our illustrative three series from Figure 6.1, but making use of all 292 surveys that we have identified. The weights ensure that the questions that were asked more frequently and of larger samples contribute more to our resulting index than do questions that were asked only a few times or in relatively small surveys.[8] The end result is a time series that captures latent attitudes toward the death penalty. We see this combined index in Figure 6.2.

Figure 6.2 replicates Figure 6.1 and adds our new index, based on all available information surveying Americans regarding their support of the death penalty. The first thing to note is that our new measure of American support for the death penalty moves in tandem with both Gallup measures and the NORC-GSS Murder measure. The new series correlates highly with each measure, $r = 0.96$ (Gallup Murder), $r = 0.86$ (Gallup Life), and $r = 0.92$ (NORC-GSS Murder), providing strong evidence that the algorithm captures latent support for the death penalty. Second, because our measure draws on more information, the series is smoother and longer – it allows us to connect the dots, start to finish, with a great deal more confidence than with the points based on either Gallup or

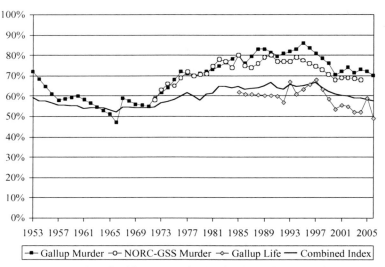

Figure 6.2. An index of public support for the death penalty, yearly from 1953 to 2006. The combined index was created by running raw death penalty survey data through the Wcalc algorithm written by James Stimson and using the optional smoothing function.

NORC-GSS alone. We see that our best estimate of the 1953 point is lower than the raw Gallup poll available for that year, given the information contained in all the other surveys, and that our measure is now on average about five percentage points less supportive than either Gallup or NORC-GSS in the 1980s to the mid 1990s. This reflects the lower levels of support voiced by the public for the death penalty in many questions that reflect specific circumstances. Yet the overall patterns are uncannily similar. Because the index is based on 292 different surveys, it is substantially more accurate than any single series could be. Each individual survey has a sampling variability associated with its sample size, usually in the range of plus or minus three points, so even if there were a single annual survey with identical questions asked repeatedly, we would still prefer to use our index. It makes the most of all the available information.

The combined index of public opinion that we construct has the value of getting the most out of all the information available to us, but it has one drawback: It is difficult to interpret. Movement of the index up or down is clearly significant, but readers should understand that the scale itself is ambiguous. Recall that the index requires that we compare questions that were posed with dozens of different question wordings so that we could note whether sentiment was moving in a pro– or anti–death penalty direction. But by combining so many questions, and taking all their values as compared with some baseline year, the actual values of our index are determined largely by which baseline we choose and what combinations

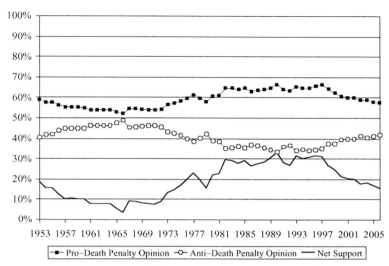

Figure 6.3. Indices of public support, opposition, and net support for the death penalty, yearly from 1953 to 2006. Support and opposition indices were created by running raw death penalty survey data through the Wcalc algorithm written by James Stimson and using the optional smoothing function. The net support index is simply the difference between these two indices (support minus opposition).

of question wordings happened to be available in the Roper survey data archive. Now, it is clear from Figure 6.2 that our overall index is not too far off the results one gets from a simple question such as "Do you support the death penalty for persons convicted of murder?" But note that it is consistently lower than this number. Further, it is consistently higher than the number received when Gallup has asked the question specifying the alternative possibility of life without the possibility of parole. In any case, we caution the reader not to make too much out of the absolute levels of our index of public opinion (e.g., 67 percent in 1997, 58 percent in 2005) but to focus instead on the direction and speed of its movement over time.

With these checks (and caveats) in place, we consider the more interesting substantive and statistical features of attitudes over time. First, what does our new series look like? We actually create three key series: Figure 6.3 shows our estimates of pro- and anti–death penalty opinion and net support, or the difference between these two opinions.[9]

The stability of public opinion surrounding the death penalty is remarkable. Many public opinion scholars are familiar with presidential approval ratings. Graphed over time, these series vary tremendously, sometimes trending downward in long slopes as a given president slowly loses public support, but often spiking sharply in one direction or another as particular events of the day cause Americans in large numbers to rally around the president in times of crisis or to distance themselves from him when events are negative. Here, we see something very different. Public opinion stands today virtually where it was fifty years ago, with just over half the population supporting the death penalty, just as in the beginning of the series. According to our combined index, opinion in 1953 was 59 percent pro–death penalty; in 2006 this number was 57 percent.[10] At first glance, looking at pro–death penalty sentiment, for example, there appears to be little action here. For the first twenty years of our series, opinions were sporadically surveyed but appear to have fluctuated little.[11] Opinion slowly drifted downward from the beginning of the series until the late 1960s. After the *Furman* decision of 1972, when executions became unconstitutional, opinion started driving in the other direction, in a slow drift toward greater support for the death penalty that lasted for more than twenty years. (Stimson found the same in his more general survey of the public mood: As government became more liberal, opinion became more conservative.) Shifts in public opinion were not massive, even during these times; the index ranges from about 60, down to just above 50, then up to the high 60s, not very substantial movement in an absolute sense.

This highly inertial and seemingly permanent level of support is consistent with our understanding of individual-level attitudes on moral issues. Issues that touch readily on core values onto which people hold fast are not expected to change in response to each item in the news, and here we see this phenomenon very clearly. Theory tells us that when attitudes are tied to core values, no amount of new information should produce attitude change (Alvarez and Brehm 1995, 1997, 1998, 2002) unless respondents are ambivalent (see also Zaller 1992). This suggests that in the aggregate we should see only very small amounts of change.

The upward drift in opinion regarding the death penalty shifted again, however, in the mid-1990s, reversing a trend toward greater acceptance that had lasted for a generation. Support for the death penalty began to fall in 1996 on the cascade of legal action based on DNA evidence and concerns about the possible innocence of death row inmates and the fallibility of the system. At the very end of our series, we see public support for the death penalty continuing to decline, slowly but steadily.

Figure 6.3 presents pro–death penalty opinion separately from anti– simply to demonstrate that, calculated as percentages of the total number of pro or anti responses, the two series mirror each other exactly. The third series in the figure is net support, or the difference between the two series. Positive values indicate a net pro–death penalty advantage in public opinion, and negative values indicate stronger numbers for the anti–death penalty series. The net support series reached a peak in 1990 with a value of 33 percent then declined by more than fifteen points in the last ten years of the series, the period of the innocence debate. We will use this

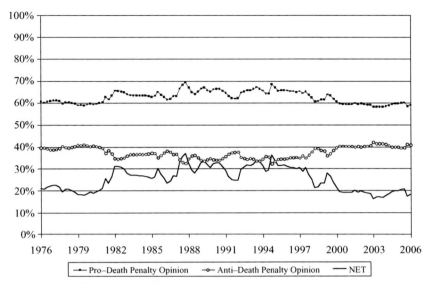

Figure 6.4. Public opinion indices, quarterly from 1976q1 to 2006q1. Support and opposition indices were created by running raw death penalty survey data through the Wcalc algorithm written by James Stimson and using the optional smoothing function. The net support index is simply the difference between these two indices (support minus opposition).

net support series as the simplest and most straightforward indicator of public opinion toward the death penalty.

Because our index is based on so many surveys, we can measure public opinion on a quarterly basis for the past forty years, not only on an annual basis as we have shown so far. This more fine-grained analysis will allow us to make a much more detailed assessment of movement in public opinion over this period. Only a few surveys were conducted in the early years of our series, so we have considerably more confidence in our analysis of the later part of the series than in the early part. Figure 6.4 presents this series.

Figure 6.4 shows the same general patterns as the annual series presented in Figure 6.3, but also more nuanced movements that reflect important shifts in media frames that often occur without warning, bursting onto the scene. We begin looking at the quarterly series in 1976 (the point at which quarterly homicide data become available), when public support for the death penalty hovered around 60 percent, according to our index. The net support series is positive throughout this period, ranging between values in the mid-20s and 30s in the 1980s and 1990s before declining quickly after 1999. During the first seven years of the new century, net support has averaged just over 18 percent – marking a dramatic reduction in public support for the death penalty. The quarterly series is less smooth than the annual series partly because the annual series is based on more observations per year, and so the random fluctuations due to sampling error are spread out more. But it also varies because there are true signals in the data, fluctuations in public opinion in response to particular events that may come to light at one point in time but may not have a lasting impact or may be cancelled out by other events occurring later in the same year. So although moving to the quarterly analysis requires that we accept a little more measurement error, it also allows us to study movement in public opinion in greater detail. As we are interested in the impact of the new innocence frame, the availability of a greater density of survey information for the recent historical period is particularly welcome. In our statistical treatment that follows, we use the quarterly data series because these allow us to track shifts in public opinion most closely. The reader can see from Figures 6.3 and 6.4 that both series tell a similar story – remember that Figure 6.3 begins in 1953, whereas Figure 6.4 begins much later, in 1976. This parallel movement makes sense, of course, as the yearly and quarterly indices are ultimately based on the same underlying surveys.

Both annual and quarterly time series are informative for our purposes. The first gives us a broad look at trends in public opinion on the death penalty, helping us to put the more recent movements in public opinion in historical perspective. The second provides a detailed look at the recent post-moratorium period and, in particular, at the effects of the innocence frame in a time in which attitudes have undergone unprecedented amounts of change in a short time period. We use the latter data to test our hypothesis that media framing influences public opinion on the death penalty. We turn to this task next.

ANALYZING PUBLIC OPINION

Public opinion on the death penalty, as we have shown, is highly stable over the long run; public opinion today looks a lot like it did yesterday. The inertial quality of aggregate public opinion means that we simply cannot expect dramatic shifts in public opinion on this topic in short periods of time. Unlike public opinion toward the president, which responds quickly to current events, aggregate sentiment on this topic is much more stable. There are two reasons for the slow, drifting quality of public opinion in this area. First is that the issue has limited salience. That is, every member of the public is not necessarily paying attention when events occur in relation to the death penalty. In contrast, say, to presidential decisions to take the nation to war, aggregate public opinion on the death penalty moves slowly partly because many Americans are not paying much attention. In

Chapter 4 we review *New York Times* coverage of the issue, and we make clear that there was, indeed, substantial coverage on the death penalty, especially during certain periods, such as those surrounding the 1972 to 1976 moratorium and when the innocence frame first "broke" in 2000, when there were 235 articles published on the topic. As we noted, 235 articles a year translates into several articles a week. But let us put this in some context – not to say that Americans do not know or care much about the death penalty, but simply to note the difference between an issue such as this and a more salient topic of discussion. Although the death penalty is familiar, it is not constantly in the news so much that members of the general public (in contrast, say, to readers of this book or to those who follow the death penalty debate with any particular interest) would continually be bombarded with news, events, and opinions on the topic to such an extent that their views might shift rapidly. One simple point of comparison is how often the issue appears on the front pages of the nation's newspapers. As we see in Chapter 4, since 1960, 254 death penalty stories have appeared on the front page of the *New York Times*. Although there is some upward trend there as we demonstrated, the total number of stories averages out to fewer than six per year, or one front-page article every two months. In stark contrast, Figure 6.5 shows front-page *New York Times* coverage of the U.S. war on terror.

Since September 2001, the war on terror has dominated the nation's headlines in a way that abortion, the death penalty, and other issues never have nor ever will. Everyone has reactions to this issue, and millions of Americans are directly affected by it, both by having family members serving overseas and by personally experiencing various commemorations and inconveniences associated with increased security. More than 35 percent of all the front-page stories in the *Times* for the past six years have been on the war. Since September 11, 2001, this number has rarely dropped below 25 percent in any given month, and in the first months of the U.S. invasion of Iraq, the war consumed more than 60 percent of front-page attention. By contrast, the death penalty, which is by no means obscure, generates nothing remotely close to this level of coverage – the series differ by orders of magnitude. So one reason public opinion moves only very slowly with respect to the death penalty is that, like most issues, it simply is not in the news very often and does not directly affect the lives of most Americans. It is easy to think that many people are or should be interested in issues such as the death penalty, especially if, like the readers of this book, one takes some particular interest in it. But the issue is remote for most Americans. People's views on the president or on issues such as the war in Iraq or the war on terror may be more volatile because people are much better informed about events that are, after all, much more dramatic than the typical courtroom drama associated with criminal appeals.

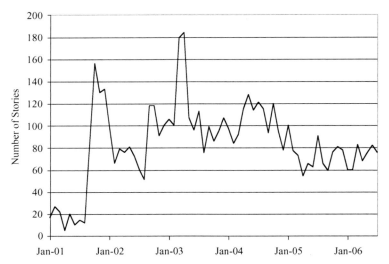

Figure 6.5. Front-page *New York Times* coverage of the war on terror, monthly from 2001 (January) to 2006 (December). The figure shows the number of articles appearing on the front page of the *New York Times* containing the words *terror, Iraq, Afghanistan,* or *al-Qaeda* anywhere in their text. Articles were collected from the Lexis-Nexis Academic Universe archives. During this period, the total number of front-page stories averaged 263 and ranged from a low of 218 to a high of 315. One hundred stories, therefore, represents about 40 percent of the total.

The second reason for the slowly evolving nature of public opinion on the death penalty is that, as we have discussed, most Americans' views on the death penalty are closely linked to their moral or religious sentiments. For any given individual, these attitudes do not change much over time. This notion rings especially true when we consider the ways in which public opinion is measured. The vast bulk of the 292 death penalty survey questions we employ have an abstract or a theoretical character. One could easily support the death penalty in the abstract, and say so in response to a survey question, even if one had strong qualms about the possibility of errors in particular cases. Because the impact of the innocence movement is partially dependent on pushing individuals to move away from the abstract and toward the specific case – questioning whether we can be sure that each specific court procedure was flawless – this shift may not be fully reflected in public opinion surveys. Yet despite these caveats, we do see movement in U.S. public opinion on the death penalty, and there is nothing that requires that public opinion remain within any particular bounds. Rather, opinion clearly moves in response to events (and interpretations of those events).

Now we move to a systematic analysis of what causes opinion to move and of the role of media framing as compared with other factors. A simple correlation between net tone, our media framing variable, and net support for the death penalty suggests that the two are related (the correlation is r = 0.57 over the period of our analysis). But simple correlations may be misleading. To test the hypothesis that media framing influences opinion on the death penalty, we estimate multivariate time series regression models of opinion. Although the effects of media frames are central to the analysis ahead, we test the additional hypothesis that attitudes toward the death penalty will respond to violent crime. Consistent with the literature that comes before us, we hypothesize that violent crime rates and support for the death penalty should be positively related.[12] As crime rates go up, citizens prefer a law and order approach to crime. Descriptive data indicate that support for harsher punishments in general increases when crime goes up, and support for the death penalty can be seen as part of this same get-tough-on-crime reaction (see Rankin 1979). Our indicator of violent crime is the number of homicides as reported in the FBI Uniform Crime Reports.[13]

In addition to homicide rates, we want to examine the effects of extraordinary events that focus public attention on the death penalty. By including extraordinary events in our analysis, we allow events to influence opinion beyond the effect of the news coverage that they generate and similarly also ensure that any measured effects of media framing are not simply picking up events, but reflect media coverage of them. The inclusion of major events is common in the literature on presidential approval, and the techniques of doing so are quite simple: One identifies the events that might be hypothesized to affect public opinion (i.e., any potentially substantial event) and includes a variable in the model that takes a value of 0 for all time periods except for when an event occurred, in which case the variable takes a value of 1. In our case, we complicate this slightly because we have some events that would be expected to increase support for the death penalty and some that would work in the other direction. So our events series consists of values of 0, +1, and −1. We considered six events: The bombing of the federal building in Oklahoma City on April 19, 1995 (+1); the January 30, 2000, declaration by Illinois governor George Ryan of a moratorium on executions in Illinois (−1); the September 11, 2001, terrorist acts (+1); the 100th exoneration of a death row prisoner on April 8, 2002 (−1); the beginning of the killing spree of the so-called D.C. snipers on September 9, 2002 (+1); and the January 11, 2003, blanket grant of clemency given all death row prisoners in Illinois (−1). The result is a single time series composed of 1s, −1s, and 0s. The estimated effect of this variable will tell us the average effect for any pro–death penalty event (with the effect of an anti–death penalty event being the inverse of this number). Although any selection of extraordinary events is somewhat arbitrary, these are clearly important events in the history of public attention to the issue. In addition, we also separately considered the effect of each of the six events individually, as we discuss below.

Armed with our time series of death penalty sentiment (net support), the net tone of media coverage from Chapter 4, homicide levels, and events, we begin our analysis. The analysis covers the period from 1976 to the first quarter of 2006, and the analysis is not annual but quarterly. So for each quarter, we want to know if we can predict public opinion on the basis of the other variables mentioned and the relative importance of each of the variables in explaining opinion. The historical window we cover is limited by the availability of homicide data, unavailable quarterly before 1976.

The general story we wish to test empirically is that public opinion on the death penalty is tied to violent crime rates and the tenor of media coverage. Given the slowly evolving nature of attitudes on the death penalty, we have expectations about the nature of the dynamic relationships we will find in the data. In particular, we expect most of the effects of homicides and media coverage to be met with initial resistance in the short run and to work their way slowly through the system, exerting their full influence on public opinion in the long run, as time passes. In statistical models, long-run effects are found in the equilibrium relationships of *levels* of homicides and net tone with *levels* of opinion. So we expect that high numbers of murders and pro–death penalty stories will be linked to more pro–death penalty opinions, whereas lower numbers of murders and anti–death penalty stories will be tied to more anti–death penalty sentiment. If this hypothesis is correct, opinion should move in tandem with levels of violent crime and the tone of media coverage as time passes. In contrast, we would not expect to see, for example, large proportions of the public opposed to the death penalty in the face of high murder rates and a barrage of media coverage supportive of capital punishment.

Short-run effects can be found in statistical models in the responsiveness of public opinion – *changes* in public opinion – to *changes* in the values of homicides and net tone. Given the solidifying role of tightly held moral values in determining death penalty opinion, we expect that short-term increases or decreases in murder rates and changes in the tone of media coverage will have little or no effect on short-term movements in opinion. Importantly, though, short-term changes in homicides and media coverage also disturb the long-run link with opinion so that opinion needs to move, or adjust, to stay linked with the harbingers of death penalty sentiment in the long run. We expect that adjustment will be slow, as opinion is highly inertial, but we expect it nonetheless to occur if indeed opinion is linked to violent crime and the tenor of media coverage in the long run.

To capture these dynamic relationships and test for their existence, we estimate an error correction model, a regression model in which *changes* in opinion are regressed on *changes* in both the number of homicides and media tone (assessing the short-run effects), and a term capturing how far out of synch the *level* of opinion is with the *level* of homicides and media tone based on their values in the previous period (assessing the long-run effects).[14]

Analysis

We present our analysis of death penalty sentiment in Table 6.1. We focus here on explaining net support, or the difference between the percentages of support for and opposition to the death penalty. This is the solid black line in Figure 6.4. (The appendix to this chapter shows the same analysis for support and opposition separately; the reader can see that the results are highly consistent with those for net support, so we focus on just one series here.)

The results from our model are presented in two columns in Table 6.1. The first column reports the long-run equilibrium relationship of levels of opinion with levels of homicides and net tone.[15] These results show that levels of opinion are positively related to levels of homicides and pro–death penalty media coverage. More specifically, each entry in column 1 tells how much net support increases for each additional 1,000 homicides or single media story. So, for example, for every 1,000 homicides in the country, the level of opinion in equilibrium goes up by an average of 3.4 percentage points. Similarly, for every ten additional net pro–death penalty stories, we expect the level of opinion to move 1.5 percentage points in the pro–death penalty direction. These are long-run effects, the amount that public opinion changes as time passes. The numbers in parentheses are standard errors; these show the level of confidence we have, statistically, in each of these coefficients. If the standard error is very small compared with the regression coefficient, this means we have a great deal of confidence in the results. If the numbers are similar in size to each other, then we have less confidence. Footnotes to the table indicate the precise degree of confidence we have in each coefficient.

Column 2 tells us how opinion moves in the short run in response to a) deviations from the long-run equilibrium relationship, b) changes in homicides and net tone, and c) the experience of major death penalty–related events. We consider these in order.

When the long-run link among levels of homicides, media coverage, and public opinion demonstrated in column 1 is disturbed, this means that public opinion is too high or too low relative to homicides and media coverage in the previous period and cannot be maintained. The "deviation from long-run equilibrium" coefficient presented in column 2 assesses

Table 6.1. *Explaining public opinion on the death penalty, quarterly from 1976q1 to 2006q1*

	Long-run (equilibrium) opinion	Short-run (change in) opinion
Net tone$_{t-1}$	0.149^a	
	(0.049)	
Homicides$_{t-1}$ (in thousands)	3.412^b	
	(0.753)	
Constant	8.949^b	−0.025
	(3.865)	(0.168)
Deviation from long-run equilibrium$_{t-1}$		−0.173^b
		(0.045)
Change in net tone$_t$		0.032
		(0.020)
Change in homicides$_t$		−2.206
		(1.883)
Death penalty events$_t$		0.809
		(0.750)
N	120	119
R-squared	0.446	0.126
RMSE	4.063	1.831
StDev	5.44	1.924

Note: Data are quarterly from the first quarter of 1976 to the second quarter of 2006. Entries are regression coefficients (standard errors in parentheses). The dependent variable is the net support series from Figure 6.4.

^{a} $p < 0.05$.
^{b} $p < 0.001$.

the quickness with which public opinion adjusts to correct this type of disequilibrium. The coefficient, −0.17, tells us two things. First, the negative sign tells us that the direction of change in opinion will counter the disequilibrium; when levels of public opinion are too strongly pro–death penalty for homicide levels and media coverage, public opinion will move in an anti–death penalty direction. And when public opinion is too strongly opposed, it must move in a pro–death penalty direction, so the system has a built-in self-correcting mechanism. Second, the coefficient tells us how quickly public opinion adjusts to return to equilibrium. Specifically, about 17 percent of the disequilibrium is corrected in each quarter. This is relatively slow; the system may be relatively far from its long-run equilibrium for quite some time, a finding consistent with the character of public opinion on the death penalty as we know it. Consistent with our understanding of opinions on entrenched moral issues such as this, the public is willing to maintain levels of support out of synch with homicides and media coverage for some number of quarters – five or more years' worth – before fully correcting the disequilibrium. Put differently, over 80 percent of the equilibrium error in public opinion levels is tolerated in each subsequent quarter after the long-run relationship is disturbed. Public support for the death penalty is highly resilient, even in the face of new and contradictory information as to its appropriateness. It is not completely unchanging with respect to new information, but it adjusts only slowly.

In addition to this error-correction effect, we assess the short-run effects of changing numbers of homicides and changing numbers of toned media stories. We find that quarter-to-quarter changes in these variables exert no independent effect on changes in opinion. The standard errors on these estimated coefficients in column 2 are so large that we cannot dismiss the possibility that the coefficients are only different from zero by chance. Once we account for the effects of any disequilibrium in the level of opinion as it is related to media coverage and homicides, changes in media coverage and numbers of homicides have no short-run effect. Given the inertial character of public opinion, we expect short-term changes to have limited influence on its short-run dynamics, and in fact we find no evidence of any effects. But given that the effects of media coverage and homicides work their way through the long-run equilibrium, the effect of net tone and homicides on public opinion is nonetheless very real (as we see in column 1).

Finally, we mention briefly our findings with regard to highly visible events such as the Oklahoma City bombing, the Washington sniper shootings, and significant events associated with the innocence movement. Considered jointly, the effect of major events is insignificant, but when we consider the separate effects of pro– and anti–death penalty events (not reported), we see that anti–death penalty events exerted a marginally significant depressant effect on net support, reducing support for the death penalty by an average of nearly two percentage points per event. When each event was entered into the model separately (again, not reported here) only Governor Ryan's grant of clemency to all death row prisoners in the first quarter of 2003, just before leaving office, is significant ($p = 0.09$). The governor's temporary moratorium on the death penalty in 2000 also increased opposition, but the effects were not significant ($p = 0.27$). None of the events that we might expect to increase support for the death penalty – the Oklahoma City bombing, the D.C. sniper attacks, and the September 11 terrorist attacks – exerted a significant effect on sentiment. We should remember, though, that these events are themselves covered by the media and may have an indirect effect through net tone. In the case of all events we considered, there was newspaper coverage – in some cases, extensive coverage. Events, then, may have both an independent effect and one mediated by the news. Finally, it is worth noting that some events, such as proof that we wrongly executed an innocent person, could have yet a larger effect, particularly if media coverage of the event was extensive.

Overall, the model explains a modest amount of variation in short-run changes in opinion. The standard for assessing the adequacy of the model fit is, however, unclear. Any time we seek to explain change, model fit will not be as impressive as when we explain levels of opinion. Calculating predicted levels of opinion based on the estimates in Table 6.1 shows that we explain the bulk of the variation in levels of opinion. So our model explains levels of opinion quite well. The model also stands up well to diagnostic tests and performs well when we look at shorter sub-periods rather than the entire period, so the model is quite robust to minor changes in specification. We now consider the effects of each variable in detail in turn.

Imagine that homicides increased by 1,000 in some quarter. Our results indicate that this would have no immediate effect on public opinion; changes in the number of homicides do not produce an immediate (lagged one period) change in public opinion. (The coefficient on lagged changes in homicides is not significantly less than zero.) However, this change in the number of homicides disturbs the long-run equilibrium relationship between homicide levels and levels of public opinion. To maintain equilibrium, public opinion must increase by 3.41 in the long run (3.41 × 1, homicides are measured in thousands and the coefficient here is that on homicides in column 1). But only a portion of this effect is realized in the next period, a portion given by the coefficient on the long-run equilibrium component in column 2 (0.17), as we noted earlier. Tracing out the effect of our increase in homicides, we expect to see 17 percent of that long-term change take place in the following quarter, and then 17 percent of the remaining disequilibrium amount in each quarter thereafter until the full impact of 3.41 points is reached. This means we would see a change of 0.59 (0.17 × 3.41) in the pro–death penalty direction in the quarter following the shock to homicides. There would be a continuing, but gradually decreasing, effect of this shift in homicide rate so that the first time period would see an impact of 0.59; the second, an impact of 0.17 × (3.41 − 0.59), or 0.49; the third, 0.17 × (3.41 − 0.59 − 0.49), or 0.40; and so on. In each successive period, 17 percent of the remaining disequilibrium would be corrected. This would continue for about twenty quarters, the amount of time it takes until the 3.41 change in public opinion is achieved.[16]

We can similarly track the effects of a shock in the net tone of *New York Times* articles, introduced in Chapter 4 – that is, the number of pro– minus the number of anti–death penalty tone articles in a given period.

High numbers reflect more pro–death penalty coverage. Here we choose to examine a five-point change in the anti–death penalty direction, where this is the average quarterly value of net tone in the time period from 1995 to the end of the series. Once again, the change in media coverage has no immediate effect (note the insignificant effect of change in net tone in column 2). As in the previous case, the effects on public opinion are all felt via the long-run relationship. Here a 5-point decrease in net tone leads to an expected 0.75-point decrease in death penalty support in the long run (0.15 × 5). As in the case of increases in the homicide level, this effect does not happen all at once, but in stages over several quarters, in fact several years. The dynamic is exactly the same as that for homicides, with just over 17 percent of the equilibrium error corrected in the quarter after it occurs, 17 percent of the remaining equilibrium error corrected in the quarter after that, and so on until the new equilibrium value of public opinion has been reached.

If we look at how net tone has actually varied over the period covered in this analysis, from January 1976 to the end of 2005, we find that there was one period – the second quarter of 1990 – in which there were sixteen more pro– than anti–death penalty stories in the *New York Times*. Similarly, in the second quarter of 2001, there were forty-three more anti– than pro–death penalty stories. So there is quite a lot of movement; net tone, in fact, ranged from +16 to −43, or a swing of almost sixty points. Based on the estimates reported in Table 6.1, we can calculate the equilibrium or expected value of public opinion for each case, holding the number of homicides constant at 5,000, its approximate mean quarterly value over the full period (homicides numbered nearly 6,000 in 1990 and dipped below 4,000 in 2001). The equilibrium value of public opinion given sixteen pro–death penalty stories and 5,000 homicides is given by the long-run equation in column 1, substituting values of net tone and homicides into the equation: $8.95 + (0.149 \times 16) + (3.41 \times 5) = 28.38$, for a net pro–death penalty opinion heavily in favor of capital punishment. Compare this with the equilibrium value of opinion associated with a net tone of −43 assuming the same 5,000 homicides. Now the equilibrium level of opinion is given by $8.95 + (0.149 \times -43) + (3.41 \times 5) = 19.59$. In just over a decade, the equilibrium value of public opinion shifted by 8.79 percentage points. Although in both periods death penalty supporters outnumber opponents, the public opinion altered dramatically. These are strong effects indeed.

A comparable look at the effect of homicides across its full range of values presents one way of assessing the relative importance of homicides and net tone over this historical period. During the period of our study, the number of homicides per quarter in the United States ranged from a high of 6,179 to a low of 3,845, or by a total of 2,334. We hold net tone at a neutral value to explore the consequences of homicide levels absent any media coverage of the death penalty (or equal amounts of pro– and anti–death penalty coverage) and to simplify the equilibrium calculations. Under this scenario, the equilibrium value of opinion for the lowest observed homicide level is given by $8.95 + (0.149 \times 0) + (3.41 \times 3.845) = 22.06$. The corresponding equilibrium value of net support at the peak homicide levels was $8.95 + (0.149 \times 0) + (3.41 \times 6.179) = 30.02$. Across the range of the data, then, we see comparable effects on the change in equilibrium levels of net support for the death penalty due to net tone and to homicides, about eight percentage points in each case.

The statistical evidence so far supports two conclusions. First, public opinion on the death penalty is indeed linked to homicide levels and net tone, but the linkage is apparent over the long run; there are no significant short-term effects. Second, related to the first point, public support for the death penalty is highly resilient. We see evidence of its resilience in several ways. First, we have no evidence that changes in either the number of homicides or net tone produce short-term changes in public opinion. Additionally, the responsiveness of public opinion is limited in the long run both in the overall size of the effects of homicides and net tone and in the speed with which public opinion reacts to equilibrium errors, as measured by the error correction coefficient in column 2; change comes in small increments and unfolds only slowly over time. What all this means in plain English is that public opinion does indeed respond to homicide levels and to the net tone of media coverage about the death penalty. But the change is sluggish not immediate. Opinion slowly drifts in response to important changes to the tenor of the debate as expressed in the media and to the violent crime rate. This opinion shift is sensible and important, but it is not immediate. Americans are not constantly paying attention to each and every news article or event related to the death penalty. In the aggregate, however, public opinion does indeed respond to changing circumstances in very sensible ways. Over the last forty years, violent crime rates and media coverage have varied dramatically and with that variation has come limited but important changes in public opinion. These shifts in public opinion, as we will see in Chapter 7, are linked in turn to important changes in public policy.

The results we present in Table 6.1 are highly robust. We considered various ways of modeling these results and tested many different specifications to ensure that our results were not sensitive to small details of our statistical specification before settling on the model we presented. One particular possibility that we tested was that increasing numbers of executions and exonerations themselves, rather than media coverage of them, could explain death penalty sentiment. Mounting numbers of executions may have made the public react with either complacency (becoming more accustomed to increasing numbers of executions as they increased during the 1980s and 1990s) or outrage (perhaps responding to a more routine use of a punishment previously reserved only for extraordinary circumstances). But there is no evidence in favor of either hypothesis. Executions have no effect on death penalty sentiment. Similarly, the number of exonerations may have affected public sentiment, so we considered that possibility by including the actual number of exonerations in the model. Media coverage may lead us to think that exonerations are a recent occurrence so that media attention is merely translating the effect of actual exonerations. But this possibility is easily dismissed. We see some weak statistical evidence that the number of individual exonerations has a short-run effect on public opinion. But if we take the full range of exoneration counts across the historical period we have studied, the expected change in public opinion is only 1.4 percentage points, and there is no long-run effect. Importantly, our earlier findings with regard to the net tone of media coverage did not change when we added exonerations to the model. It is not the occurrence of executions that influences opinion, it is media coverage, specifically its tone, that matters. And although exonerations may exert some direct effect on short-run opinions, they do not affect public opinion in the long run, and the short-term effect is substantively trivial. In sum, the model we present in Table 6.1 is highly robust.

The complicated short-term and long-term effects of each of the variables in Table 6.1 make it hard to understand how public opinion moves, because in the real world, all the variables are shifting at the same time. That is, public opinion at any given time is partly affected by previous changes in homicide rates, media coverage, and dramatic events. But in each period, there are further changes in each of these variables, some working to reinforce each other, some working in the opposite direction, and so the net impact on public opinion of immediate and historic events is very difficult to parse out. We can take our statistical model and substitute hypothetical values for one or another independent variable to see what public opinion *would have been* under different scenarios. That is, we can take our statistical model and set homicides to some level and not allow them to change. Or we can set media coverage to a set level and leave it there. By doing this carefully and one variable at a time, we can see how public opinion would have changed if one variable, and one variable alone, were changing over time. In the real world, everything changes at the same time, but in a computer simulation we can simplify things. Figure 6.6 shows two such scenarios.

The solid line in Figure 6.6 shows our predicted value of net support.[17] The line with black squares (called scenario 1) shows what net support *would have been* if media coverage had never changed from its actual value of +14 in 1993. Under this alternate scenario, public opinion continues to grow more supportive of the death penalty until 1995. It declines after that (largely as the result of observed declines in the number of homicides), but much less sharply than in reality. The series ends with a value

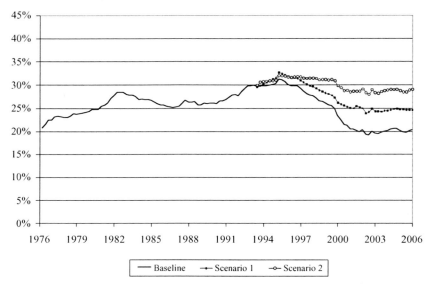

Figure 6.6. Simulating public opinion on the death penalty I, quarterly from 1976q1 to 2006q1. The figure shows simulated public opinion compared with our baseline prediction. Scenario 1 shows the predicted level of net support if the net tone of media attention had achieved its actual value of +14 in the third quarter of 1993 and then remained constant at that level. Scenario 2 shows predicted net support under the case in which homicides reached their value of 6,613 in that same period and then never changed. In each scenario, values for all the other variables in the model retain their actual observed values.

about five points higher than that of the actual observations. The largest gap in the two series comes after 2000, when the net tone of media coverage in fact declined precipitously. Holding our net tone variable constant at its highest value allows us to see what would have happened if these changes had not occurred. Public opinion would have been significantly more pro–death penalty, but it still would have declined from its peak because of the decline in homicides. Because the hypothetical series ends up, several years later, at a level five points higher than the actual series, we can attribute this difference solely to the impact of the observed changes in media coverage. In fact, the net tone of media coverage went down, then up, over this time. If it had reached its high point in 1993 and stayed there, public opinion in 2006 would have been five points higher than in fact it was.

    The line with empty circles in Figure 6.6 (scenario 2) presents the case in which media coverage follows its actual course, but we hold the number of homicides constant at 6,132, the value it actually reached in the third quarter of 1993, and very close to its all-time maximum. Comparing the

Table 6.2. *The impact of various scenarios on public opinion,*
quarterly

Hypothetical scenario	Projected impact on net support
Reduce net tone of media coverage by 50	−7.46
Reduce homicides by 2,000	−6.80
Have an event twice as powerful as the mass commutation by Ill. governor Ryan	−1.62
Both 1 and 2	−14.27
All three events	−15.89

Note: The table shows the long-term impact on net public opinion of each change in the independent variables (net tone and homicides) as listed. Individual events, occurring just once, have only a short-term impact that deteriorates after several quarters, and so we show only the short-term impact of the mass commutation in Illinois. All the impacts are symmetrical, so the impact of net tone, homicides, or events moving opinion in the pro–death penalty direction would be equal in size to those shown here.

distance between this line and the dark solid line allows one to see the impact of declining homicides on public opinion. In all, had homicides not been on the decline from 1993 onward, we would expect net support in 2006 to be nine points higher in a pro–death penalty direction than we in fact observe.

We can, of course, manipulate our hypothetical model of public opinion in any way we want to consider a variety of counterfactuals. Table 6.2 shows some alternative scenarios and the resulting impact on net support.

Table 6.2 shows the impact of various possible changes to the tone of media coverage surrounding the death penalty, the number of homicides, and significant events. All these events are symmetrical, so when the table shows that a movement of fifty points toward more critical news coverage would lead to a decline in net support of about seven and a half points, that also means that the opposite would be true: Opinion would move in the pro–death penalty direction by the same amount if media coverage shifted by the equivalent amount in that direction. It is impossible to say, of course, what are the most reasonable possible scenarios to consider. However, the movements we illustrate here are all within the realm of what has occurred in the past. The net tone of media coverage, as we noted, has in fact shifted quite dramatically, by more than sixty points, in the past twenty years, and the number of homicides has shifted by well over the 2,000 murders we illustrate in the table. Only the events series has been manipulated more significantly than what we have observed. This is because each event is unique, and in any case, most of the impact of these events is reflected in the change in the tone of media coverage. The impact of an event twice as strong as the most powerful one we have yet observed would be just two points, over and above its impact on media coverage.[18] Of course, that effect would probably be quite substantial because such an event would be highly newsworthy.

What would be the overall effect of the various counterfactual scenarios we have considered? It could easily move net support by twenty points in one direction or another. Looking back at Figure 6.3, which shows this series over the past forty years, it is clear that if opinion shifted by twenty points in the downward direction, overall opinion would be significantly below zero; a majority would oppose the death penalty. This number would be even more substantially biased in the anti–death penalty direction if the question posed to the public specified the option of life without parole, which as we noted, is available in forty-eight of the fifty states. Public opinion on the death penalty changes only slowly. But it does change, and it changes predictably in response to changes in the environment. It is impossible to say what developments might occur with regard to homicide rates and media coverage of the death penalty in the years to come. Opinion could shift toward a pro–death penalty direction. But we have shown a combination of forces here that could easily move American public opinion in a way that would support a drastic reduction in the use of the death penalty, if not its complete elimination.

Figure 6.7 illustrates two alternative scenarios. This is largely the same information from Table 6.2, but graphing it over time shows the slowly evolving nature of the trends. The simulations are very simple. We picked an arbitrary time period, in this case 1992, and substituted alternative values for the observed figures for homicides and net tone. In the first scenario, we added fifty points to whatever the actual net tone of media coverage was in each quarter. So if the net tone in any given period was +15, we made it +65. We did the same to homicides, adding 2,000 to each value. Comparing scenario 1 with the baseline, our actual predicted values, shows that the events take some time to reach their impact, but that after several years the two series are perfectly parallel to each other. The series are fifteen points apart.

Scenario 2 in Figure 6.7 represents the opposite case, with media coverage fifty points more negative in tone and homicides 2,000 cases lower than actually observed. Like the first series, this one takes several years to allow these manipulations to reach their full impact, but after that time, it is consistently fifteen points lower than the baseline.

The scenarios we present may appear unrealistic. Public opinion does not move that much; over the period of our quarterly analysis, after all, net support has remained within a range of +17 to about +35. But in fact, what we really know about public opinion is mostly that it moves *slowly*. Over the forty-year period at which we have looked, net support has ranged from just below 0 (in 1967) to 35 (in 1994). If other factors were to change, in particular the nature of political and media-related

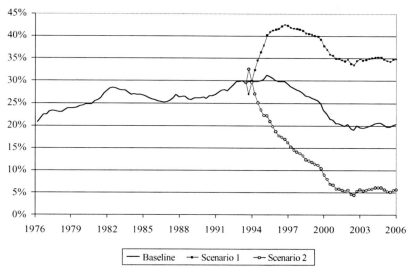

Figure 6.7. Simulating public opinion on the death penalty II, quarterly from 1976q1 to 2006q1. The figure shows simulated public opinion compared with our baseline prediction. Scenario 1 shows the trace that public opinion would have followed if, in 1992 and thereafter, media coverage was fifty points more positive than actually observed, there were 2,000 more homicides per quarter, and the Illinois mass clemency in January 2003 had not occurred. Scenario 2 presents the opposite: media coverage fifty points more negative, 2,000 fewer homicides, and the Illinois event having twice its observed impact.

discussions of the death penalty, then we could easily see changes in public opinion. It would take some time for these changes to affect aggregate public sentiment, but sustained movement can have a strong impact.

CONCLUSIONS

In this chapter, we construct a new measure of public opinion on the death penalty, the most comprehensive assessment of trends over time in public sentiment on the topic ever assembled. The results of this survey analysis show that public opinion is highly inertial. The American public supports the death penalty, by and large. But public sentiment has waxed and waned gradually over time, moving toward greater support during the 1970s and 1980s and in the first several years of the 1990s, as media coverage and the number of homicides both also trended in the direction of pro–death penalty positions. An important shift occurred in the mid-1990s, however, as the idea of "innocence" began to have a significant impact on the nature of public discussion surrounding this topic, and as the number of homicides began a long decline. Today, more Americans support than oppose the death penalty when queried using the standard survey questions. However, these numbers are significantly lower when the question offers the option of life without parole. Our analysis here has suggested that public opinion, in the aggregate, responds in a meaningful, logical, and consistent fashion to changes in the environment surrounding this issue. Facts matter. Newspaper coverage matters. The tone of discussion matters. Significant events matter. The public responds to these things in the aggregate, and aggregate public opinion therefore shifts in response to these trends.

One interesting element about public opinion regarding the death penalty is how hypothetical the questions are concerning it. In the next chapter, we move from looking at public opinion in general to the actual behavior of prosecutors, defense attorneys, judges, and juries in America's courtrooms, and we do so in a form that directly parallels the analysis presented in this chapter. The people involved in courtroom drama associated with the death penalty are faced with anything but a hypothetical, theoretical discussion; rather, they deal literally with questions of the life and death of an individual sitting in front of them. As we see in Chapter 7, many of the same factors that we have seen to affect public opinion in this chapter also affect the behaviors of juries and therefore the annual number of death sentences imposed across the country, but the degree of change we have witnessed in response to the rise of the innocence frame is much more substantial. Change comes quicker when the question moves from the theoretical to the individual, and there is reason to expect that the innocence frame would have its greatest impact here. Many could truthfully say they support the death penalty in response to a generically worded survey question, but not impose it in a case before them because of doubts about the perfection of the system. We turn to this question in the next chapter when we examine the effects of framing on policy.

APPENDIX

Table 6.A1. *Explaining public opinion on the death penalty, quarterly from 1976q1 to 2006q1*

	Opposition to the death penalty		Support for the death penalty	
	Long-run (equilibrium) opinion	Short-run (change in) opinion	Long-run (equilibrium) opinion	Short-run (change in) opinion
Net tone$_{t-1}$	−0.068[a]		0.081[a]	
	(0.023)		(0.026)	
Homicides$_{t-1}$ (in thousands)	1.677[b]		1.735[b]	
	(0.355)		(0.399)	
Constant	45.403[b]	0.012	54.352[b]	−0.014
	(1.824)	(0.079)	(2.050)	(0.090)
Deviation from long-run equilibrium$_{t-1}$		−0.172[b]		−0.175[b]
		(0.045)		(0.045)
Change in net tone$_t$		−0.015		0.017
		(0.009)		(0.011)
Change in homicides$_t$		0.915		−1.304
		(0.885)		(1.010)
Death penalty events$_t$		−0.506		0.304
		(0.351)		(0.403)
N	120	119	120	119
R-squared	0.453	0.131	0.438	0.124
RMSE	1.917	0.859	2.155	0.985
StDev	2.583	0.905	2.863	1.034

Note: Data are quarterly from the first quarter of 1976 to the first quarter of 2006. Entries are regression coefficients (standard errors in parentheses). The dependent variables are from Figure 6.4.
[a] $p < 0.05$.
[b] $p < 0.001$.

7 THE RISE AND FALL OF A PUBLIC POLICY

IN CHAPTER 6, we demonstrate powerful framing effects on aggregate public opinion – specifically, how the innocence frame led to a slow but steady and cumulatively important decrease in public support for the death penalty over the last decade. In that chapter, our focus is fine-grained; we use quarterly data to measure short- as well as long-term opinion responsiveness to the shifting foci of media attention. In doing so, we eliminate counterexplanations for the decline in death penalty support that we have observed since the mid-1990s; in particular, neither executions nor exonerations help to explain this change. Homicides and the cascade of attention paid to the new innocence frame together explain the decline in support for the death penalty. The changes in public opinion that we note in Chapter 6 are not spectacular; many people continue to view the death penalty in the same way they always have. All members of the public have not been affected by the innocence frame, and the survey questions about the topic tend to elicit, we think, relatively general or generic reactions to the issue. We will see here that public policy and the behaviors of juries have been much more greatly affected by the innocence frame than aggregate public opinion. Further, even the modest shifts in public opinion that we document in Chapter 6 have a powerful impact on public policy. In this sense, public opinion itself contributes to the positive feedback mechanisms that are at the heart of an attention cascade. As more Americans come to question the logistics and the mechanics of the death penalty, slowly this begins to affect their neighbors, even if some "opinion leaders" are quicker to be affected by the general trend than are others. As more members of the public look at the issue in this new way, public policy is also affected; these effects are also reciprocal, so we see the development of a positive reinforcement system.

In this chapter, we focus on explaining changes in the annual number of death sentences handed down by judges and juries across the nation, and we look particularly at public opinion, media coverage, and the number of homicides to explain these shifts; our model of public policy parallels very closely the one we use for public opinion. Our analysis is unusual because we have a very clear measure of the state of public policy; in the political science literature on framing and policy outcomes, it is often difficult to measure policy outcomes clearly, but here we have a clear indicator. Although many who are initially sent to death row are later released, have their sentences commuted, or are not executed for other reasons, the decision by a jury to sentence someone to death is a powerful policy statement, one of the most powerful our government ever makes. It reflects both legal mores and social concerns. For these reasons, we find the number of death sentences to be a singularly appropriate gauge of public policy in this area, and we use this measure as the dependent variable in our analysis.

We proceed by following the strategy employed in the previous chapter so that the structure of Chapter 7 parallels that of Chapter 6. We begin by recapping the history of death sentences in the United States. Then we analyze these trends systematically to determine the relative importance of media framing and homicide levels. We also assess the role of public opinion and events related to the death penalty – in particular, the constitutional ban on death sentences. We show that the number of death sentences, like the balance of public opinion that we examine in Chapter 6, is strongly influenced by each of these pieces of the death penalty system. Further, we show that the effects of the net tone of media coverage are substantively much bigger than homicide levels. Public opinion, which we show in Chapter 6 to be affected strongly by net tone, further drives death sentences, over and above the direct impact we observe. Our results provide strong support for the social cascade model. With more pro–death penalty media coverage come more death sentences; and with more popular support for the death penalty come more death sentences as well. Of course, the effects work both ways, so our analysis helps explain both the rise and the decline of the death penalty over the past several decades.

ANNUAL DEATH SENTENCES

Approximately 100 Americans were sentenced to death on average in each year from 1961 to 1972. The numbers varied widely during the years immediately surrounding the four-year constitutional moratorium on executions from 1972 to 1976. In the years following the reinstatement of capital punishment, annual sentencing rates rose in a regular progression from 137 in 1977 to 320 in 1996. Since 1997, however, death sentences have dramatically declined, reversing a twenty-year trend. Only 128 Americans were sentenced to death in 2005, less than half the number of nine years before. Part of our job in this chapter, as we have said,

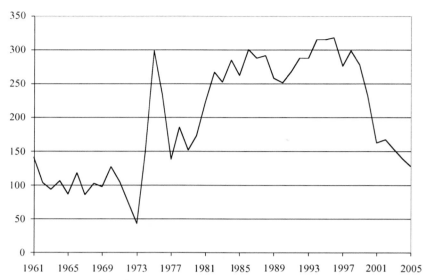

Figure 7.1. Annual death sentences, 1961 to 2005. (*Source*: Snell 2005.)

is to explain the variance in sentencing rates for the entire time period of our data, from 1961 to 2005. And in parallel with Chapter 6, we are particularly interested here in determining whether the dramatic decrease in sentences over the last decade can indeed be attributed in part to the redefinition of the debate that we have observed in the media. We further assess the role of public opinion in determining the number of death sentences delivered in the United States each year, controlling for media framing and the number of homicides.

Figure 7.1 provides a detailed view of how sentencing rates have changed over time. We see in Chapter 2 that the number of executions per year across America was high in the early parts of the century, reaching a peak in the 1930s and just before World War II. In the more recent period, however, Figure 7.1 makes clear that there were approximately 100 new death sentences per year before the 1972 to 1976 moratorium and that these constitutional decisions induced huge changes in sentencing. First, the decline in sentences directly before the moratorium indicates state anticipation of the concerns with the death penalty system that the Supreme Court would officially censure in 1972. Then, when the national tide turned quickly and strongly back in favor of the death penalty immediately after the moratorium was instituted, the states pushed an unprecedented number of sentences through the system, resulting in the spike we see in 1975. Following this spike, there was a steady and large increase in the use of the death penalty in the 1980s, leveling off at around 250 to 300 cases per year until 1996, when the series reached a peak of 320. In stark contrast to the previous three decades, since 1997 sentences have decreased such that by 2005 there were only 128: a decline of more than 60 percent. In the world of policymaking, this is a decline of dramatic proportion.

The late 1960s and early 1970s were momentous times in U.S. politics and social history, with riots, assassinations, antiwar protests, rising crime rates, and a law-and-order reaction to many of these events. Rising crime rates and President Nixon's federal "war on crime" led to a dramatic shift in policy, reversing trends that had lasted more than a generation toward less use and support of the death penalty. The new politicization of crime policy led to both parties advancing "tough-on-crime" policies. These attitudes as well as increasing use and support of the death penalty would themselves last a generation, before being reversed, in turn, in the mid-1990s with the rise of the innocence frame. In the long-term perspective, which we present in Chapter 2, it could well be that the period from the early 1970s to the mid-1990s will appear to be the anomaly.

ANALYZING DEATH SENTENCES

The number of death sentences per year over the last forty years varies quite a lot, considerably more than what we see for public opinion in Chapter 6. This discrepancy between sentencing dynamics and opinion dynamics results, we think, from the hypothetical and abstract nature of the public opinion questions as opposed to the practical and concrete nature of decision-making on capital cases before juries. Citizen opinions on the death penalty are theoretical, based on relatively fixed core values applied to questions about capital punishment that are necessarily abstract and usually quite vague. As we see in Chapter 6, the most common question used to gauge Americans' views on capital punishment asks respondents if they favor the death penalty "in the case of murder." Without being pressed for specifics, people tap into their core values. These general opinions, as we discuss in Chapter 6, are difficult to budge. In contrast, citizens in a jury box are exposed to two kinds of information that influence the opinion formation process. First, jurors are asked to consider the death penalty not in the general "case of murder" but in the very specific case before them. The nature of the crime, aggravating and extenuating circumstances, and live testimonies – in addition to the experience of having personal responsibility for a defendant's fate – provide information that allows jurors to pinpoint their opinion in a specific case, not in general. Although people's opinions in specific cases often mirror their abstract views, under the right circumstances specific and general opinions may differ in important ways. Second, jurors receive informational cues from prosecuting and defense attorneys alike that serve as education about the state of the criminal justice system and capital punishment in particular – a "crash course" in sentencing policy that average citizens do not receive. In times when the death penalty is accepted in the nation (and in legal communities) as just punishment, cues to this effect come through in the way each side of a criminal sentencing case presents itself. When the death penalty is under question, as it has been throughout the last decade, prosecuting attorneys may back off from calling for the death penalty (or call for it with less conviction), and defense attorneys may highlight popular criticisms about the system to spark doubts of innocence in jurors' minds, even though the defendant has already been convicted. Thus, if we think of death penalty sentencing as "applied" opinion, we see why opinion in sentencing decisions has wider variance than opinion in the abstract, because jurors equipped with these additional pieces of information will respond more quickly to changes in – and framing of – the death penalty system than will Americans on average.

In this chapter, we assess the responsiveness of death sentences to homicides and media framing, comparing these effects with those we find on public opinion in Chapter 6, and additionally we assess the role of public opinion. Along the way, we account for the effects of the constitutional ban on executions, which – as we noted earlier – affected death sentences as well. The correlation between net tone, our media framing variable, and sentences is positive but modest, $r = 0.24$. Still simple correlations are misleading if either another variable – perhaps the number of homicides – influences both media framing and the number of death sentences or if the relationship holds only under certain conditions. We test the hypothesis that media framing influences death sentences using a simple multivariate time series regression model to deal with both of these problems and to estimate death sentences. In parallel with Chapter 6, we hypothesize that as violent crime rates increase, the number of death sentences should increase. Not only do the numbers of potential capital cases before juries increase with the number of murders, but also concern about crime increases with crime rates, leading to the view that more should be done to be tough on crime – namely, sentencing more people to death. As we note in Chapter 6, exercising the death penalty is part of a tough-on-crime strategy. Also as in Chapter 6, we use the number of homicides (measured in thousands) as reported in the FBI Uniform Crime Reports as our indicator of violent crime rates.

New to this model is public opinion. Public opinion has been linked to political behavior and public policy in a variety of settings (Erikson et al. 2002; Page and Shapiro 1983). As individual opinions shift to favor new policy positions, behavior changes to reflect those opinions. In the aggregate, change in the opinions of a small number of people can produce dramatic change in overall behavior or policy. The conditions required for this shift to happen are that the individual changes in the citizenry systematically favor one policy position and that the policy itself be clearly linked to individual opinions. The former condition is met in the case of the death penalty in periods of time in which public opinion is moving systematically in a pro– or anti–death penalty direction. So in Chapter 6, we see that especially beginning in the mid-1990s there was a relatively large amount of systematic change in public opinion; it became more opposed to the death penalty. The second condition is met in the death penalty case as well. Support of the death penalty in the general case is very clearly linked to support of the death penalty in a particular case. Although, as discussed earlier, it is possible to support the death penalty in the abstract case and to oppose it in a particular case as a juror, both opinion and policy deal explicitly with a policy position. Shifts in aggregate public opinion are noted in the media, by politicians, and by others involved in the advocacy process; when they are shifting as they have been in the past ten years, they provide another element in the social cascade.

Public opinion is shown in Chapter 6 to be influenced by both media framing and homicide levels. So at a very basic level, we hypothesize that the effects of both of these variables may be in part direct – that is, they may exert a straightforward influence on death sentences – and in part indirect – they may influence the number of death sentences annually by influencing opinion, which in turn influences death sentencing behavior. It is easy to imagine that as more of the public is opposed to the death penalty, fewer and fewer prosecutors choose to pursue it. Not only do more prosecutors themselves find it unpalatable, they also anticipate that the likelihood of getting the death penalty is low enough that the time, effort, and political capital expended may not be worth it. Further, jurors themselves are more likely to be tentative in support of the death penalty because of the ownership they have over the sentencing verdict. In particular, they may be more open to the innocence argument. So, although generally not opposed to the death penalty – by law, would-be jurors who are categorically opposed to capital punishment may be eliminated during *voir dire* proceedings – jurors may be open to doubt in specific cases.[1] Defense attorneys, for example, may focus their arguments on instilling doubt about possible imperfections in the process, taking advantage of generally greater social awareness of the innocence frame among the general public. Our measure of public opinion is the annual time series created in Chapter 6.[2]

The machinery of the death penalty unsurprisingly responded to the constitutional ban on and reinstatement of the death penalty in 1972 and 1976, so we must incorporate these dynamics into our model. Legal restrictions on death penalty statutes associated with the constitutional ban on executions temporarily forced changes in the death penalty system. In the immediate aftermath of *Furman v. Georgia*, the number of death sentences fell in 1973, and with the anticipation of its reversal in *Gregg v. Georgia*, death sentences spurted in 1975, a year before the death penalty was reinstated. We account for the beginning and end of the moratorium period with variables measured 1 in those periods to which they refer and 0 in all other time periods.

Our analysis covers the time period from 1961 to 2005. This gives us forty-five years of data with which to work in testing our hypotheses. For each year, we want to know whether we can predict the number of death sentences and the relative role of each of the variables in explaining the number of death sentences. Our analysis in this chapter relies on annual data – the unit of time in which death sentence data are reported – and covers a longer historical window than that of public opinion in Chapter 6. This allows us not only to assess the effect of the innocence frame, but more generally to assess the effects of media framing, including during periods in which an "eye-for-an-eye" and constitutionality were the main topics of attention.

The model we estimate is a simple regression analysis of the number of death sentences as a function of the number in the previous period – recognizing the inertial nature of the number of death sentences each year – and the previous years' media framing, homicide level, and opinion, accounting as well for both the beginning and end of the moratorium period.[3] As such, the modeling enterprise is simpler than in the previous chapter. We can, however, once again calculate long- and short-run effects and see how the effects of our variables play out over time.

Analysis

The results are presented in Table 7.1. As in Chapter 6, we focus our attention on the influence of media framing, comparing the magnitude of the estimated effects with those of the number of homicides. The entries in the table show the expected change for each unit-change in the row variable, this time on the number of annual death sentences.

Overall, the model results look much like we expect them to. As is the case in the Chapter 6 analysis of public opinion, our model of death sentences shows significant inertia, here directly assessed by the size of the coefficient on the number of sentences in the previous year. The first coefficient tells us that when large numbers of people were sentenced to death in the previous year, it is likely that a large number will be sentenced to death in the present year. In this case, the number of sentences in the previous year propagates forward at the rate of 0.316. The inertia has two important implications. First, the estimated effects of media framing and homicides presented in Table 7.1 represent only a portion – the short-term portion – of the effect each variable has on death sentences. To calculate the full effect, we need to multiply the short-term effect by

Table 7.1. *Explaining the number of annual death sentences, 1963 to 2005*

	Annual death sentences[a]
Sentences$_{t-1}$	0.316[b]
	(0.097)
Net tone$_{t-1}$	0.453[b]
	(0.137)
Opinion$_{t-1}$	5.059[c]
	(1.069)
Homicides$_{t-1}$ (thousands)	0.817
	(1.437)
1973	−67.80[b]
	(25.80)
1975	129.49[c]
	(25.34)
Constant	22.92[d]
	(19.20)
R-squared	0.930
RMSE	23.97
StDev	83.70

[a] Entries are regression coefficients; standard errors are in parentheses.
[b] $p < 0.05$.
[c] $p < 0.001$.
[d] $p < 0.10$, one tailed.

1.46 $(1/(1 − 0.316))$. Second, it will take about four years for effects to reach their full impact. Why might this inertia occur? As we noted earlier, death sentences vary substantially in number over time, and yet these changes evolve slowly from year to year. We can think of at least two reasons that might be the case. First, the prosecutors making decisions about whether to pursue the death penalty tend to be the same from one year to another; only slowly are prosecutors replaced. Second, standard operating procedures in place in the justice system mean that the process is sticky, changing only slowly. These two facts contribute to the likelihood that the number of death sentences handed down in a given year will look something like that in the previous year. However, it is also clear that inertia is far from the full story here; change does occur. Further, the inertial factor here is significantly less than what we saw for public opinion in the previous chapter. (This is also clear from glancing at Figure 7.1, which shows less inertia than Figure 6.4 on public opinion.)

Consider next the effect of a change in net tone, our media-framing variable. The coefficient associated with net tone is 0.453 and is statistically significant. For every ten more pro–death penalty articles in a given year, we expect more than four more death sentences. But about 32 percent of this effect is carried forward in the next period and 32 percent of the remaining effect carried forward into the next year, and so on. The long-run effect ends up being about 1.46 times the short-term effect. The total estimated effect associated with a ten-point swing in the pro–death penalty direction of the tenor of media framing produces an average of about 6.5 death sentences ($(10 \times 0.453) \times 1.46 = 6.61$) after about four years. Note that this dynamic effect is considerably larger in numeric terms than that associated with public opinion. In that model (see Chapter 6), the long-term effect of ten additional positive stories was about a 1.5 percentage point movement in the pro–death penalty direction in public opinion; here the full impact is nearly seven death sentences. Further, there was no immediate effect of change in net tone on public opinion. Here net tone exerts a significant – and substantively meaningful – effect immediately.

We can compare this effect to that of homicide levels, which also significantly predict the number of death sentences.[4] Let's say that homicides increased by 1,000 in one year, a typical amount. With this increase in the number of homicides in a given year, the results suggest less than one additional death sentence the following year (1×0.817). Multiplying by 1.46, the total effect is estimated to be just one more death sentence ($0.817 \times 1.46 = 1.19$). These are very small substantive effects. Homicides show a significant and powerful impact on public opinion in Chapter 6, but here we see no such direct impact.

As we do in Chapter 6, we consider the effect of changes in the tenor of media coverage of the magnitude associated with interesting periods in history. Pro–death penalty coverage topped out in 1973 with the constitutional ban and again in 1992, with thirty-six more pro– than anti–death penalty stories in that year, before turning around and beginning a steady march in an anti–death penalty direction. In contrast, in 2000 there were 105 more anti– than pro–death penalty stories in the *New York Times*. The range of net tone was thus 141. Multiplying this observed shift by the coefficients in Table 7.1, we see that the turnaround predicts a swing of nearly sixty-four death sentences in the short term and just over ninety-three in the long run. That is, the shift in net tone that we observe from 1992 to 2000 corresponds to a decline of more than ninety death sentences per year. These are large numbers indeed.

But how do these effects compare with those of homicides? Consider that the mean number of annual homicides is about 18,115, with a low of 8,530 (in 1962) and a high of 24,703 (in 1991). This range spans 16,173. We compute the short-term effects first, multiplying the range by the coefficient ($0.817 \times 16,173 = 13.65$) to get about fourteen death sentences.

The long-run effect is twenty death sentences ($13.65 \times 1.46 = 19.9$). This effect is not trivial, but it is far smaller than that of net tone.

We can compare the relative effects of homicides and media framing more precisely by comparing how comparable shifts in each influence the number of death sentences. But what is a comparable change? Because homicides and media stories are counted on vastly different scales and their variation is significantly different, we cannot simply compare the effect of adding one more pro–death penalty story with one more homicide. Instead, we compare the effects of a standard deviation change in each on the number of death sentences. A standard deviation change in media framing produces an expected change in sentences of more than twenty, whereas the comparable change in homicides produces an expected change of only five death sentences.[5] We see that net tone has an effect almost four times larger than that of homicides, using equivalent measures of each.

Public opinion also plays a role in determining the number of death sentences in a given year.[6] The estimated short-term effect of a one-point shift in net public opinion is to change the number of death sentences by more than five (5.06). The long-term effect of this change is more than seven additional death sentences ($5.06 \times 1.46 = 7.39$). When public opinion becomes more pro–death penalty, on average we experience more death sentences. When it becomes less pro–death penalty, we experience fewer death sentences on average, as hypothesized. In fact, what we present provides the upper bounds on the effects of opinion on sentences and we do not draw out the dynamic implications of these shocks because of the mutual effects of sentences on opinions. The positive and significant finding provides further evidence for the social cascade theory. Media-framing effects build momentum in the death penalty system, influencing sentencing directly as well as indirectly through public opinion.

In addition to the effects of media framing, homicides, and opinion, Table 7.1 models the effects of the constitutional ban on death sentences. We find that the estimated effects of the onset and end of the constitutional ban on the death penalty were to drop death sentences by about 68 (estimated as 1×-67.80) and to increase death sentences by 129, respectively, controlling for the levels of homicides, net tone, and opinion that existed at that time (1×129.49). These are contemporaneous effects and so again underestimate the total effect. The total effect is the now familiar 1.46 times the contemporaneous effect; for the onset of the moratorium, that is -98.99, and for the end of it, that is 189.06. That structural changes to the death penalty system exert such big effects should come as no surprise. One reason to include these effects in the model is so we know that the other effects we measure are in addition to these effects, not simply a reflection of them.

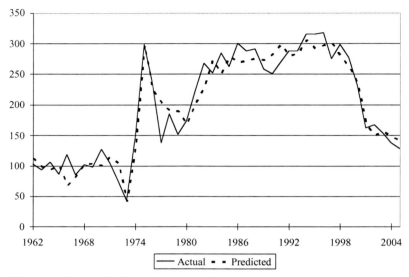

Figure 7.2. Annual death sentences: actual versus predicted values, 1962 to 2005.

Figure 7.2 shows the predicted and actual values of death sentences. Our average error in predicting the number of death sentences is about twenty-four. In some years, we overestimate the number of death sentences – in the period from 1978 to 1982. In this period of mounting death sentences in the aftermath of the reinstatement of the death penalty, our model does not do quite as well as during the remainder of the last forty years. In other years, we underestimate the number of death sentences – in the mid-1980s and mid-1990s. But overall, the model is quite strong. As we noted earlier, the model explains 93 percent of the variance in the number of death sentences per year. The general trends in death sentencing are well captured by the model, and at no point does our estimated number of death sentences wander too far from those actually observed.

Having succeeded in modeling the system, next we follow the strategy of Chapter 6 to make further sense of the results. Specifically, we consider the values of death sentences predicted by our model under some alternative scenarios. We begin with values of sentences, homicides, public opinion, and net tone that the world has dealt us as a baseline and compare this to different scenarios. We ask: What would the number of death sentences have looked like if history had been just a little bit different?

Figure 7.3 shows the predicted number of death sentences from our model – the solid line – and that from two hypothetical scenarios (the first shown with black squares, the second with empty circles). We take the two scenarios of the last chapter and play them out here. In Chapter 6, we ask: How would public opinion have looked if net tone had not moved

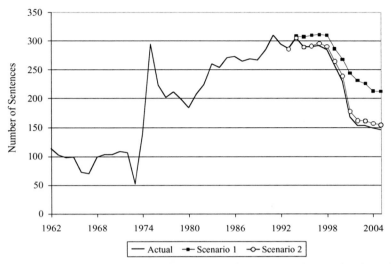

Figure 7.3. Simulating death sentences I. The figure shows the simulated number of death sentences compared with our baseline prediction from Figure 7.2. Scenario 1 shows the predicted level of annual sentences if the net tone of media attention had achieved its actual value of +36 in 1992 and then remained constant at that level. Scenario 2 shows predicted sentences under the case in which homicides reached their value of 23,760 during that same period and then never changed. In each scenario, values for all the other variables in the model retain their actual observed values.

from its 1992 value? We ask this same question here but now with regard to the effect on annual death sentences: What would death sentencing have looked like in 1993, 1994, and so on through 2005 if media coverage had remained fixed at its 1992 value? Media framing of the death penalty in 1992 had a substantial pro–death penalty tenor, with thirty-six more pro– than anti–death penalty stories. Under this hypothetical scenario (the line marked with black squares), Figure 7.3 shows that the number of sentences would have been much greater than we have actually observed and that over time the gap between actual and predicted death sentences would have grown. This growth comes in part from the dynamic effect of sentences – the multiplying effect of lagged sentences on current sentencing behavior – and in part from the fact that actual media framing grew first less pro–death penalty and then increasingly anti–death penalty in nature from 1992 onward so that the gap between the hypothetical and actual values of net tone grew. Because all other variables continue to take their actual values, the observed difference is entirely the result of the difference between the actual and hypothetical values of net tone and the dynamics of the model. The numbers would have declined (because homicides and public opinion moved), but not by as much. By 2005, the gap between

Table 7.2. *The impact of various scenarios on annual death sentences*

Hypothetical scenario	Projected impact on sentences
Reduce net tone of media coverage by 50	−33.13
Reduce homicides by 8,000	−9.56
Both 1 and 2	−42.69

Note: The table shows the long-term impact on the number of annual death sentences of each change in the independent variables (net tone and homicides) as listed. Note that we estimate the effects of a reduction in yearly homicides by 8,000 to match the quarterly reduction of 2,000 we use in Chapter 6. All the impacts are symmetrical, so the impact in the pro–death penalty direction would be equal in size to those shown here.

observed and simulated is 67. From 1992 to 2005, holding net tone at +36 would have yielded a total of 516 more death sentences (the sum of the gap across all thirteen years).

The second scenario is given by the line with empty circles in Figure 7.3. Here, we hold the number of homicides constant at its 1992 value – 23,760 – nearly the highest recorded. The difference between this second scenario and the solid line of the baseline reflects the effect of the difference between the actual and hypothetical values of homicides. Although the hypothetical values stayed near record highs, the actual value of homicides dropped in each year, hitting a low of 15,522 in 1999 before slowly increasing back to 16,692. Because the observed number of homicides was lower than under our alternative scenario in every year, the predicted number of death sentences in this hypothetical case was always more than that predicted by the observed data. Note, though, that this line is much closer to that based on the observed data. Here the predicted values under scenario 2 differ from the predicted values given the observed data by about nine death sentences in 2005. The cumulative effect over the thirteen-year period of our simulation is seventy-three death sentences. This is a small number based on such large differences between actual and hypothetical values of homicides, and it is a much smaller number than that due to our hypothetical shift in net tone.

When we manipulate one variable at a time, the distance between predicted values based on observed and hypothetical values represents the effect of a single variable. In other words, the effect size that we see depends on the difference between the hypothetical values and the actual values of the variable as they unfold over time, as well as the estimated coefficients in Table 7.1. As an alternative, we want to consider what happens when we manipulate more than one variable at just one point in time. These results are presented in Table 7.2, which parallels Table 6.2. The entries in the table tell us the projected effect of a reduction in net

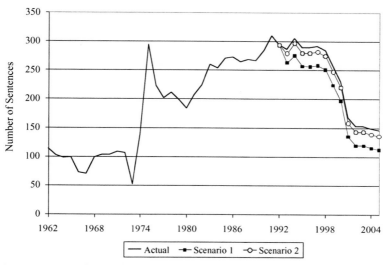

Figure 7.4. Simulating death sentences II. The figure shows the simulated number of death sentences compared with our baseline prediction from Figure 7.2. Scenario 1 shows the trace that the sentencing rate would have followed if, in 1992 and thereafter, media coverage was fifty points more negative than actually observed. Scenario 2 shows the trace that sentences would have taken if, in 1992 and thereafter, there were 8,000 more homicides per year than actually observed.

tone and homicides on the number of death sentences. The effect of a shock is symmetric so that the projected effect of an increase is the same size as that of a reduction, but in the other direction.

We calculate the effect of a reduction in net tone of 50, exactly the same as in Chapter 6, and just under half its minimum value of −106 (and two thirds the size of the largest annual change, −78). We want to emphasize that this is a change of the kind we see in the data; it is reasonable to expect to see this type of change in media framing in the real world. In Chapter 6, we found the effect to be −7.45 in opinion. Here the effect is −33.13 sentences. Both effects are substantively large, although it is not obvious which effect is more so. The homicide manipulation is 8,000 – four times that of Chapter 6, an equivalent number as we move from quarterly to annual data. This swing in annual terms would be quite large in a single year but reasonable over a three- to four-year period. Yet the effect on numbers of death sentences is much smaller than that of media framing, here just over 9.56 fewer death sentences. The combined effect of both shocks simultaneously occurring is the sum of the separate effects, or about forty-three death sentences.

In Figure 7.4, we graph the effects of our two manipulations had they occurred in 1992, showing the predicted number of death sentences had the net tone of media coverage been fifty points lower than its observed values (in scenario 1) and had homicides been reduced by 8,000 from the actual values (in scenario 2). The total impacts, once the long-run effects are reached, are the numbers reported in Table 7.2: 9.56 fewer death sentences associated with the reduction in homicides, and 33.13 fewer associated with the manipulation of net tone. The media coverage effect is almost four times greater than the homicide effect.

CONCLUSIONS

Death sentences are a very important indicator of public policy, one that has changed a lot over this period, ranging from 50 to 327. In this chapter, we show that this variation is highly predictable. We know that it responds in parallel fashion with public opinion to the tenor of media attention and to homicide levels. It is particularly responsive to the tenor of media framing. In particular, the sentencing rate is almost four times more responsive to net tone than to homicides. Public opinion in turn also influences the number of death sentences. Each of these findings supports the theory that attention cascades may lead to dramatic policy change.

Taken with our knowledge of actual media coverage, we can say a lot about the nature of policy change with respect to the death penalty. The paths that homicides, media framing, and public opinion have followed in recent time periods have produced a dramatic decrease in the number of people sentenced to death. Declines in the number of homicides carried out and a consistent anti–death penalty tenor in media framing have pulled opinion in an anti–death penalty direction and both directly and indirectly – via public opinion – led to a reduction in the number of death sentences. They help us to understand the decline in the number of death sentences handed down by juries from 320 to 128. This conclusion is meaningful and, moreover, it is sensible. It also supports the attention cascade model by linking media framing to death sentences.

The innocence movement documented in Chapter 3 appears to have led to a shift in the focus of the death penalty debate, as we document in Chapters 4 and 5. This redefinition in turn led to opinion shifts as documented in Chapter 6. Here in this chapter, we see the direct and indirect effects of the shift documented in Chapters 4 and 5 on policy outcomes. The story we tell draws first on real events and then on the media's presentation of them, what we have referred to variously as net tone, media framing, issue-definition, and attention cascades. The consequence of these events and media framing, as we have shown, is fundamentally, but slowly, to alter public opinion as well as public policy. This is a straightforward story, told with many tables and figures.

In Chapter 8, we pull the story together still tighter. We bring together each of the chapters and talk about their implications when taken together.

We draw general lessons for our understanding about media attention and public opinion and policy. We also talk about the implications for the future of the death penalty. Here the implications may be large indeed as media attention and homicide levels move in an anti–death penalty direction.

8   CONCLUSION

Chapter 1 lays out four goals for this book: to understand the development and evolution of the death penalty in America, how it has changed and why; to understand the nature of policy change more generally, in particular the role of framing; to learn about the power of various social groups in American democracy, who can create policy changes and who cannot; and finally to develop and explain some new methodologies for the study of framing, policy change, public opinion, and the linkages among these factors. We have reviewed a tremendous number of facts and figures in the previous pages. What does it all add up to? The most important substantive and theoretical finding of our book is how ideas matter.

A small group of students and activists defending the rights of a reviled population in the face of active hostility from large segments of the population and the political leadership set in motion a positive-feedback system. The social cascade reverberated through the system not on the basis of money and power, but simply by bringing attention to an aspect of the criminal justice system that has been known for hundreds of years: It is not perfect. This is completely uncontroversial in that no one has claimed that it is perfect, totally immune from error. (People certainly argue that it is fair, in that each side has an equal opportunity to present their case, but fair is different from perfect.) With attention focused so strongly on the possibility that innocent people could wrongfully be executed, suddenly those who were exonerated became more newsworthy. Innocence projects and journalistic and legal research teams proliferated, leading to more investigations. Government officials took notice and were sometimes shocked at what they saw. Popular culture shifted as well, with more attention to forensics and the possibility of fraud and errors in the nation's crime labs. In sum, each element of the system affected the others, producing an explosive rise in attention to innocence. Innocence, however, had always been around us. It took a social cascade of tremendous proportions to make us "discover" something that we had known all along.

THE RISE AND DECLINE OF A PUBLIC POLICY

The death penalty is in historic decline. In 2006, the number of death sentences declined to 114, continuing a steady decline from more than 300 in 1998. The number of executions declined, the population of death row was smaller, and several states had enacted moratoria related to innocence questions or problems in the lethal injection process itself. Public opinion, as we have seen, also shifted. For the first time, Gallup reported that equal numbers of Americans supported the death penalty as life without parole for persons convicted of murder; the number supporting life without parole rose from 38 to 48 percent from 1998 to 2006, whereas the number supporting capital punishment declined from 56 to 47 percent (DPIC 2006f).

Just ten years before, the situation was quite different. In 1996, there were 320 death sentences, and the number had been rising steadily since 1977, when there were 137 sentences nationwide. Public opinion was largely supportive and the general tenor of media coverage was more pro– than anti–death penalty. Over the past forty-five years, we saw a decline in the death penalty until it was virtually extinguished (from 1968 to 1977, as we note in Chapter 2, there were no executions in America); a surge in its use that went on for more than twenty years, reaching a peak in the mid-1990s; and then a rapid decline.

How did all this occur? Our focus has been on the development of new ways of thinking about this old question. Beginning in the 1980s, innocence movements developed around the country, slowly at first but more rapidly in the 1990s. By the late 1990s the debate had been transformed by the intrusion of the new innocence argument, displacing the previously dominant constitutionality and morality frames. Once established, the innocence frame affected not only public opinion and the news media, but the policy itself. A system of positive feedback set in whereby movement away from the death penalty made each subsequent step that much easier: a slippery slope. We saw, for example, that exonerations have played a major role in the development of the innocence argument but that media coverage of exonerations is highly unequal – some exonerees get no coverage whatsoever whereas a few become the object of scores or hundreds of newspaper articles. As the innocence argument gained steam, journalists had a ready-made frame, a story line that could easily be adapted to the next example of exoneration or miscarried justice. Before the frame became so prominent, the same events may have been ignored or described in ways that made no linkage to broader issues of public policy: A lucky inmate was released from death row, nothing more. The result of this, as we show in Chapter 3, is that there is much more attention to each exoneration today than there was before the rise of the innocence frame. As these stories have become familiar, Americans have come to understand the death penalty in a wholly different light, and they do not like what they see. Juries in particular have become much less willing to impose the sentence, and states have adopted life-without-parole alternatives, another part of the positive-feedback system. Politicians have taken notice, acting with much less relish to expand death penalty statutes and in some cases strongly expressing the view that the system is irretrievably broken; in early 2007, the governor of Maryland backed not a moratorium but the abolition of the death penalty in the state that sentenced Kirk Bloodsworth to death for a crime he did not commit. In Texas, a proposal to expand capital punishment to repeat child sexual offenders has been stalled after Republican state lawmakers expressed concern about expanding a punishment that is not working perfectly. These developments would have been quite unlikely twenty years ago, but they make sense today in the context of the innocence frame. A self-reinforcing dynamic thus created a strong momentum pushing public policy in the same direction year after year. Politicians, prosecutors, jurors, and defense attorneys all can see the same trends simultaneously and are all affected by them. In turn, their own behaviors then reinforce the trends of which they are a part.

The case of the death penalty is important for its own sake. Whether or not we execute in the name of justice sends powerful signals about who we are as a nation. We address some of the substantive issues about the death penalty in the last section of this chapter. But we can draw some more general lessons about the nature of policy change as well. The death penalty is one of the most entrenched public policies imaginable. People traditionally have thought about it in moral terms, based their views on their understanding of their own religious traditions, and been relatively uninformed about the specific facts and procedures associated with it. Political leaders have known that the issue is emotional among the public and that most members of the public strongly support a hard moral stance on punishing criminals. And yet, things have changed, even in this "most difficult" case. The reasons for this have entirely to do with attention-shifting – by raising a new dimension, by focusing attention and discussion on innocence rather than on morality, the debate has been transformed.

Attention-shifting, or exploiting the multidimensional nature of public policy debates, is a topic we discuss in Chapter 1 and one that theorists have considered for decades. But very few have shown how the process works. One important element of what we have shown is that in spite of the power of the innocence movement and the impact of the rise of the innocence frame, this process was not controlled by any single individual or actor. In a social cascade, no single event or participant in the process may determine the outcome. Rather, as each actor affects the actors around him or her, the system as a whole responds, sometimes dramatically, but no single actor can be said to have caused the change, single-handedly.

The innocence frame may be extremely frustrating to those who support the death penalty. After all, there are other important questions to consider, such as whether the death penalty deters crime and how cruel and vicious criminals should be made to pay for their deeds. Frames are always frustrating to those on the losing side of a debate, but in one sense critics have a very strong point. The innocence frame, like any frame, is incomplete. By discussing innocence, we focus our attention on only one element of a very complicated set of trade-offs relating to the policy. In this regard, the death penalty is typical of public policies more generally. Virtually every substantial issue of public policy is tremendously complicated, with various perspectives on the issue and various bits of evidence about what policy solutions to the problem are most effective. Poverty, the energy crisis, environmental degradation, globalization, racism, immigration, the war in Iraq, any number of issues show this same characteristic. The underlying issues are tremendously complex, but attention gets focused for long periods of time only on certain dimensions, an incomplete set of them. It is happening now with the innocence frame just as it happens regularly in other cases and just as it happened with the death penalty in previous periods when problems of innocence were routinely ignored.

Bryan Jones and Frank Baumgartner (2005) argued that the incomplete nature of public discussion was both inevitable (because of the complexity of social problems) and full of consequence. The most important consequence of the partial nature of public consideration of complex public policies is that the policies themselves are inherently unstable. The death penalty has waxed and waned in this country because at different periods we have focused on different elements of it. The current focus on innocence is long overdue because, as we discuss in Chapter 1, people have known of examples of errors in the criminal justice system for hundreds of years. It is indeed inevitable that an institution of this size and scope would be imperfect. And yet, for most of our history, this important question was never the object of much focus or discussion. Today it is the focus of a lot of discussion, but this discussion, like those before it, is also incomplete. The incomplete nature of public debate is a major source of policy change. As the focus shifts to topics that had previously been ignored, different outcomes follow logically as a consequence. A continued focus on innocence and problems in the criminal justice system can be expected to lead to a continued decline and the possible abandonment of the death penalty. The cause of this tremendous change in public policy will not be a single event, the speech of a single leader, the actions of Governor George Ryan, or any other single item. Rather, it will be an attention-shift and the social cascade surrounding it.

THE IMPACT OF FRAMING

Besides understanding better why the death penalty has shifted and how policies change more generally, we show the impact of framing here. Our review of media coverage of the death penalty makes clear that shifts in the topic of discussion are strongly related to changes in the tenor of that discussion. Thus the shift in attention to innocence has led to a massive amount of bad news from the perspective of supporters of capital punishment. This shift in the frame of the debate, of course, has in turn affected both public opinion and public policy. As the policy has shifted and public opinion has turned more critical, the frame itself has been strengthened, so we see here the same kind of positive reinforcement system as above. Framing effects may be strongly self-reinforcing, as is apparent in our analysis in Chapter 3 of media coverage of exonerations.

We cannot point to a single source of the new frame, however. Further, we know that for every actor attempting to push a new frame, there may logically be one attempting to suppress the new way of thinking about the issue. Those who support the status quo, after all, have no reason to sit back and watch as the new frame gains momentum. And in fact, for most public policies most of the time, the frames associated with them are quite stable. The stability in public policy that we observe most of the time, the status quo bias of American politics, stems in part from the difficulty of reframing issues.

There is much more to learn about how political leaders can be most effective in raising new elements of debate or in getting the public to focus attention on one dimension rather than another. But we take some important steps in this book. The exhaustive coding of every argument we could identify in media discussion of the death penalty allows us to show clearly that attention shifted in important ways over time and that these shifts later translated into opinion and policy responses. It also allows us, in Chapter 5, to develop some new statistical approaches that allow us to measure the resonance, salience, and persistence of the various frames that have been associated with capital punishment over time. This discussion enables us to reconstruct the history of the debate and to show the rise of the different frames at different periods of history. Finally, in Chapters 6 and 7, we are able to demonstrate statistically the impact of shifting frames on public opinion and public policy, and to compare directly the relative impact of media framing, specific real-world events, and other plausible alternative explanations. Our framing variables show the most powerful impacts. The net tone of media coverage, for example, has had about four times more impact on the number of death sentences nationally than the number of homicides. We all know that framing matters, but in Chapters 6 and 7 we can assign some precise estimates about the degree of policy change that can be attributed to framing as opposed to other factors. This suggests some important avenues for other scholars to follow in their studies of other policy debates.

By far the greatest number of analyses of public attitudes toward the death penalty have focused on the individual. Factors such as race, ideology, partisanship, and area of residence are known to affect people's attitudes toward capital punishment, as we review in Chapter 6. We address very different questions in this book. We contribute to a newly developing literature that focuses on macro-level changes in public opinion, elite behaviors, and public policy (see Erikson et al. 2002). In this work, the question is how the system evolves through time. It is of course clear that at any given time, different individuals have different attitudes, but we also know that there are temporal trends toward greater or lesser support in the aggregate. We hope we show some of the value of this approach here, but at the same time we must recognize that many issues cannot be addressed at the high level of aggregation that we have adopted, dealing with national trends typically on a yearly basis. Further studies into the individual-level psychology of how people respond to framing effects would be important extensions. Similarly, we observe that fewer death sentences are being imposed. Is that because prosecutors are not seeking death or because juries are not imposing it? Do defense attorneys make explicit reference to the innocence argument in their closing statements? There are many details that we have not addressed, many areas where future work could lead to much better understanding of the mechanism of policy change.

NECESSARY CONDITIONS, SUFFICIENT CONDITIONS, AND COMPLEXITY

Throughout this book, we emphasize both the dramatic rise in the innocence frame and the complex and self-reinforcing interactions that pushed it forward so dramatically. But are there not perhaps some simple causes of the rise of this frame, or at least some necessary conditions that allowed it to take off? Could it have taken hold as it did if homicide rates had not decreased during the late 1990s? What if DNA evidence had not become available around the same time? What if the Chicago police scandals had not occurred or if the governor of Illinois had not looked so carefully into the process or if he had not come to his conclusion about the errors pervading the system? Can we point to any single cause, any necessary or sufficient conditions for the shift in framing that we have observed? It is tempting to think that we could easily construct a model of the necessary combination of factors for a new frame to emerge. Reality, however, may be more complex.

In Chapter 1 we discuss the concept of tipping points, momentum, and self-reinforcing processes. Scholars from a range of disciplines, from engineering to physics to sociology, have noted that processes that are "linked" or "networked" often show dynamics different from those in which each individual operates independently of the others (for general overviews, see Ball 2004; Barabasi 2003; Watts 1999, 2003). A process is linked if the behaviors of individuals in the system are not completely independent from one another, but rather have some degree of connection. Many people may make up their minds about the death penalty based on what their friends say, for example. Or they may watch the same news programs, all simultaneously being affected by the same small number of events. Journalists themselves, in deciding what is newsworthy, may look to see what other journalists do. In processes that are linked, in contrast to those that are totally independent, a change in one case can make change in the next case that much more likely. (Where the events are independent, by definition, there is no correlation between the first and subsequent events; people make up their minds independently based on their own distinct experiences.) Linked or networked processes are subject to cascade effects and may be extremely stable for long periods, as the mutual connections among the various individuals act to reinforce the status quo. However, when a process of change does begin – when a few individuals are affected by some new information or a new frame emerges – the spread of change may be surprisingly quick. But the cause of the shift in frame is multiple and complex, not simple. Like a hurricane that builds up speed over a warm spot in the ocean, we can understand the general processes that caused it, but pinpointing the individual causes is difficult. Not all warm spots or tropical storms develop into hurricanes, after all, even if they have many of the requisite characteristics. The same is true for policy cascades.

There is no question that new technologies and declining homicide rates in the 1990s set the stage for the new innocence frame. There is no doubt that DNA mattered, no question that extensive public relations efforts by opponents of the death penalty were effective in getting more news coverage of the innocence idea, and no doubt that this redefinition would have been more difficult in a period with rising rather than declining homicide rates. On the other hand, one might have thought that the war on terror and the federal support for tough-on-crime policies would have overtaken the growing innocence movement, stopped it in its tracks after September 11, 2001, if not before. Americans in 2000 elected a president who as governor had overseen 146 executions, more than any other governor in

U.S. history (Gross and Ellsworth 2003, 52). And since the 9/11 attacks, Americans arguably have been more tolerant of limits on defendants' civil rights, at least in the case of suspected terrorist detainees. All things considered, the innocence frame has found extraordinary success despite a number of trends that militate against it.

In fact, it is virtually impossible to isolate the precise causes of the redefinition of the death penalty, or any redefinition for that matter. Rather, we know that a cascade has occurred and that Americans, especially those serving on juries, increasingly raise questions about the application of the death penalty in individual cases. As all cases relate to individuals and the possibility of error is always there, this shift in jury response has the possible result of eliminating the death penalty altogether. So we can understand the process without understanding each of the individual factors that led to it. In fact, their interaction and mutual reinforcement is more important than the strength of any one of the contributing factors. Such is the nature of a complex system.

Because there are so many factors working potentially to affect the collective framing of an issue as complex as the death penalty, new frames only rarely emerge – the combination of so many factors rarely aligns in one direction. During the period from World War II to the mid-1960s, in fact, declining use of the death penalty seemed to be putting the United States on track to be at the forefront of what is now a long list of countries having abolished the death penalty. But rising crime rates, terrible urban riots, shocking political assassinations that riveted the country, a partisan political conflict about being "tough on crime," and a Supreme Court decision that was largely seen as a question of federalism rather than one about abolition led most American states to revise their death penalty statutes rather than to abandon them when they were declared unconstitutional in 1972. Over a generation, public policy was pushed in a single direction: toward greater and greater use of the death penalty (though in a more geographically isolated set of states). A generation later, through a very different process, the stars aligned again: Innocence projects, new DNA evidence, public skepticism about police labs and documented evidence tampering in those same labs, declining homicide rates, the efforts of many activists working closely with journalists, and some terrible police scandals in Chicago led to the reversal of these trends. What factors were sufficient, and which were necessary? We cannot pinpoint the answers to these questions. The key is in the linked, or connected, nature of the contributing factors, not in any one of them in isolation.

From humble beginnings in the 1980s, individual academics and university-based innocence projects documented examples of egregious miscarriages of justice. Attention built up slowly at first to the various practical problems in the administration of the death penalty. As more cases were discovered, a wider range of actors got involved. As more actors got involved, more cases were discovered and more publicity flowed to this new concept. And nearly all the while, homicides were slowly dropping. The combination of these many factors, each reinforcing the other as in an echo chamber, illustrates well the nature of dramatic policy change in America.

THE (OCCASIONAL) POWER OF THE WEAK

The model of policy change that we have described here, with its focus on positive feedback and attention-shifts, points to the possibility that even the most entrenched public policies may be dramatically altered. After all, as we discuss in Chapter 1, the constellation of forces cool to the idea of criminal justice reform includes many of the most powerful actors in American government. Those seeking change include none of the leading corporations or financially powerful actors in American politics and yet these changes have occurred. As we noted, we cannot point to a single actor and say that it caused the policy to change. But it is clear that the policy is changing, and those who have been at the forefront of the push for change can rightly be considered political underdogs.

John Kingdon quoted Victor Hugo in trying to understand the power of framing: "'Greater than the tread of mighty armies is an idea whose time has come'" (quoted in Kingdon 1984, 1). This suggests that any actor, if it can cause attention to focus on a new element of debate, may unleash tremendous forces, more powerful forces than those controlled even by the supposedly most powerful actors in American politics. Innocence is clearly an idea whose time has come. The transformation of the debate has been remarkable not only because of its speed and effects, but also because of where it came from. Public defenders, journalism students, law students, and the dedicated individuals in a small number of citizen groups have changed the nature of public policy in a contentious area not by making campaign contributions, not by mobilizing vast sums of money, not by demonstrating and protesting by the hundreds of thousands on the steps of the Capitol, not by any of what are often considered to be the classic tactics of interest-group mobilization. Rather, they have created change by raising a new element of debate.

The power and impact of the innocence movement is no evidence that the weak typically do very well in American politics. But it clearly demonstrates that the weak *can* sometimes do well in politics. Social cascades, new ideas, and positive-feedback processes can combine to create such momentum that whole policy areas are transformed. We hope to have pushed our understanding of these processes further here, but there is obviously much more that we need to do to know why sometimes these processes catch on whereas typically they do not. Most policies, after all, are strongly resistant to change. But our analysis clearly suggests that an overly pessimistic assessment of American democracy, where the status quo supports moneyed interests and cannot effectively be challenged except by coalitions of equally well-endowed political actors, is not completely accurate. Policies, because they are based on partial rather than comprehensive approaches, are inherently unstable. Although they may be stable for long periods and although there certainly is a bias toward actors with greater access to the corridors of power, even the most entrenched policies supported by powerful actors are vulnerable to the mobilization of new ideas. Ideas matter in politics. Sometimes ideas matter more than anything else.

THE DEATH PENALTY IN AMERICA

The decline in the application of the death penalty that we have observed since 1996 was by no means inevitable. Shortly after the September 11, 2001, attacks, Washington, D.C., was riveted with an anthrax scare whose perpetrators were never found and a series of deadly sniper shootings. This violence, which left ten people dead and three others seriously wounded, took place over a period of three weeks in October 2002. When John Muhammad, a deranged army veteran, and Lee Malvo, his young accomplice, were apprehended, Maryland, Virginia, and other states as well as the U.S. Department of Justice vied over who would gain jurisdiction to try them first. In announcing that the two would first be tried in Virginia (the number two state in the nation for executions; see Figure 2.3), U.S. attorney general John Ashcroft said, "We believe that the first prosecutions should occur in those jurisdictions that provide . . . the best range of available penalties. . . . It is imperative that the ultimate sanction be available for those who have committed these crimes" (CNN 2002). Though Malvo was seventeen years old at the time of the crimes, prosecutors sought the death penalty for him as well (though this possibility was precluded after the *Roper* case was decided in 2005). Muhammad was indeed sentenced to death in Virginia and faces additional charges in several other states.

The Washington snipers are far from the only high-profile capital cases to follow the rise of the innocence movement. Zacarias Moussaoui was charged with a capital offence for his alleged involvement in the September 11 terrorist plot but was eventually sentenced to life in prison after a lengthy trial in which he showed serious signs of mental illness. Several governors allowed executions to proceed despite substantial pressure to commute sentences in high-profile cases, such as that of Stanley "Tookie" Williams, executed in December 2005 by lethal injection in California; Governor Arnold Schwarzenegger refused multiple appeals to spare the life of the former Los Angeles gang leader despite pleas that he had changed while in prison, had renounced violence, and had become an anti-gang campaigner.

The possibility of innocence seems to have no relevance in high-profile cases, such as those of the Washington snipers, certain captured terrorists, or Timothy McVeigh, the Oklahoma city terrorist whose destruction of the Alfred P. Murrah Federal Building killed scores of victims, a crime for which he proudly accepted responsibility and for which there was no doubt about his guilt. Cases such as these, vicious and highly publicized crimes, consistently attract attention to public support for the death penalty, and some notorious criminals, some proudly admitting their crimes as a badge of honor, become poster children for pro–death penalty arguments. District attorneys and law enforcement personnel, sometimes up to the level of the attorney general of the United States, line up to show their support for execution in these high-profile cases. Recently proposed legislation in Texas would expand eligibility for the death penalty to some convicted of child sexual abuse short of murder.

In sum, everyone does not agree with the idea of abandoning the death penalty, and America's leading political figures often support it publicly in the most highly visible cases. Periodically, of course, terrible crimes come to the public attention and leaders do indeed push for the harshest penalties, including death. Attention, in other words, is not uniformly focused on the innocence frame to the exclusion of all else. The same forces that have made the death penalty attractive to many public officials and members of the public in the past continue to exert influence. Trends toward the greater use of capital punishment throughout recent periods include the security focus of the war on terror, the personal views of President George W. Bush (who as governor of Texas commuted only 1 out of more than 140 scheduled executions during his time in Austin), and other factors, as we review in Chapter 1. There are many reasons to believe that the innocence movement should never have happened; certainly it bucks some important trends.

And yet, public policy has changed. In this book, we do not pay much attention to the pro–death penalty side of the equation; our focus is on documenting and explaining the rise of the "innocence movement." This is not because there has not been continued support for the death penalty, and our review of public opinion in Chapter 6 should make clear that although the numbers in support have declined, this movement has been gradual and incomplete. Depending on the question posed, a majority of Americans support the death penalty. (This number is lower if alternative punishments are made available, but as we note in response to an abstract and theoretical question about the proper punishment for murder, many Americans continue to express support for the eye-for-an-eye view of things.) It is unclear whether the innocence movement will lead to the abolition of the death penalty or to its continued reduction in use so that it becomes a smaller and smaller factor in the U.S. criminal justice system (a possibility that could itself have constitutional import), or if the trends we document here might be reversed in the future. But it is already clear that dramatic changes have already occurred with relation to public understanding and discussion of the death penalty. This is not because we have had no more vicious criminals; indeed the period since September 11, 2001, has featured a public mood of substantial anxiety along these lines, and some horrific events.

But the innocence movement remains strong and all trends point in the direction of less use of capital punishment. In late 2006, substantial controversy swirled around the future use of lethal injection as a botched execution in Florida led Governor Jeb Bush to halt all executions in the state pending a review of procedures and a federal judge halted all executions in California and issued a scathing critique of state corrections procedures. Details that have emerged during these and similar controversies have added to the general impression that the death penalty system is poorly managed and prone to error, even in the final act of execution itself. The particular remedies available to states seeking to "perfect" the mechanism may involve a requirement that licensed medical officials participate in the process, and it is possible that associations of medical professionals will take a strong moral stand that the healing professions should not be involved. On the other hand, there are many other means of execution, not all of which require a medical professional. There are solutions to the specific issues of how to put an inmate to death. However, the lethal injection controversies of 2005 and 2006 have certainly contributed to the general feeling that the system itself is far from perfect, far from a flawless bureaucratic machine. It is often operated by poorly trained and poorly supervised individuals who occasionally make gross errors. There is no solution to this; imperfection is inevitable.

Writing in the landmark 1972 case that outlawed the death penalty in America, Justice Thurgood Marshall hypothesized that public support for capital punishment was largely based on a lack of knowledge about how the punishment is administered. With greater public education, he argued, support would decline. (He also noted that public support for the death penalty based on the idea of retribution would *not* be subject to such knowledge or education effects.) In certain ways, the analysis presented in this book can be seen as a validation of the Marshall hypothesis, although an indirect one. We document here not so much an overall net increase in knowledge about the death penalty, but rather a surge in attention to an aspect of the punishment that Marshall certainly had in mind: how well it works in individual cases. The shift in public discussion from the general and theoretical to the details of the application of the death penalty in particular cases has indeed led to decreased public support (most dramatically in the behaviors of juries, but also in general public opinion surveys). Similarly, Marshall's idea that individual views based on the concept of retribution would be less resistant to change is certainly valid. As the innocence frame has risen, attention has shifted from the morality/retribution dimension to a more practical set of issues, and in this sense, our analysis suggests that Marshall was correct on all counts.

Frustrated by repeated evidence of the fallibility of the system, more and more state legislatures are considering laws that would abolish the death penalty – or at least suspend further executions until improvements can be made.[1] As we note in Chapter 2, New York's state supreme court declared the death penalty to be unconstitutional in 2006, and there is no movement toward passage of a new law; effectively, New York is now an abolitionist state. Three states – Illinois, New Jersey, and Tennessee – have imposed moratoria on executions in response to rising concerns about innocence and problems with the lethal injection process. At time of publication, abolition or moratorium legislation is being considered in at least eighteen states. In February 2007, the Montana senate voted to abolish the death penalty; the measure will go next to the Montana house for consideration. Also in February 2007, New Mexico's house of representatives approved legislation that would repeal the death penalty and replace it with a sentence of life without parole (though passage in the state senate is far from certain), and in Colorado, the house judiciary committee also voted to abolish the state's death penalty, replacing it with life without parole. Maryland also faces strong pressure, including the support of the governor and a former governor, for repeal legislation being considered in February 2007. In North Carolina, the death penalty was thrown into doubt when, in response to a state regulation requiring medical participation in any execution, the state medical board voted to punish any doctor who participates in such a procedure. And in Dallas, District Attorney Craig Watkins announced in February 2007 that he will open his case files to the Texas Innocence Project and work alongside the group to revisit the last thirty years' worth of cases to see whether DNA evidence may reveal instances of wrongful conviction. Dallas has one of the highest rates nationally of overturned convictions.

Other efforts are under way to "perfect the mechanism" of the death penalty, and in recent years, the courts have incorporated important safeguards into the process, rendering unconstitutional the execution of juveniles and the mentally handicapped and providing greater access to appeal. Congress provided funds for post-conviction DNA testing in the Innocence Protection Act of 2004 and made other changes designed to improve the quality of legal representation for the accused. These and other improvements to the mechanisms of judicial process can only move in one direction, that of increased resources for the defense. This will logically lead to lengthier trials and more costly prosecutions as the state is not likely to respond to greater defense resources with fewer for the prosecution. Already in the United States, many commentators have noted that the cost of capital punishment, per execution, is several million dollars. In California alone, the state has spent hundreds of millions of dollars on an extensive system of capital punishment, but has executed only thirteen inmates since 1976. Similarly in New York, costs of the system were recently estimated at over $20 million per death sentence. Given the availability of life-without-parole sentences, many people question whether the high cost of the death penalty system represents money that could better be spent on police officers, crime prevention, and other purposes. One interesting element in any political debate is how those previously not particularly involved may become so because of the budgetary implications reflected in these staggering numbers. In rural areas in particular, the high costs of a single capital prosecution may have lasting effects on local government budgets. As the costs continue to rise, political leaders may conclude that rarer is better.

Rare may mean unconstitutional. In both the *Atkins* and *Roper* decisions, majority opinions in the Supreme Court made reference to "evolving standards of decency" reflected in such things as public opinion and state legislative actions barring the execution of the mentally handicapped (in *Atkins*) and those who were juveniles at the time of their crimes (*Roper*). The death penalty is already rare in many states, more common just in a few. One possible indirect effect of the innocence movement, by increasing resources to the defense and providing them with significantly greater access to DNA and other technologies, and by making juries more accepting of arguments that police crime labs cannot always be trusted, would be that costs would rise so much that capital cases would be significantly more rare. They have already declined by over 60 percent since 1996. If these trends were to continue, and more states were to follow New York and impose a permanent moratorium on the practice, one possible outcome would be to open the "evolving standards of decency" argument to capital punishment in general. If it is applied so rarely as to be "unusual," then it may well be deemed unconstitutional, even by a Supreme Court that has no moral qualms about the punishment whatsoever.

The scenarios we lay out above may or may not occur; we cannot predict the future. We can say some things with much greater certainty, however. Most important is that the innocence movement has caused Americans to consider the death penalty as a bureaucratic institution dealing with real cases and making life-and-death decisions. Although a majority of Americans have a moral or religious view that supports capital punishment, when they are exposed to stories such as those of Kirk Bloodsworth and Ray Krone – completely innocent individuals who were sentenced to death for crimes they did not commit – when they see the poor training and flagrant misconduct associated with the administration of lethal injections in many recent cases, when they see the high cost of the capital punishment system, and when they couple all this with their own understanding of how efficient most government bureaucracies are, they do not like what they see. With all due respect to former senator Denton, who we quote in Chapter 1, the idea that a "few errors" are perfectly acceptable even in the context of the death penalty does not sit well with most Americans. Most Americans would rather avoid the topic than admit that they are comfortable with the execution of "a few" innocent people if that is the price to pay for capital punishment. For most of American history, we have indeed avoided the topic. But with attention focused on the issue as never before, people recoil at the thought of calculating how many innocent deaths would be few enough to make the system worthwhile. It is a calculation that people simply refuse.

From 1973 to 2006, 123 individuals were exonerated after having been sentenced to death. This reflects in large measure the impact of the innocence movement. But the impact of the movement is many times greater than that. Before the powerful forces of positive feedback associated with the innocence movement set in during the 1990s, executions and death sentences were trending upward in a regular progression; 320 individuals were sentenced to death in 1996 as compared with 137 in 1977. If that number had remained constant (i.e., even if there had been no further upward movement in the trend), from 1997 to 2006 we would have seen 3,200 individuals sentenced to death. But in fact, 2006 saw just 114 death sentences nationwide, and the total number from 1977 to 2006 was 1,944. More than 1,250 individuals were *not* sentenced to death who otherwise might have been if the changes we describe in this book had not occurred. As we have said, it is impossible to foretell what will happen from this point forward. But we can say that the discovery of innocence has upended the American debate on capital punishment and that it has already saved hundreds of lives. For capital punishment in America, the "discovery" of innocence may well be the beginning of the end.

Epilogue

INDIVIDUALS EXONERATED FROM DEATH ROW

One hundred twenty-four individuals have been released from prison after having served time on death row in the modern era (1973 to 2007). Here we provide a list of each of these individuals along with the date of their exoneration (information from the Death Penalty Information Center [DPIC]). The average number of years between being sentenced to death and exoneration is 9.2. Among the 124 individuals listed here, DNA evidence played a substantial role in establishing the innocence of fifteen. For inclusion on DPIC's Innocence List, defendants must have been convicted and sentenced to death, and one of the following two conditions must apply:

a) the defendant's conviction was overturned *and*
  i. the defendant was acquitted at retrial *or*
  ii. all charges were dropped
b) the defendant was given an absolute pardon by the state's governor based on new evidence of innocence.

Of course, hundreds of other individuals have seen their death sentences commuted to life in prison or have been sentenced to prison in a retrial after their death sentence was invalidated; these commutations and retrials are not listed here. This group of 124 individuals includes only those who have been set free.

For a more complete description of the criteria used to compile this list and the reasons why these criteria were chosen, or for fuller description of each exoneration case, visit the DPIC at http://www.deathpenaltyinfo.org/.

1973
David Keaton

1974
Samuel A. Poole

1975
Wilbert Lee
Freddie Pitts
James Creamer
Christopher Spicer

1976
Thomas Gladish
Richard Greer
Ronald Keine
Clarence Smith

1977
Delbert Tibbs

1978
Earl Charles
Jonathan Treadway

1979
Gary Beeman

1980
Jerry Banks
Larry Hicks

1981
Charles Ray Giddens
Michael Linder
Johnny Ross
Ernest (Shuhaa) Graham

1982
Annibal Jaramillo
Lawyer Johnson

1985
Larry Fisher

1986
Anthony Brown
Neil Ferber
Clifford Henry Bowen

1987
Joseph Green Brown
Perry Cobb
Darby (Williams) Tillis
Vernon McManus
Anthony Ray Peek
Juan Ramos
Robert Wallace
Richard Neal Jones

1988
Willie Brown
Larry Troy

1989
Randall Dale Adams
Robert Cox
Timothy Hennis
James Richardson

1990
Clarence Brandley
John C. Skelton
Dale Johnston
Jimmy Lee Mathers

1991
Gary Nelson
Bradley P. Scott
Charles Smith

1992
Jay C. Smith

1993
Kirk Bloodsworth
Federico M. Macias
Walter McMillian
Gregory R. Wilhoit
James Robison
Muneer Deeb

1994
Andrew Golden

1995
Adolph Munson
Robert Charles Cruz
Rolando Cruz
Alejandro Hernandez
Sabrina Butler

1996
Joseph Burrows
Verneal Jimerson
Dennis Williams
Roberto Miranda

Gary Gauger
Troy Lee Jones
Carl Lawson
David Wayne Grannis

1997
Ricardo Aldape Guerra
Benjamin Harris
Robert Hayes
Christopher McCrimmon
Randall Padgett
James Bo Cochran

1998
Robert Lee Miller, Jr.
Curtis Kyles

1999
Shareef Cousin
Anthony Porter
Steven Smith
Ronald Williamson
Ronald Jones
Clarence Dexter, Jr.
Warren Douglas Manning
Alfred Rivera

2000
Steve Manning
Eric Clemmons
Joseph Nahume Green
Earl Washington
William Nieves
Frank Lee Smith
Michael Graham
Albert Burrell
Oscar Lee Morris

2001
Peter Limone
Gary Drinkard

Joaquin Jose Martinez
Jeremy Sheets
Charles Fain

2002
Juan Roberto Melendez
Ray Krone
Thomas Kimbell, Jr.
Larry Osborne

2003
Aaron Patterson
Madison Hobley
Leroy Orange
Stanley Howard
Rudolph Holton
Lemuel Prion
Wesley Quick
John Thompson
Timothy Howard
Gary Lamar James
Joseph Amrine
Nicholas Yarris

2004
Alan Gell
Gordon Steidl
Laurence Adams
Dan L. Bright
Ryan Matthews
Ernest Ray Willis

2005
Derrick Jamison
Harold Wilson

2006
John Ballard

2007
Curtis McCarty

Photographer Loren Santow has produced a series of portraits of fifteen individuals who have been exonerated from death rows in the United States. A selection of these portraits appears in the pages that follow.

Rolando Cruz

Jay Smith

Joseph Green Brown

Joe Burrows

Alex Hernandez

Randall Dale Adams

Carl Lawson

Darby Tillis

Verneal Jimerson

Anthony Porter

Steve Smith

Ron Jones

Gary Gauger

Dennis Williams

Perry Cobb

Appendix A

NEW YORK TIMES CAPITAL PUNISHMENT COVERAGE, 1960 TO 2005

The aim of this data collection project was to track media framing of capital punishment over time. To accomplish this task, we collected and coded paper copies of all abstracts of articles on the death penalty as listed under the heading "capital punishment" in the *New York Times Index* for the years 1960 through 2005, a total of 3,939 abstracts. Two coders (Feeley and Boydstun) worked independently to code the bulk of this data (1960 to 2002), with intercoder reliability of approximately 98 percent at the first level of coding (seven main categories plus one "other" category) and 92 percent at the second level of coding (sixty-five distinct arguments). One of these coders (Boydstun) then worked alone to update the dataset through 2005.

We assigned each abstract one and only one code to capture the overall tone (i.e., pro–death penalty, anti–death penalty, or neutral) as well as one and only one code for the type of article being summarized (i.e., news, editorial, op-ed, or letter to the editor). Additionally, we coded each abstract according to its component arguments, whether it mentioned victim and/or defendant characteristics, and any characteristics of the crime. The same abstract could receive multiple codes for those variables. Finally, we coded each abstract for the presence of any of sixty-five distinct arguments about the death penalty – pro–death penalty arguments, anti–death penalty arguments, and neutral arguments – as described below. These arguments are divided into seven predefined main dimensions – efficacy (100s), morality (200s), fairness (300s), constitutionality and popular control (400s), cost (500s), mode of execution (600s), international issues (700s) – plus an "other" category (code 900). Within each category, the –00 code (e.g., 100) is used for general references to that dimension of neutral or uncodeable tone. The next set of codes (e.g., 101, 102, 103, etc.) is used to capture specific arguments within that dimension that have a pro–death penalty valence, and the –09 code (e.g., 109) is used

for miscellaneous "other" pro–death penalty arguments. Similarly, codes
–10 and on (e.g., 110, 111, 112) are used for specific anti–death penalty
arguments, and the –19 code (e.g., 119) is used for other anti–death
penalty arguments in that dimension.

It is important to remember that many abstracts discuss victims, defendants, or dimensions of the capital punishment debate in a future-
oriented or hypothetical sense. For example, the topic of an abstract could
be proposed legislation that seeks to handle a specific crime (e.g., the
murder of police officers) or future defendant (e.g., a juvenile) in a certain
way. No crime has occurred; the crime or defendant is "theoretical" or
"potential," but these topics and characteristics are still coded in the same
way as if the abstract were speaking about a death penalty case dealing
with a murder of a police officer that has already occurred or a case
dealing with a juvenile defendant who has already committed a crime
(receiving codes 31 and 10 in the former instance and 25 in the latter
instance).

TONE

Tone refers to the direction or implication of an article – whether the
article reports on activities or opinions that support or advance the death
penalty on the one hand, or activities or opinions that oppose or restrict
the death penalty on the other. Note that the coding need not be related
to the opinions of the author of the article; tone does not necessarily
reflect journalistic slant. Tone may refer to an opinion suggested by the
author of the article or to the activities that are reported. Thus, the pro–
death penalty code would be used for an article reporting on any of the
following: a death sentence being carried out, a defendant being arraigned
on capital charges, a legislature passing a bill to expand the application of
the death penalty, a study finding a link between capital punishment and
deterrence, or a political figure announcing his or her support for the death
penalty. Similarly, any reports of actions or opinions tending to make the
death penalty less likely to be carried out or placing restrictions on it
would be coded anti–death penalty. In a case in which an abstract contains
multiple arguments or statements of fact, we code by the predominance
of focus. If there is equal focus, it is coded neutral.

1. Pro–death penalty
2. Anti–death penalty
3. Neutral or uncodeable – used if the abstract mentions an equal
   number of points in favor and arguments opposing the death penalty
   or if the tone cannot be assessed

ARTICLE TYPE (CODE ONLY ONE)

1. News
2. Editorial
3. Op-ed
4. Letter to the editor

MENTIONS OF DEFENDANT/VICTIM CHARACTERISTICS (CODE AS MANY AS APPLY)

10. Victim police officer/criminal justice enforcement figure – prison guard, patrol officer, and so forth
11. Victim child
12. Multiple victims
13. Victims' families mentioned
14. Victim woman
19. Other humanizing characteristic of victim – elderly, mentally or physically handicapped, and so forth
20. Defendant terrorist/security threat – includes spies, assassins, and threats to national security
21. Defendant racial minority
22. Defendant mentally handicapped
23. Defendant woman
24. Defendant motherhood/fatherhood
25. Defendant juvenile
27. Defendant is humanized in other way (defendant has found God, detailed descriptions of last minutes on death row, description of defendant crying in the courtroom, etc.)
29. Other vulnerability of defendant – defendant is war veteran, foreign national, and so on

MENTIONS OF CRIME, MODE OF EXECUTION, AND LEGISLATION (CODE AS MANY AS APPLY)

30. Mode of execution mentioned – for example, electric chair, lethal injection, firing squad
31. Type of crime committed mentioned – for example, murder, armed robbery; reference must state the crime by name (i.e., an abstract referring to "certain crimes" does not receive this code); any abstract that receives a 32 must also receive a 31
32. Violence of crime mentioned – for practical purposes, all abstracts that mention a second crime in addition to murder should receive

this code (e.g., "rape and murder," "murdered victim while rob-bing a convenience store"), but this code may also be used to cap-ture more subtle inflections of violence, such as the choice of verbs (e.g., "slaying" as opposed to "murder") at the discretion of the coder

40. Legislation issues – used for abstracts that signal *upcoming, cur-rent*, or *recent* movement within a legislature to affect change in the status of the death penalty (e.g., new legislation, proposed leg-islation, a desire in a legislature to introduce new legislation – often in effort to comply with new Supreme Court rulings, etc.); examples of items that would *not* receive this code include "death sentence falls in line with California state law that mandates cap-ital punishment for rapists," "Supreme Court limits role of state legislatures in deciding fate of death penalty cases," "California legislature abolished death penalty in 1985"

DIMENSIONS OF DEBATE – ARGUMENTS
(CODE AS MANY AS APPLY)

Efficacy Arguments

100. General efficacy arguments – effectiveness of capital punishment as a system of punishment and deterrent; for example, "new study examines effectiveness of capital punishment as crime deterrent"
101. Deterrence – the use of capital punishment deters crime
102. Incapacitation – capital punishment makes the United States safer by removing dangerous criminals from society
103. Problems with other methods – other methods are ineffective or not strong enough
109. Other pro–death penalty efficacy arguments – for example, "edito-rial argues death penalty is effective and thus should remain intact"
110. Non-deterrent – capital punishment does not deter crime
111. Alternate systems – alternate systems (e.g., life without parole) could be as effective or more effective in achieving the same results of punishment and/or deterrence
119. Other anti–death penalty efficacy arguments – for example, "edi-torial argues death penalty to be ineffective," "capital punishment perpetuates more killing through a culture of violence"

Morality Arguments

200. General moral arguments – for example, "Bush's death penalty record offers insight into his distinct views of mercy and justice"

201. Retribution – retribution is good; a person should be punished in the same way, or in equal amount as he/she punished another (i.e., "eye for an eye")
202. Family wants/deserves justice or vengeance – families of the victims should be able to feel avenged for losing a loved one
203. A particular type of crime warrants the death penalty – for example, "rapists like John Smith should be killed," "legislation proposed that would make terrorism capital offense," "extension of capital punishment for arson and kidnapping in California," "legislation is being proposed that would make legal or mandatory the death penalty for certain crimes"
209. Other pro–death penalty moral arguments – for example, "death penalty is morally justified"
210. Killing/vengeance is wrong – killing is always immoral and capital punishment is no exception; for example, "death penalty promotes vengeance and hatred," "the death penalty is barbaric"
211. Family opposed – the family of the victim does not want the defendant executed
219. Other anti–death penalty arguments – for example, "the pope denounced the death penalty"

Fairness Arguments

300. General fairness arguments – questions about the fairness of the legal system or the judicial process, general discussion of issues of innocence or a moratorium
301. Proceedings are fair – for example, "Sen. John Smith argues that capital punishment trials have the most safeguards in place of any trials"
302. Abbreviate the process – the system cannot work because the (appeals) process is too long
303. Wrong convictions overstated – death penalty opponents exaggerate the number of wrong convictions; the system does not have a propensity for making mistakes
304. No blanket regulations on members of vulnerable populations – members of vulnerable populations, like children or the mentally handicapped, should not receive special immunity for their race, age, mental retardation, and so forth
309. Other pro–death penalty fairness arguments – for example, "capital punishment is fair"
310. Inadequate legal representation – for example, "court-appointed lawyers are paid so little that competent individuals refuse work, often resulting in only older or inexperienced lawyers handling

capital cases," "there is no statewide public defender system and thus no oversight"

311. Arbitrary/capricious nature of application – the death penalty is applied in an arbitrary and capricious way (akin to lightning striking); even if factors are held constant in whether a person receives the death penalty, sentencing is not applied consistently

312a. Proceedings are racist – minority populations receive a disproportionate amount of inadequate defense lawyers, unfair trial proceedings, and/or death penalty sentencing; death penalty targets African Americans

312b. Proceedings are classist – defendants of low socioeconomic status receive a disproportionate amount of inadequate defense lawyers, unfair trial proceedings, and/or death penalty sentencing

312c. Capital punishment is unfair to other demographic groups – used for discussions linking the incidence of inadequate defense and/or unfair trial proceedings with cases involving defendants of other demographics (gender, state committed, age of defendant, locality committed, etc.)

313a. Vulnerable populations – it is unfair to subject members of vulnerable populations (juveniles, the handicapped, another population with a disadvantage) to the death penalty

313b. Mitigating factors – mitigating factors (defendant's personal circumstances/history) were not given proper consideration in a capital case; jury was given misinformation (that ended up hurting the defendant) about the defendant's history during the sentencing phase of the trial

314. Mandatory sentencing unfair – it is unfair for the system to sentence an individual to death automatically without taking the particular circumstances into account

315. No comparable punishment – many people (and jurors) would not choose to impose the death penalty if the legal system had another comparable punishment, such as life without parole

316. Access to evidence – used for arguments that evidence (specifically, DNA evidence) did not get proper consideration in a trial; the process was unfair because the trial may have turned out differently if (DNA) evidence had been allowed

317. Innocence in question – flaws lead to the possibility of falsely sentencing a person to death; as a system run by human beings, the capital punishment system cannot avoid making mistakes

318. Effectiveness in rendering justice – there are fairness problems within the system that must be examined; the death penalty system is broken and even though it may be "good" in principle, the United States should establish a moratorium on executions at least until the system is improved

319. Other anti–death penalty fairness arguments – for example, "jury was not properly instructed to consider case evidence," "trial suffered from prosecutorial misconduct"

Constitutionality and Popular Control Arguments

400. General constitutionality/popular control arguments – for example, "Supreme Court hears capital punishment case," "editorial discusses public opinion on death penalty"
401. Neither cruel nor unusual – the death penalty is neither cruel nor unusual
402. Due process and equal protection upheld – laws that act as guidelines for capital punishment proceedings do not inherently violate right to due process or equal protection
403. Popular support/sovereignty – a jury is the manifestation of popular sovereignty such that this body of peers has the right to punish as it sees fit; the will of the people should drive policy; the death penalty is supported by the people (e.g., "recent polls indicate that American approval for the death penalty has increased")
404. States' rights (pro–death penalty) – state should maintain capital punishment jurisdiction; Supreme Court should leave the fate of capital punishment to the states; there should be no blanket rulings and Supreme Court decisions should not take precedence
405. Federal jurisdiction (pro–death penalty) – the federal government has the right to step into a state's affairs to instate federal death penalty if state does not have capital punishment (in cases of terrorism, for example)
409. Other pro–death penalty constitutionality/popular control arguments – descriptions of decisions made by the Supreme Court or other court that are in favor of the death penalty in specific cases or that support the extension or maintenance of the death penalty in general; discussions of jury composition, such as who should or should not be allowed to sit on a jury; for example, "Bob Jones disagrees with Supreme Court's decision to abolish death penalty"
410. Cruel and unusual punishment – under the Eighth Amendment, the death penalty is cruel and unusual punishment
411. Violation of due process and equal protection – because it can so easily be confused with arguments in the 300 series, the abstract must make explicit reference to violation of due process and/or equal protection for this code to be applied; also used in any case in which a foreign national or citizen of another country was denied due process and cases in which international law was violated because of lack of due process

412. Popular support declining – popular support for the death penalty is declining or is lower than typically thought
413. States' rights (anti–death penalty) – states have the right not to use capital punishment; for example, "governor argues that the Supreme Court should not be able to override state supreme court decisions against the death penalty"
414. Federal jurisdiction (anti–death penalty) – it is constitutional for the federal government to step into state capital punishment decisions where necessary to disallow for or narrow the use of the death penalty
419. Other anti–death penalty constitutionality/popular control arguments – death penalty violates defendants' constitutional rights; for example, "defendants feel coerced to plead guilty to avoid the death sentence," "individuals who believe in blanket sentencing regulations should not be allowed to sit on juries," "district court upholds death sentence"

Cost Arguments

500. General cost arguments – questions or issues regarding the cost of capital punishment
502. Cost of life imprisonment – it costs too much to imprison a person for life, and thus the death penalty should be used instead
509. Other pro–death penalty cost arguments – for example, "capital punishment system is cost-effective"
510. High costs not worth it – it costs too much to put someone to death; for example, "legal proceedings can bankrupt a small town"
519. Other anti–death penalty cost arguments – for example, "the death penalty is too expensive"

Mode of Execution Arguments

600. General mode of execution arguments – for example, "state resumes use of electric chair"
601. Particular mode of execution just – there is nothing wrong with a certain mode of execution; the mode of execution does not violate the Eighth Amendment prohibiting cruel and unusual punishment
609. Other pro–death penalty mode of execution arguments – for example, "lethal injection is no more painful than a flu shot," "lethal injection is too kind, murderers should suffer painful and torturous death"
610. Particular mode of execution called into question – for example, "the electric chair is inhumane"
619. Other anti–death penalty mode of execution arguments

International Arguments

700. General international arguments – for example, "death penalty editorial raises international issues"

709. Arguments from abroad that are pro–death penalty – for example, "foreign minister applauds U.S. pledge to seek the death penalty in drug trafficking case"

710. Heat from abroad – for example, "French prime minister urges United States to abolish death penalty"

711. Complications with extradition due to death penalty – "Canadian officials refuse to return defendant to United States to face trial if possibility of death sentence exists"

712. Foreign nationals should not be executed here – foreign citizens should not be executed by nature of the fact that they should not be subject to the U.S. laws

Other Arguments

900. Other arguments

Note: Table 4.1 provides the frequencies with which each of these arguments was observed.

Appendix B

DESCRIPTION OF DATA

This appendix offers a summary description of the data sources and, where applicable, data collection procedures for the six major data series presented in this book: death row inmates, death sentences, executions, exonerations, homicides, and net support. We employ annual measures of each of these variables as well as quarterly measures of the last four. Complete datasets for these series are available at the Web site associated with this book. Additionally, throughout this book we refer to several data sources beyond these six major series. We provide citations for those data sources in notes throughout the text.

DEATH ROW INMATES

Annual Measure, 1953 to 2006: This series gives the total number of individuals under sentence of death in the United States in each year. We follow the Death Penalty Information Center in supplementing the primary Bureau of Statistics data source with the NAACP estimate for the most recent year as follows: 1953 to 2005 data from Snell 2005 (Figure 1: Persons under Sentence of Death 1953 to 2005); 2006 data from Fins 2006 (Table: Total Number of Death Row Inmates Known to LDF [Legal Defense Fund]).

DEATH SENTENCES

Annual Measure, 1961 to 2005: This series gives the number of death sentences handed down each year as provided by the following sources: 1961 to 1972 data from National Prisoner Statistics 1974; 1973 to 2005 data from Snell 2005 (Appendix Table 2: Prisoners Sentenced to Death and the Outcome Sentence, by Year of Sentencing, 1973 to 2005).

EXECUTIONS

Annual Measure, 1930 to 2006: This series gives the number of individuals executed in the United States in each year as reported by the following sources: 1930 to 2005 data from Snell 2005 (Figure 4: Persons Executed, 1930 to 2005); 2006 data from DPIC 2006c.

Quarterly Measure, 1960q1 to 2006q4: This series gives the number of individuals executed in the United States each quarter as calculated from the following sources: 1960 to 2002 data from Espy and Smykla 2005; 2003 to 2006 data from DPIC 2006c.

EXONERATIONS

Annual Measure, 1971 to 2006: This series gives the number of individuals exonerated from death row in the United States in each year as calculated from the following source: 1971 to 2006 data from DPIC 2006e.

Quarterly Measure, 1971 to 2006: This series gives the number of individuals exonerated from death row in the United States each quarter as calculated from the following source (which we supplemented with extensive research to identify the exact date, or at least the quarter, in which each individual was exonerated): 1971 to 2006 data from DPIC 2006e.

Note: The Death Penalty Information Center makes the following statement regarding the criteria for identifying exonerations: "The DPIC uses the traditional objective criteria that have determined innocence since the founding of this country. In order to be included on the list, defendants must have been convicted and sentenced to death, and subsequently either: a) their conviction was overturned and they were acquitted at a re-trial, or all charges were dismissed; or b) they were given an absolute pardon by the governor based on new evidence of innocence. The list includes cases in which the release occurred in 1973 or later."

HOMICIDES

Annual Measure, 1950 to 2006: This series gives the number of homicides committed in the United States each year as provided by the following sources: 1950 to 1985 data from Fox and Zawitz 2006 (Table of Homicide Victimization, 1950 to 2004); 1986 to 2005 data from Uniform Crime Reporting Program 2006 (Table 1: Crime in the United States by Volume and Rate per 100,000 Inhabitants, 1986 to 2005); 2006 value estimated by increasing the 2005 value by 1.4 percent in accordance with Mueller 2006 (Table 3: Percent Change for Consecutive Years January to June, 2002 to 2006).

Quarterly Measure, 1976q1 to 2006q4: This series gives the number
of homicides committed in the United States each quarter as provided by
the following sources: 1976q1 to 2001q4 data from Fox 2005; 2002q1
to 2003q4 data from Fox 2005, adjusting for a difference of twenty-
five homicides in each of 2002 and 2003 appearing in the national-level
data but not in the victim-level data; 2004q1 to 2006q4 data imputed
from yearly values (described above). For specific information about the
imputing procedure, please see our Web site.

NET PUBLIC SUPPORT FOR THE DEATH PENALTY
(ANNUAL AND QUARTERLY MEASURES)

These series give measures of public support for the death penalty as
calculated from data collected from the following source: Gallup Organization. Public opinion surveys conducted November 11, 1953, to May
5, 2006. Retrieved March 18, 2007, from the iPOLL Databank, The
Roper Center for Public Opinion Research, University of Connecticut,
http://www.ropercenter.uconn.edu/ipoll.html.

In this book, we use a variable we call "net support." This variable is
calculated simply from subtracting, at each point in time, our measure
of death penalty opposition from our measure of death penalty support
(i.e., percent pro minus percent anti). To gather these measures of death
penalty support and opposition, we began by searching on iPOLL for all
public opinion polls on "capital punishment" or "death penalty." Our
search yielded 780 survey items taken between December 1936 and May
2006. These surveys were conducted by a wide range of different survey
organizations (Gallup, CBS, Roper, etc.) and employed an even wider
range of question types ("Do you believe in the death penalty?" "Are
you in favor of the death penalty for murder?" "Do you think the death
penalty prevents crime?" "Are you in favor of the death penalty for persons convicted of rape?" etc.). Although there is significant variance across
these surveys in terms of survey house and question wording, we are able
to incorporate different questions asked by different organizations by
using the Wcalc algorithm created by James Stimson, which we describe
below.

Through use of this algorithm, questions with important differences
in question wording but with a common root subject – including those
questions listed above and many more – can each contribute information
to our overall measure of public opinion on the death penalty. Other
questions are simply off topic from the fundamental pro–death penalty
versus anti–death penalty divide and must be thrown out altogether, such
as this one:

People who are liberal in their lifestyles tend to support affirmative action for Blacks and other minorities, they are more in favor of women's liberation, and they are not so likely to condemn marijuana smoking or sexual freedom. People who are conservative in their lifestyles tend to be strongly in favor of the death penalty and more often than not, they are opposed to laws that permit abortion or homosexuality. When it comes to social matters like these, would you say you are generally very liberal, somewhat liberal, middle-of-the-road, somewhat conservative or very conservative?

The root of this question – a gauge of political ideology – is fundamentally distinct from the core issue at the heart of all questions we include in our death penalty measure, namely support for the practice of executing criminals.

In addition to throwing out all surveys not directly on topic (item 1 below), we establish the following list of requirements that must be met to include a survey in our measure. Of the full set of 780 question items we downloaded from iPOLL, 292 surveys meet our criteria for inclusion:

1. The survey question is directly relevant to the death penalty debate (as opposed to questions like the example above).
2. The survey was given to a random sample of national adults (as opposed to being asked only of registered voters, women, death penalty supporters, etc.).
3. The survey response options are polarized (pro vs. anti) or can be adjusted to be polarized through categorization into pro–death penalty and anti–death penalty clusters (e.g., the question "How strongly do you (favor/oppose) the death penalty for persons convicted of murder – very strongly or not too strongly?" provides four valenced response options (favor strongly, favor not too strongly, oppose not too strongly, and oppose strongly), and so we aggregate the favor responses and aggregate the opposition responses to calculate a single "pro" percentage and a single "anti" percentage.
4. The same question by the same survey organization was asked two or more times (a requirement of the algorithm described below).
5. The survey question was asked within reasonable proximity to the next survey question in time; two survey items were asked in 1936 but no other relevant surveys taken until 1953, and so we exclude the 1936 items from our data.

To use this dataset of 292 surveys from multiple survey houses and with multiple question types, we employed the Wcalc Public Opinion Dimensional Extraction Algorithm created by James Stimson (software retrieved March 23, 2007, from http://www.unc.edu/~jstimson/resource.html). In a manner similar to the dynamic factor analysis we describe in Chapter 5, this software program calculates how the survey marginals (i.e., percentage values) for each survey question asked by each organization change over time. Having calculated relative change scores for each individual survey question series, the algorithm extracts the latent dimension underlying the shared patterns of variance across these changes, producing a single series of public opinion data. The algorithm is also equipped with an optional smoothing function, which we choose to employ to minimize the "noise" inherent in this kind of survey data. The result: two smoothed time series, one representing aggregate support for the death penalty and the other representing aggregate opposition. Subtracting the opposition values from the support values, we obtain the final series of net support, which we employ in our Chapter 6 and Chapter 7 models.

Table B.1 shows the complete list of all the survey questions included in our set of 292 surveys comprising our net support series, with the survey house and number of surveys also indicated. In the case of minor variations in question wording, the most common question type is presented. The surveys we used represented nineteen distinct survey organizations and thirty-five distinct question wordings. In all, the data hold a total of sixty-five survey organization/question wording combinations, as shown by the sixty-five rows listed in Table B.1.

Table B.1. *List of survey questions used*

Series	Survey house	Question wording	Number of surveys
GAL_MUR	Gallup Organization	Are you in favor of the death penalty for persons convicted of murder?	42
NOR_MUR	National Opinion Research Center, University of Chicago	Do you favor or oppose the death penalty for persons convicted of murder?	25
GAL_LIFE	Gallup Organization	What do you think should be the penalty for murder – the death penalty or life imprisonment with absolutely no possibility of parole?	18
PSR_MUR	Princeton Survey Research Associates	I am going to read you a list of some programs and proposals that are being discussed in this country today. For each one, please tell me whether you strongly favor, favor, oppose, or strongly oppose it.... The death penalty for persons convicted of murder.	10
AWP_MUR	*ABC News/Washington Post* Poll	Do you favor or oppose the death penalty for persons convicted of murder?	9
GAL_OFT	Gallup Organization	In your opinion, is the death penalty imposed – too often, about the right amount, or not often enough?	7
GAL_ACC	Gallup Organization	(Next, I'm going to read you a list of issues. Regardless of whether or not you think it should be legal, for each one, please tell me whether you personally believe that in general it is morally acceptable or morally wrong.) How about...the death penalty?	6
GAL_TIM	Gallup Organization	Thinking about Timothy McVeigh, the man convicted of murder in the Oklahoma City bombing case and sentenced to death, which comes closest to your view? I generally support the death penalty and believe McVeigh should be executed. I generally oppose the death penalty, but believe McVeigh should be executed in this case. I generally oppose the death penalty and do not believe McVeigh should be executed.	6

(continued)

Table B.1 (continued)

Series	Survey house	Question wording	Number of surveys
ABC_MUR	ABC News Poll	Are you in favor of the death penalty for persons convicted of murder?	5
CBS_MUR	CBS News Poll	Do you favor or oppose the death penalty for persons convicted of murder?	5
GAL_DET	Gallup Organization	Do you feel that the death penalty acts a deterrent to the commitment of murder, that it lowers the murder rate, or not?	5
GAL_RAPE	Gallup Organization	Do you favor or oppose the death penalty for persons convicted of ...rape?	5
GAL_SKY	Gallup Organization	Do you favor or oppose the death penalty for persons convicted of ... hijacking an airplane?	5
LHA	Louis Harris & Associates	Do you believe in capital punishment (death penalty) or are you opposed to it?	5
PSR_TIM	Princeton Survey Research Associates	Do you favor or oppose the death penalty for Timothy McVeigh if he is convicted of bombing a federal building in Oklahoma City?	5
YSW_KID	Yankelovich, Skelly & White	A number of controversial proposals are being discussed these days. I'd like you to tell me for each one how you feel about it. The death penalty should be restored for certain crimes like kidnapping or hijacking.	5
AWP_LIFE	ABC News/Washington Post Poll	Which punishment do you prefer for people convicted of murder, the death penalty or life in prison with no chance of parole?	4
CBS_TIM	CBS News Poll	As you may know, Timothy McVeigh was found guilty of the 1995 bombing of the federal building in Oklahoma City, in which 168 people were killed, and was sentenced to death in 1997....He is scheduled to be executed on May 16, 2001. Do you favor or oppose the death penalty for Timothy McVeigh?	4
CNY_MUR	CBS News/New York Times Poll	Do you favor or oppose the death penalty for persons convicted of murder?	4
GAL_APP	Gallup Organization	Generally speaking, do you believe the death penalty is applied fairly or unfairly in this country today?	4

PSR_LVL[a]	Princeton Survey Research Associates	Which one of the following four statements comes closest to your opinion of who should be subject to the death penalty . . . only those convicted of murder, only those convicted of the most brutal murders, mass murders and serial killings, all those convicted of murder, other especially violent crimes and major drug dealing or do you oppose the death penalty in all cases?	4
YAN_MUR	Yankelovich Clancy Shulman	Do you, in general, favor or oppose the death penalty for individuals convicted of serious crimes, such as murder?	4
CBS_DET	CBS News Poll	Do you think that capital punishment – the death penalty – is or is not a deterrent to murder?	3
CBS_LIFE	CBS News Poll	What do you think should be the penalty for murder – the death penalty, or life imprisonment with absolutely no possibility of parole?	3
CNY_ANY	CBS News/New York Times Poll	Are there any circumstances under which you think the death penalty is justified?	3
CNY_DRGM	CBS News/New York Times Poll	Do you favor or oppose the death penalty for people convicted of controlling large drug dealing operations?	3
GAL_BLK[b]	Gallup Organization	As I read off each of these statements, would you tell me whether you agree or disagree with it . . . A black person is more likely than a white person to receive the death penalty for the same crime.	3
GAL_EVRIN5	Gallup Organization	How often do you think that a person has been executed under the death penalty who was, in fact, innocent of the crime he or she was charged with – do you think this has happened in the past five years, or not?	3
GAL_MAND	Gallup Organization	(The following is a list of some programs and proposals that are being discussed in this country today. For each one, please tell me whether you strongly favor, favor, oppose or strongly oppose.) . . . A mandatory death penalty for anyone convicted of premeditated murder.	3

(continued)

259

Table B.1 (continued)

Series	Survey house	Question wording	Number of surveys
GAL_POOR[b]	Gallup Organization	(As I read off each of these statements, would you tell me whether you agree or disagree with it)...A poor person is more likely than a person of average or above average income to receive the death penalty for the same crime.	3
GAL_PRES	Gallup Organization	Do you favor or oppose the death penalty for persons convicted of... attempting to assassinate the president?	3
GAL_SPY	Gallup Organization	Do you favor or oppose the death penalty for persons convicted of...spying for a foreign nation during peacetime?	3
HAR	Harris Survey	Do you believe in capital punishment, that is, the death penalty, or are you opposed to it?	3
HAR_DETEF	Harris Survey	Suppose it could be proved to your satisfaction that the death penalty was not more effective than long prison sentences in keeping other people from committing crimes such as murder, would you be in favor of the death penalty or would you be opposed to it?	3
LAT_MUR	*Los Angeles Times*	Generally speaking, are you in favor of the death penalty for persons convicted of murder, or are you opposed to that – or haven't you heard enough about that yet to say?	3
LHA_COP	Louis Harris & Associates	Do you feel that all persons convicted of...killing a policeman or prison guard...should get the death penalty, that no one convicted of...killing a policeman or prison guard...should get the death penalty, or do you feel that whether or not someone convicted of...killing a policeman or prison guard...gets the death penalty should depend on the circumstances of the case and the character of the person?	3
LHA_MUR	Louis Harris & Associates	Do you feel that all persons convicted of...first degree murder...should get the death penalty, that no one convicted of...first degree murder...should get the death penalty, or do you feel that whether or not someone convicted of...first degree murder...gets the death penalty should depend on the circumstances of the case and the character of the person?	3

NBC_MUR	NBC News/Associated Press	Do you favor or oppose the death penalty for persons convicted of murder?	3
ROP_MUR	Roper Organization	(Frequently on any controversial issue there is no clear-cut side that people take, and also frequently solutions on controversial issues are worked out by compromise. But I'm going to name some different things, and for each one would you tell me whether on balance you would be more in favor of it, or more opposed to it?) . . . Imposing the death penalty on those convicted of serious crimes such as murder, kidnapping, etc.	3
ABC_LIFE	ABC News Poll	Which punishment do you prefer for people convicted of murder, the death penalty or life in prison with no chance of parole?	2
CBS_PAR	CBS News Poll	What do you think should be the penalty for persons convicted of murder – the death penalty, or life in prison with no chance of parole, or a long prison sentence with a chance of parole?	2
CPS_MUR	Center for Political Studies, University of Michigan	Do you favor or oppose the death penalty for persons convicted of murder?	2
GAL_DRGN	Gallup Organization	Do you favor or oppose the death penalty for drug dealers not convicted of murder?	2
GAL_EVRIN[a]	Gallup Organization	How often do you think a person has been sentenced to the death penalty who was, in fact, innocent of the crime he was charged with? Do you think this has ever happened in the past 20 years, or do you think it has never happened?[a]	2

(continued)

Table B.1 (continued)

Series	Survey house	Question wording	Number of surveys
GAL_EXT	Gallup Organization	(Please tell me whether you would generally favor or oppose each of the following proposals which some people have made to reduce crime.)...Extending the death penalty for some serious crimes other than murder.	2
GAL_MOR	Gallup Organization	Which comes closer to your view? There should be a moratorium, or temporary halt, on the death penalty? There should be a moratorium, or temporary halt, on the death penalty until it can be better determined if the death penalty is being administered accurately and fairly in this country. There should not be a moratorium, or temporary halt, on the death penalty because there are already sufficient safeguards in the current justice system to prevent the execution of innocent people?	2
GAL_NOTEV	Gallup Organization	Suppose new evidence showed that the death penalty does not act as a deterrent to murder – that it does not lower the murder rate. Would you favor or oppose the death penalty?	2
GAL_PCT[a]	Gallup Organization	Just your best guess, about what percent of people who are executed under the death penalty are really innocent of the crime they were charged with?	2
GAL_SUS	Gallup Organization	In a recent case that received a lot of media attention, Susan Smith confessed to drowning her two young sons in her car. If found guilty of murder in this case, do you think Susan Smith should receive the death penalty, or not?	2
GAL_TRE	Gallup Organization	Are you in favor of the death penalty for persons convicted of: Treason?	2
GAL_WOM	Gallup Organization	Do you favor or oppose the death penalty for ...women?	2
HAR_MUR	Harris Survey	Do you favor or oppose the death penalty for individuals convicted of serious crimes such as murder?	2
HLEVIN	Harris Interactive	If you believed that quite a substantial number of innocent people are convicted of murder, would you then believe in or oppose the death penalty for murder?	2

HI_MOR	Harris Interactive	Do you think that there should be a temporary moratorium or halt in the death penalty to allow the government to reduce the chances that an innocent person will be put to death or do you think that there should not be a moratorium because there are already sufficient safeguards to prevent the execution of innocent people?	2
HTR	Hart and Teeter Research Companies	Do you favor or oppose the death penalty?	2
HTR_MOR	Hart and Teeter Research Companies	As you may have heard, there have been several instances in which criminals sentenced to be executed have been released based on new evidence or new DNA testing. Based on this information, would you favor or oppose a suspension of the death penalty until questions about its fairness can be studied?	2
LAT	*Los Angeles Times*	Do you approve or disapprove of the death penalty?	2
LHA_MUG	Louis Harris & Associates	Do you feel that all persons convicted of…mugging…should get the death penalty, that no one convicted of…mugging…should get the death penalty, or do you feel that whether or not someone convicted of…mugging…gets the death penalty should depend on the circumstances of the case and the character of the person?	2
LHA_RAPE	Louis Harris & Associates	Do you feel that all persons convicted of…rape…should get the death penalty, that no one convicted of…rape…should get the death penalty, or do you feel that whether or not someone convicted of…rape…gets the death penalty should depend on the circumstances of the case and the character of the person?	2

(continued)

Table B.1 *(continued)*

Series	Survey house	Question wording	Number of surveys
LHA_SKY	Louis Harris & Associates	Do you feel that all persons convicted of…skyjacking…should get the death penalty, that no one convicted of…skyjacking…should get the death penalty, or do you feel that whether or not someone convicted of…skyjacking…gets the death penalty should depend on the circumstances of the case and the character of the person?	2
LHA_TER	Louis Harris & Associates	(Now let me ask you about some solutions that have been proposed as ways of dealing with terrorism. For each, tell me if you favor or oppose that solution)…All those caught committing acts of terror should be convicted and given the death penalty.	2
PSR_ACC	Princeton Survey Research Associates	Please tell me whether you would generally favor or oppose the death penalty for murder in each of the following circumstances. If the convicted person was…only an accomplice to the person who actually did the killing, would you favor or oppose the death penalty?	2
PSR_TEEN	Princeton Survey Research Associates	If a teenager commits a crime that could carry the death penalty for an adult, do you think he or she should receive a death sentence, or not?	2
QUI_MUR	Quinnipiac University Polling Institute	Do you favor or oppose the death penalty for persons convicted of murder?	2
WP_MUR	*Washington Post*	Do you favor or oppose the death penalty for persons convicted of murder?	2
YAN_TIM	Yankelovich Partners	(I have a few questions about Timothy McVeigh, one of the men on trial for bombing the federal building in Oklahoma City two years ago.) If found guilty of murder in this case (the Oklahoma City bombing), do you think Timothy McVeigh should receive the death penalty, or not?	2

[a] We broke the response categories of these surveys in half to create one pro–death penalty response marginal and one anti–death penalty response marginal.
[b] To maintain a consistent pro/anti polarization direction across all surveys in our dataset, we treated the "yes" responses of these surveys as being pro–death penalty and the "no" responses as being anti–death penalty in nature.

NOTES

1. INNOCENCE AND THE DEATH PENALTY DEBATE

1. The account presented here is based on information compiled from several sources, including Chebium 2000, Connors et al. 1996, Junkin 2004, The Center on Wrongful Convictions (http://www.law.northwestern.edu/depts/clinic/wrongful/exonerations), The Innocence Project (http://www.innocenceproject.org), and The Justice Project (http://www.thejusticeproject.org).
2. For an excellent discussion of framing theory and a review of framing research at the individual level, see Chong and Druckman 2007.
3. When the Gallup Organization asked a random sample of national adults "Are you in favor of the death penalty for a person convicted of murder?" the percentage of respondents who answered "yes" was 79 percent in September 1988, 76 percent in June 1991, and 80 percent in September 1994. In June 2000 this number dropped to 62 percent. Minor fluctuations have followed, but support remains at this significantly decreased level: 64 percent in October 2005 and 65 percent in May 2006.

2. THE DEATH PENALTY IN AMERICA

1. Because of missing data for eight countries (for which we do not know the precise date on which they abolished the death penalty), the figure includes just seventy-nine countries.
2. The following is a list of all countries and territories that retain the death penalty for ordinary crimes (Amnesty International 2006): Afghanistan, Antigua and Barbuda, Bahamas, Bahrain, Bangladesh, Barbados, Belarus, Belize, Botswana, Burundi, Cameroon, Chad, China, Comoros, Congo (Democratic Republic), Cuba, Dominica, Egypt, Equatorial Guinea, Eritrea, Ethiopia, Guatemala, Guinea, Guyana, India, Indonesia, Iran, Iraq, Jamaica, Japan, Jordan, Kazakhstan, Korea (North), Korea (South), Kuwait, Laos, Lebanon, Lesotho, Libya, Malaysia, Mongolia, Nigeria, Oman, Pakistan, Palestinian Authority, Qatar, Rwanda, Saint Christopher and Nevis, Saint Lucia, Saint Vincent and Grenadines, Saudi Arabia, Sierra Leone, Singapore, Somalia, Sudan, Syria, Taiwan, Tajikistan, Tanzania, Thailand, Trinidad and

Tobago, Uganda, United Arab Emirates, United States of America, Uzbekistan, Viet Nam, Yemen, Zambia, and Zimbabwe.

3. Source: European Commission (http://ec.europa.eu/comm/external_relations/human_rights/adp/index.htm).

4. Data in this section include the fifty states as well as the District of Columbia, the U.S. military, and the U.S. federal courts. The federal and military death penalties have been extremely rare; the District of Columbia does not have capital punishment.

5. The federal government makes rare use of the death penalty; like most aspects of criminal law, it is mostly a state function. Still, forty-eight individuals have been sentenced to death since the first case in the modern era, in 1991. There have been three federal executions: Timothy McVeigh (the Oklahoma City federal building bomber) in 2001; Juan Raul Garza (a drug kingpin) in 2001; and Louis Jones, Jr. (the army master sergeant – honorably discharged – convicted of kidnapping, raping, and murdering Army Private Tracie Joy McBride) in 2003. The U.S. military has not executed any of its servicemen or women since 1961, though under President Ronald Reagan, capital punishment was reinstated for fifteen different military crimes. There were nine individuals on military death row as of 2007. There is some chance that federal and military uses of the death penalty will increase, perhaps dramatically, in the future. Congress has passed legislation increasing the range of crimes (including that of being a "drug kingpin") subject to federal capital prosecution. However, the death penalty remains largely a state function.

6. Readers may note slight differences in the numbers of executions by state depending on the source, which we note at the bottom of our tables and figures. The Department of Justice Bureau of Justice Statistics and the Death Penalty Information Center (DPIC) together provide the most up-to-date information we have been able to find, and we use these sources where available. Espy and Smykla 2005 is the most comprehensive database of executions available over a longer historical period, containing a record of every execution for which information was available going back to the 1600s. However, it has some missing values and coverage extends only through 2002. Together, these factors explain the few slight but substantively inconsequential discrepancies between the numbers quoted for executions by jurisdiction in this section.

7. Florida, the fifth state with large numbers of post-1976 executions, had eighty-nine executions in the earlier period followed by sixty-four in the later one, so like most states, it in fact reduced its use of executions.

8. Data taken from Liebman et al. 2002, Figure 8a.

9. We do not explore in detail the differences in framing or public opinion across states; our analysis is focused on national-level trends over time. However, Figure 2.8, as well as data presented in Chapter 4 comparing various newspapers around the country (see Figures 4.15 to 4.17), makes clear that trends over time are similar. Even if there are significant differences in how the death penalty is framed in different areas around the country, our evidence suggests that chronological trends are similar. Of course, it is always possible that a local event such as the exonerations and police scandals in Chicago, or a brutal crime wave such as the sniper shootings in suburban Washington,

D.C., can affect public opinion in a local area without affecting the national debate. However, over the long run, our evidence suggests that the trends we document here, especially the rise of the innocence movement, have not been particular to any one area of the country; the entire system has been affected by these shifting terms of debate. In any case, a detailed state-by-state analysis of these events is simply beyond the scope of our analysis.

10. DNA testing, or genetic fingerprinting, was developed by Sir Alec Jeffreys at the University of Leicester and announced in 1985. On November 6, 1987, Tommie Lee Andrews became the first American to be convicted as a result of DNA evidence; he was convicted of rape and aggravated burglary and sentenced to twenty-two years in prison. Although during the late 1980s and early 1990s DNA evidence led to several U.S. convictions and exonerations, the technology gained widespread attention in 1994 during the highly publicized double murder trial of O. J. Simpson. The Simpson trial and its media coverage illustrated, among other things, Americans' fascination with forensic evidence and the laboratory difficulties and evidence-handling misconduct that may occur.

3. A CHRONOLOGY OF INNOCENCE

1. We encourage readers interested in a more complete history of the innocence movement, and the death penalty in general, to visit the Death Penalty Information Center (http://www.deathpenaltyinfo.org).

4. THE SHIFTING TERMS OF DEBATE

1. Thanks to Cheryl Feeley for doing the bulk of this work for her senior thesis and for allowing us to use and update the data she collected.

2. Appendix A displays the full codebook containing a description of the coding procedures, a complete list of the dimensions and arguments used, and coding examples. Intercoder reliability was estimated at approximately 98 percent at the first level of coding (seven main categories plus one "other" category) and 92 percent at the second level of coding (sixty-five distinct arguments).

3. Some articles mention *both* the victim and the defendant, and these are included in both totals above. If we limit ourselves to the 308 stories with tone that mention the defendant but have no mention of the victim, only 22 percent have a pro–death penalty tone. Looking only at the 505 stories with tone that mention the victim without mentioning the defendant, 71 percent are pro–death penalty in tone.

4. Specifically, to capture all relevant articles, we searched for stories containing reference to the death penalty, capital punishment, and/or death row.

5. For nine of these ten newspapers, Lexis-Nexis offers data for the last fifteen years or so, beginning in most cases around 1990 and running consistently through 2005, when our data collection finished. However, for one newspaper – the *Miami Herald* – the data series begins and ends approximately five years earlier; stories are archived from 1980 through 1999. From 1980 through 1999, the *Herald* contains far fewer stories about the death penalty

than its peer papers present from 1990 through 2005; it has less than half as many as the next, *Denver Post*, which in fact is only archived in Lexis-Nexis for eleven years, from 1994 through 2005. Presumably, this discrepancy in total counts is the result of the major events that occurred in the death penalty debate between 2000 and 2005. Because our primary aim is to test whether other national papers gave the same level of treatment to the innocence frame in these most recent years, we exclude the *Herald* from our analysis; however, it makes little difference.

6. The number of articles listed annually for this Lexis-Nexis search of the *Times* is substantially higher than what we report throughout the earlier sections of this chapter and in particular in Figure 4.1. This is because the electronic search is not limited only to those articles for which the death penalty was the predominant theme of the article, as is the case in using the printed indices, as we have done. The trends are similar, of course. As there are no printed indices for most of the other newspapers, however, for comparability we used the electronic search in each case, so the numbers in Figure 4.15 are comparable.

7. We used standard principal-components factor analysis and then adjusted the results through orthogonal varimax rotation.

8. Center for Media and Public Affairs press release, "Networks Set Pace for Green Mile: By June 2000, Death Penalty Coverage Exceeds All Years in Past Decade," June 29, 2000.

5. INNOCENCE, RESONANCE, AND OLD ARGUMENTS MADE NEW AGAIN

1. Similarly, if an innocence argument is made by a defendant or a defense attorney, or if these same individuals raise issues of fairness of the judicial system, source credibility comes into play. The listener may react by recognizing that the source of the complaint has a vested interest and discount the new information substantially.

2. This argument, incidentally, is empirically false, at least in recent times, because capital trials themselves are so expensive.

3. As we note in our more detailed discussion of the EFA method in the appendix to this chapter, we exclude from our analysis all arguments in a given five-year time window that appeared in fewer than five stories during that period. How is it possible, then, that argument 309 is listed here as contributing only one story? Following our EFA rules as described in the appendix, we identify argument 309 as contributing to the 1971, 1972, and 1975 periods (i.e., it loads above our threshold of |.85| in the factor analysis performed on the 1969 to 1973, 1970 to 1974, and 1973 to 1977 time windows). This argument was included in the factor analyses of all these windows because, with one story in 1971, eight stories in 1973, four stories in 1974, and two stories each in 1976 and 1977, the argument was used in more than five stories in each five-year window. But the values we display in parentheses in Table 5.1 show the total number of stories using each argument summed across the years during which the argument contributed to the evolutionary frame. So for argument 309, which was part of the eye-for-an-eye evolutionary frame during the time windows centering on 1971, 1972, and 1975, only one story (the one in 1971) is counted. It is for this same reason that two component

arguments – argument 719 (anti international – other) in the "innocence" evolutionary frame and argument 309 (pro fairness – other) in the "popular support down" evolutionary frame – can be listed as contributing zero stories to their evolutionary frames although, in fact, each one contributed a small handful. Whereas the decision to measure argument salience in Table 5.1 in this way may underestimate the contribution of smaller, more "noisy" arguments, such as argument 309 here, alternate counting approaches such as summing the number of stories using each argument across the moving five-year windows would do much worse in inflating the contribution of each argument. Because the arguments that are the driving force of each evolutionary frame are usually used in approximately the same high number of stories from one year to the next during their contribution to the frame, measuring salience as a count of the stories just in the central year of each time window offers a much more accurate depiction of attention.

4. In this way, performing EFA on the death penalty data we have already examined in raw frequency form in Chapter 4 data uses *confirmatory*, or theory-driven factor analysis. Having demonstrated EFA's ability to produce basic results consistent with those yielded by the frequency approach, we hope other researchers will feel confident using EFA based on *exploratory* factor analysis to study the framing of even those issues with which the researcher has little familiarity. And having demonstrated EFA's ability to produce additional and compelling insights into the framing of the death penalty debate beyond those afforded by taking counts of newspaper stories alone, we hope researchers will consider using EFA as an improved method of framing analysis in particular.

5. There are simply not enough stories in most months or quarters to warrant aggregating reliably at a more detailed level of time. Some datasets, however, might lend themselves to a more fine-grained temporal analysis, in which case, a day, week, or month time window may be employed.

6. To have the most complete coverage in time possible, the windows at the very beginning and end of our series are truncated, with just four years of data for the penultimate data points and three years of data for the first and last windows. Unlike the standard five-year windows, which are centered on the year in question, these tapered windows must by necessity use data primarily after or before the final years. At the end of our data, for example, we analyze 2003 through use of a normal five-year window (2001 to 2005), then for 2004 we use a four-year window (2002 to 2005), and for 2005 we use a three-year window (2003 to 2005).

7. This fact in itself is quite remarkable because, theoretically, there could be as many factors as there are series, sixty-five in our case. It means that there are typically just a handful of themes "out there" at any given time, and each one of these factors may be associated with a number of individual arguments.

8. We refer here to absolute values, so we would also retain as part of a frame any argument that loaded –0.85 or below as well as any loading at +0.85 or above; the former category would be arguments that systematically move in the *opposite* direction as the latter in the frame: fewer articles mentioning these arguments appear in years when more articles appear mentioning other articles in the frame. We choose to include the negative as well as the positive loading arguments because for two arguments to move in direct opposite tandem

tells us that the arguments share as much of a thematic connection as two arguments that move in direct tandem, except that in this case, the presence of one argument predicts the absence of the other. There are relatively few such negative loadings in our dataset, however – less than one quarter of all the factor loadings above |.85| that we use.

9. We allow one rare exception to this rule by allowing an argument previously part of an evolutionary frame to contribute again to that frame if it appears in the same factor after lapsing for no more than two windows. In our analysis, this exception occurs only twice: first, when argument 309 rejoins the "eye-for-an-eye" evolutionary frame in 1975 and, second, when argument 302 rejoins the "innocence" evolutionary frame in 2002. In both cases, allowing the argument in question to rejoin the ongoing frame stays true to our understanding of how these frames evolved in the real-world debate.

6. PUBLIC OPINION

1. For example, in March 2000 an *ABC News/Washington Post* survey asked 1,083 national adults: "How important will handling the death penalty issue be to you in deciding how to vote in the 2000 presidential election in November – very important, somewhat important, not too important or not important at all?" A full 72 percent of respondents said the death penalty would be at least "somewhat important" in determining their vote (37 percent answered "very important," and 35 percent answered "somewhat important"; see *Roper*, question ID# USABCWP.040300.R04N).

2. There is, of course, substantial debate about whether the death penalty is effective in reducing violent crime. One reason for the continued nature of the debate in the face of evidence that the penalty does not reduce crime rates could be that areas with higher crime rates see more emphasis on "getting tough" with the ongoing crime problem. So the crime rate drives the death penalty, not the converse. If the death penalty were effective and reduced the crime rate, there might be less support for the death penalty, paradoxically. In any case, scholars have found that high crime rates are typically associated with greater popular support for the death penalty.

3. Fan et al. (2002) offer evidence that the sudden shift in death penalty opinion in the late 1990s occurred in direct proportion to increased media coverage on exonerations from death row, but their analysis lacks the systematic treatment of framing that we offer here. Besides this single study, the role of framing has been limited to the framing effects of question wording used to measure public opinion, as we discussed earlier. And even here, some have noted: "It seems that most Americans know whether they 'favor' or 'oppose' the death penalty and say so in response to any question that can reasonably be interpreted as addressing this issue" (Ellsworth and Gross 1994).

4. The high levels of support for the death penalty by representative samples of Americans contrast sharply with the much lower rates at which juries impose the sentence in actual cases. This discrepancy is in spite of the fact that Americans who disagree with the concept of the death penalty are excluded from serving on capital juries. In its 1968 *Witherspoon v. Illinois* (391 U.S. 510) decision, the Supreme Court ruled that "death-qualified" juries – juries composed

only of individuals who are willing to consider imposing a death sentence – are constitutional, and in 1986, the Court again upheld the use of death-qualified juries in *Lockhart v. McCree* (476 U.S. 162). So there are substantial differences between abstract thoughts about the death penalty in response to a survey question and its possible use in a particular case, as discussed in the jury room.

5. In earlier surveys, respondents were not given the "don't know" response option, so the marginals are not comparable. Average sample size is more than 1,000, making sampling error average approximately ± 3 percent.

6. The assumption we make is not that all or even most of the variation in each component series is shared, but that some part of the variance is shared. The remainder is composed of error variance and variance unique to that input series. For example, questions about the appropriateness of the death penalty for Timothy McVeigh no doubt capture both general attitudes toward the death penalty (shared variance) and variance associated specifically with the appropriateness of the death penalty for acts of domestic terrorism or reflecting people's feelings toward McVeigh in particular (unique variance). Because they are based on opinion polls and samples, they also include random sampling error (error variance). With enough observations, the shared variance will be apparent. The unique variance associated with each individual series will be reduced by accumulating many series and taking an average among them. The error variance associated with random sampling will be reduced by having multiple polls, allowing the random fluctuations associated with any single poll to cancel out.

7. Technically, we analyze covariance across *ratios* of change in the survey responses within questions. The ratios are calculated relative to some baseline time point, say 2002. We arbitrarily rescale the value of the series to a value of one in this year, and then for each survey item, we compute support for each time point as a ratio relative to that baseline value. When the baseline year is missing for a given survey item – as will inevitably be the case for some questions – a new baseline is selected and calibrated with respect to the old baseline, and ratios are computed for all items that contain observations for that baseline. This process is repeated over and over again until ratios are computed for all items. (See Stimson 1991, Appendix 1 for details.) These ratios, unlike the raw component series values, are comparable across survey items and thereby provide a solution – a common metric – for dealing with the unique mean value associated with each survey house and question wording. This technique amounts simply to comparing each series to its value at a common point in time. With all the series recalibrated so that they are all measured on the same scale, we can move forward.

8. Formally, the series is calculated according to the formula:

$$\text{Support} \quad t = \sum_{i=1}^{n} \sum_{j=1}^{t} \left[\frac{ui^2 \left(\frac{question_{ij}}{question_{ib}} \right) metric_b}{n} \right],$$

where i is all available questions at time t and j is all available dyadic comparisons for question i, b is the base period for computing the ratios, *metric b* (here 100) is the value of the metric for period b, and ui^2 is the estimate of the common variance of question i and the estimated support for the death penalty. The final series is exponentially smoothed and the metric is defined to have a mean and standard deviation that is a weighted average of the component series where weights are equal to the estimated common variance. The more an item contributes to the measure, the more weight that item will be given in determining the metric of the final series.

9. We estimated anti–death penalty attitudes using Stimson's algorithm by inputting the marginals for the anti–death penalty categories of the response options to the same questions used for the support series. In both cases, values were calculated as a percentage of the summed pro– and anti–death penalty responses; we eliminated the "neutral" and "don't know" responses. The pro– and anti–death penalty series were also smoothed during the algorithm process. The net support measure is simply the difference between the percent supporting and opposing the death penalty (pro minus anti).

10. Remember, of course, that these index values themselves are somewhat arbitrary; what we can draw from these numbers is that whatever support for the death penalty is today, it has returned to the same level it was a half-century ago.

11. The stability of opinion in the early years is in part an artifact of missing and therefore interpolated data. We have no survey data in 1954, 1955, 1958, 1959, 1961 through 1964, 1968, or 1970. After 1970, survey data on the death penalty is much more complete.

12. Although most research on public sentiment and the death penalty has modeled opinion as a function of homicides, as we do here, some researchers argue that opinion responds to perceptions of crime rather than crime itself. We choose to use actual homicide numbers because, although we do not contend that most Americans could quote the year's homicide rate from the Bureau of Justice Statistics, we believe that rising (and falling) crime rates have real manifestations in social life. So although citizens may not know the numbers, they are very aware of the trends. (For discussion of the accuracy of the public's perceptions of crime, see Kleinman and David 1973, Lewis and Salem 1986, McPherson 1978, Stafford and Galle 1984, and Warr 1980 and 1982; although see Janson and Ryder 1983 for the argument that some social categories and ethnic groups are more accurate at perceiving crime than others.)

13. Quarterly data exhibit seasonal fluctuations. In particular, more murders are committed in the summer and fewer in the winter. Because we do not want these patterns in homicides to influence opinion, we smooth the quarterly homicide data, creating a four-quarter moving average of homicide levels.

14. Net support, homicide levels, and net tone each behave as a unit root process, necessitating this treatment. Dickey-Fuller tests indicate that a unit root null hypothesis cannot be rejected. Tests for cointegration confirm that the series are cointegrated and an error correction model is thus appropriate and necessary.

15. The independent variables are lagged one period to ensure, for example, that surveys used to create the public opinion measure in one quarter cannot

predate media stories assumed to drive opinion, thus preserving the causal ordering of the variables.

16. The total effect is asymptotic. After twenty quarters, approximately 98 percent of the total effect will have been corrected: $(1 - 0.17)^{20} = 0.024$.

17. Predicted values of net support (shown in Figure 6.6) are much smoother than actual values of net support (shown in Figure 6.4). The difference arises because predicted values are calculated as a function of past predicted values – as well as observed values of homicides, net tone, and major events – with no reliance whatsoever on observed opinion values. This process inherently produces a smoother picture of net support.

18. The estimated effect is based on the coefficient on the effect of the Illinois clemency grant by Governor George Ryan in a model in which each event was separately included. Results are not reported here.

7. THE RISE AND FALL OF A PUBLIC POLICY

1. In its 1968 *Witherspoon v. Illinois* (391 US 510) decision, the Supreme Court ruled that "death-qualified" juries – juries comprised only of individuals who are willing to consider imposing a death sentence – are constitutional. In 1986, the Court again upheld the use of death-qualified juries in *Lockhart v. McCree* (476 US 162).

2. We choose to analyze annual data here because although death sentences are handed down at a specific date – and thus theoretically available quarterly – they are not in fact recorded quarterly at the national level. We chose not to analyze the public opinion series annually for two main reasons. First, the annual data average across interesting variation in opinion, and we were able to assess that with high-quality quarterly estimates only since 1977. Second, the annual data require us to model opinion during the moratorium period, but the relation between these Supreme Court interventions and public opinion (as opposed to sentencing) is unclear.

3. The number of death sentences is large enough that the variable is approximately normally distributed so that ordinary least squares (OLS) regression, rather than models designed especially for the unique problems associated with count data, is appropriate for the analysis.

4. We estimated statistical tests – Granger causality tests – that allow us to test the null hypothesis that each of the processes we care about predicts the others. We find that homicide levels are predicted by the number of death sentences that occur in a given year. This finding means that the estimated effect of homicides on death sentences is, strictly speaking, biased. We find, however, that in estimating the full system of equations and interpreting effects in the context of a vector autoregression (VAR), we draw inferences almost identical to those produced by the simple regression analysis that we report here. Of particular note, net tone *is* weakly exogenous and, thus, unbiased. Given the complexities of the VAR, we choose to present the single equation in Table 7.1.

5. The standard deviation of net tone is just over thirty stories, that of homicides 4,508.

6. As with homicides, we find that we cannot rule out the possibility that the number of death sentences influences opinion when we test that hypothesis using Granger causality tests. This finding means that our estimated coefficient on public opinion is biased. Using more statistically sophisticated techniques that handle this possibility – again the VAR – we find that the dynamic effects we report overestimate the effect of opinion somewhat.

8. CONCLUSION

1. Reports of state-level legislation in this section come from the StandDown Texas Project (http://standdown.typepad.com/) and from the Death Penalty Information Center (http://www.deathpenaltyinfo.org/).

REFERENCES

Althaus, Scott L., Jill A. Edy, and Patricia F. Phalen. 2001. Using Substitutes for Full-Text News Stories in Content Analysis: Which Text Is Best? *American Journal of Political Science* 45 (3): 707–723.

Alvarez, R. Michael, and John Brehm. 1995. American Ambivalence Towards Abortion Policy: Development of a Heteroskedastic Probit Model of Competing Values. *American Journal of Political Science* 39 (4): 1055–1082.

Alvarez, R. Michael, and John Brehm. 1997. Are Americans Ambivalent Towards Racial Policies? *American Journal of Political Science* 41 (2): 345–374.

Alvarez, R. Michael, and John Brehm. 1998. Speaking in Two Voices: American Equivocation about the Internal Revenue Service. *American Journal of Political Science* 42 (2): 418–452.

Alvarez, R. Michael, and John Brehm. 2002. *Hard Choices, Easy Answers: Values, Information, and American Public Opinion.* Princeton, N.J.: Princeton University Press.

Amnesty International. 2006. Abolitionist and Retentionist Countries. Retrieved March 13, 2007, from http://web.amnesty.org/pages/deathpenalty-abolitionist1-eng.

Arrow, Kenneth. 1970. *Social Choice and Individual Values.* New Haven, Conn.: Yale University Press.

Associated Press. 2004. Justice Dept. Reports a 30-Year Low in Death Sentences and Fewer Inmates on Death Row. *New York Times* 15 November.

Atkins v. Virginia, 536 U.S. 304 (2002).

Ball, Philip. 2004. *Critical Mass: How One Thing Leads to Another.* New York, N.Y.: Farrar, Straus, and Giroux.

Banner, Stuart. 2002. *The Death Penalty: An American History.* Cambridge, Mass.: Harvard University Press.

Barabasi, Albert-Laszlo. 2003. *Linked: How Everything Is Connected to Everything Else and What It Means.* New York, N.Y.: Plume.

Baumgartner, Frank R. 1989. *Conflict and Rhetoric in French Policymaking.* Pittsburgh, Pa.: University of Pittsburgh Press.

Baumgartner, Frank R., and Bryan D. Jones. 1993. *Agendas and Instability in American Politics.* Chicago, Ill.: The University of Chicago Press.

Bedau, Hugo Adam, ed. 1997. *The Death Penalty in America: Current Contro-versies.* New York, N.Y.: Oxford University Press.

Bedau, Hugo Adam, and Michael L. Radelet. 1987. Miscarriages of Justice in Potentially Capital Cases. *Stanford Law Review* 40 (1): 21–179.

Berinski, Adam J., and Donald R. Kinder. 2006. Making Sense of Issues through Media Frames: Understanding the Kosovo Crisis. *Journal of Politics* 68 (3): 640–656.

Bohm, Robert M. 1987. American Death Penalty Attitudes. *Criminal Justice and Behavior* 14 (3): 380–396.

Bohm, Robert M., Louise J. Clark, and Adrian F. Aveni. 1991. Knowledge and Death Penalty Opinion: A Test of the Marshall Hypothesis. *Journal of Research in Crime and Delinquency* 28 (3): 360–387.

Borchard, Edwin M. 1932. *Convicting the Innocent.* New Haven, Conn.: Yale University Press.

Bowers, William. 1993. Research Note: Capital Punishment and Contemporary Values: People's Misgivings and the Court's Misperceptions. *Law & Society Review* 27 (1): 157–176.

Branch v. Texas, 408 U.S. 238 (1972).

Carroll, William K., and R. S. Ratner. 1999. Media Strategies and Political Projects: A Comparative Study of Social Movements. *Canadian Journal of Sociology* 24 (1): 1–34.

The Center on Wrongful Convictions. Last modified March 11, 2005. The Mary-land Exonerated: Kirk Bloodsworth. Retrieved November 24, 2006, from http://www.law.northwestern.edu/depts/clinic/wrongful/exonerations/.

The Center on Wrongful Convictions. 2007. A Constituency for the Innocent. Retrieved August 3, 2007, from http://www.law.northwestern.edu/wrongfulconvictions/History.htm.

Chebium, Raju. June 20, 2000. Kirk Bloodsworth, Twice Convicted of Rape and Murder, Exonerated by DNA Evidence. CNN.com. Retrieved November 24, 2006, from http://archives.cnn.com.

Chong, Dennis, and James N. Druckman. 2007. Framing Theory. *Annual Review of Political Science* 10: 103–126.

CNN. November 8, 2002. Sniper Suspects Sent to Virginia for Trial. Retrieved December 16, 2006, from http://archives.cnn.com/2002/US/11/07/sniper.case/index.html.

Connors, Edward, Thomas Lundregan, Neal Miller, and Tom McEwen. June 1996. Convicted by Juries, Exonerated by Science: Case Studies in the Use of DNA Evidence to Establish Innocence after Trial. National Institute of Justice (U.S. Department of Justice, Office of Justice Programs). Retrieved December 15, 2006, from http://www.ncjrs.gov/txtfiles/dnaevid.txt.

Crampton v. Ohio, 402 U.S. 183 (1971).

Cullen, Francis T., Bonnie S. Fisher, and Brandon K. Applegate. 2000. Public Opinion about Punishment and Corrections. In Michael Tonry, ed., *Crime and Justice: A Review of Research*, Volume 27. Chicago, Ill.: University of Chicago Press, pp. 1–79.

Dardis, Frank, Frank R. Baumgartner, Amber E. Boydstun, Suzanna De Boef, and Fuyuan Shen. 2007. *Mass Communication and Society* 10 (4). Forth-coming.

Dieter, Richard C. 2000. The Death Penalty in 2000: Year End Report. Washington, D.C., Death Penalty Information Center. Retrieved March 19, 2007, from http://www.deathpenaltyinfo.org/article.php?scid=45&did=488.

DPIC (Death Penalty Information Center). 2006a. Clemency. Retrieved March 13, 2007, from http://www.deathpenaltyinfo.org/article.php?did=126&scid=13.

DPIC. 2006b. Death Row Inmates by State. Retrieved March 13, 2007, from http://www.deathpenaltyinfo.org/article.php?scid=9&did=188#state.

DPIC. 2006c. Searchable Database of Executions [Database]. Retrieved March 13, 2007, from http://www.deathpenaltyinfo.org/executions.php.

DPIC. 2006d. Death Sentences in the United States from 1977 to 2005. Retrieved March 13, 2007, from http://www.deathpenaltyinfo.org/article.php?scid=9&did=847.

DPIC. 2006e. Innocence: List of Those Freed from Death Row. Retrieved March 13, 2007, from http://www.deathpenaltyinfo.org/article.php?scid=6&did=110.

DPIC. 2006f. The Death Penalty in 2006: Year End Report. Retrieved December 17, 2006, from http://www.deathpenaltyinfo.org/2006YearEnd.pdf.

Druckman, James N. 2001a. On the Limits of Framing Effects: Who Can Frame? *Journal of Politics* 63 (4): 1041–1066.

Druckman, James N. 2001b. The Implication of Framing Effects for Citizen Competence. *Political Behavior* 23 (3): 225–256.

Druckman, James N. 2004. Political Preference Formation: Competition, Deliberation, and the (Ir)relevance of Framing Effects. *American Political Science Review* 98 (4): 761–786.

Druckman, James N., and Kjersten R. Nelson. 2003. Framing and Deliberation: How Citizens' Conversations Limit Elite Influence. *American Journal of Political Science* 47 (4): 729–745.

Durham, Alexis M., H. Preston Elrod, and Patrick T. Kinkade. 1996. Public Support for the Death Penalty: Beyond Gallup. *Justice Quarterly* 13 (4): 705–736.

Elder, Charles D., and Roger W. Cobb. 1983. *The Political Use of Symbols.* New York, N.Y.: Longman.

Ellsworth, Phoebe, and Samuel R. Gross. 1994. Hardening of the Attitudes: Americans' Views on the Death Penalty. *Journal of Social Issues* 50 (2): 19–52.

Ellsworth, Phoebe, and Lee Ross. 1983. Public Opinion and Capital Punishment: A Close Examination of the Views of Abolitionists and Retentionists. *Crime and Delinquency* 29 (1): 116–169.

Erikson, Robert S., James A. Stimson, and Michael MacKuen. 2002. *The Macro Polity.* New York, N.Y.: Cambridge University Press.

Espy, M. Watt, and John Ortiz Smykla. 2005. Executions in the United States, 1608–2002: The Espy File [Computer File]. 4th ICPSR ed. Compiled by M. Watt Espy and John Ortiz Smykla, University of Alabama. Ann Arbor, Mich.: Inter-university Consortium for Political and Social Research [producer and distributor], updated 11/04/05.

Fan, David P., Kathy A. Keltner, and Robert O. Wyatt. 2002. A Matter of Guilt or Innocence: How News Reports Affect Support for the Death Penalty in the United States. *International Journal of Public Opinion Research* 14 (4): 439–452.

Festinger, Leon. 1957. *A Theory of Cognitive Dissonance.* Evanston, Ill.: Row, Peterson, and Co.

Fins, Deborah. 2006. Death Row U.S.A.: Fall 2006. Washington, D.C.: NAACP Legal Defense and Education Fund, Inc. Retrieved March 13, 2007, from http://www.naacpldf.org/content/pdf/pubs/drusa/DRUSA_Fall_2006.pdf.

Fox, James Alan. 2005. Uniform Crime Reports (United States): Supplementary Homicide Reports, 1976–2003 [Computer File]. Compiled by Northeastern University, College of Criminal Justice. ICPSR04351-v1. Ann Arbor, Mich.: Inter-university Consortium for Political and Social Research [producer and distributor], 2005–11-22.

Fox, James A., Michael L. Radelet, and Julie L. Bonsteel. 1991. Death Penalty Opinion in the Post-Furman Years. *New York University Review of Law and Social Change* 28: 499–528.

Fox, James Alan, and Marianne W. Zawitz. 2006. Homicide Trends in the United States. Washington, D.C.: U.S. Department of Justice, Bureau of Justice Statistics. Retrieved March 16, 2007, from http://www.ojp.usdoj.gov/bjs/homicide/tables/totalstab.htm.

Frisbie, Thomas, and Randy Garrett. 1998. *Victims of Justice*. New York, N.Y.: Avon Books.

Furman v. Georgia, 408 U.S. 238 (1972).

Gallup Organization. Public opinion surveys conducted November 11, 1953 to May 5, 2006. Retrieved March 18, 2007, from the iPOLL Databank, The Roper Center for Public Opinion Research, University of Connecticut, http://www.ropercenter.uconn.edu/ipoll.html.

Gilliam, Franklin D., Jr., and Shanto Iyengar. 2000. Prime Suspects: The Influence of Local Television News on the Viewing Public. *American Journal of Political Science* 44 (3): 560–573.

Gladwell, Malcolm. 2002. *The Tipping Point*. New York, N.Y.: Little, Brown and Co.

Granovetter, Mark S. 1978. Threshold Models of Collective Behavior. *American Journal of Sociology* 83 (6): 1420–1443.

Grasmick, Harold G., Elizabeth Davenport, Mitchell B. Chamlin, and Robert J. Bursik, Jr. 1992. Protestant Fundamentalism and the Retributivist Doctrine of Punishment. *Criminology* 30 (1): 21–45.

Grasmick, Harold G., and Ann McGill. 1994. Religion, Attribution Style, and Punitiveness toward Juvenile Offenders. *Criminology* 32 (1): 23–46.

Gregg v. Georgia, 428 U.S. 153 (1976).

Grisham, John. 2006. *The Innocent Man*. New York, N.Y.: Doubleday.

Gross, Samuel R. 1998. Update: American Public Opinion on the Death Penalty – It's Getting Personal. *Cornell Law Review* 83 (6): 1448–1475.

Gross, Samuel R., and Phoebe C. Ellsworth. 2003. Second Thoughts: Americans' Views on the Death Penalty at the Turn of the Century. In Stephen P. Garvey, ed., *Beyond Repair? America's Death Penalty*. Durham, N.C.: Duke University Press.

Gross, Samuel R., Kristen Jacoby, Daniel J. Matheson, Nicholas Montgomery, and Sujata Patil. 2005. Exonerations in the United States 1989 through 2003. *Journal of Criminal Law and Criminology* 95 (2): 523–560.

Haddock, Geoffrey, and Mark P. Zanna. 1998. Assessing the Impact of Affective and Cognitive Information in Predicting Attitudes toward Capital Punishment. *Law and Human Behavior* 22 (3): 325–339.

Halim, Shaheen, and Beverly L. Stiles. 2001. Differential Support for Police Use of Force, the Death Penalty, and Perceived Harshness of the Courts. *Criminal Justice and Behavior* 28 (1): 3–23.

Hancock, Ange-Marie. 2004. *The Politics of Disgust: The Public Identity of the Welfare Queen*. New York, N.Y.: New York University Press.

Herrera v. Collins, 506 U.S. 390 (1993).

Holmes v. South Carolina, 547 U.S. 319 (2006).

House v. Bell, 126 S.Ct. 2064 (2006).

The Innocence Project. (n.d.) Kirk Bloodsworth Case Profile. Retrieved November 24, 2006, from http://www.innocenceproject.org/.

Jackson v. Georgia, 408 U.S. 238 (1972).

Jacobs, David, and Jason T. Carmichael. 2002. The Political Sociology of the Death Penalty: A Pooled Time-Series Analysis. *American Sociological Review* 67 (1): 109–131.

Janson, Philip, and Louise K. Ryder. 1983. Crime and the Elderly: The Relationship between Risk and Fear. *Gerontologist* 23 (2): 207–212.

Jones, Bryan D., and Frank R. Baumgartner. 2005. *The Politics of Attention: How Government Prioritizes Problems*. Chicago, Ill.: University of Chicago Press.

Junkin, Tim. 2004. *Bloodsworth: The True Story of the First Death Row Inmate Exonerated by DNA*. Chapel Hill, N.C.: Algonquin Books.

Jurek v. Texas, 428 U.S. 153 (1976).

The Justice Project. (n.d.) The Problem: A Broken System, Kirk Bloodsworth. Retrieved November 24, 2006, from http://www.thejusticeproject.org/press/bloodsworth/.

Kahneman, Daniel, and Amos Tversky. 1985. Prospect Theory: An Analysis of Decision-Making under Risk. *Econometrica* 47 (2): 263–292.

Kansas v. Marsh, 547 U.S. 1037 (2006).

Kellstedt, Paul M. 2000. Media Framing and the Dynamics of Racial Policy Preferences. *American Journal of Political Science* 44 (2): 245–260.

Kim, Jae-on, and Charles W. Mueller. 1978a. *Introduction to Factor Analysis: What It Is and How to Do It*. Newbury Park, Calif.: Sage Publications.

Kim, Jae-on, and Charles W. Mueller. 1978b. *Factor Analysis: Statistical Methods and Practical Issues*. Newbury Park, Calif.: Sage Publications.

Kingdon, John W. 1984. *Agendas, Alternatives, and Public Policies*. Boston: Little, Brown and Co.

Kleinman, Paula H., and Deborah S. David. 1973. Victimization and Perception of Crime in a Ghetto Community. *Criminology* 11 (3): 307.

Lawrence, Regina. 2000. *The Politics of Force: Media and the Construction of Police Brutality*. Berkeley: University of California Press.

Lewis, Dan A., and Greta Salem. 1986. *Fear of Crime: Incivility and the Production of a Social Problem*. New Brunswick, N.J.: Transaction Books.

Liebman, James S., Jeffrey Fagan, Andrew Gelman, Valerie West, Garth Davies, and Alexander Kiss. 2002. A Broken System, Part II: Why There Is So Much Error in Capital Cases, and What Can Be Done about It. Columbia University Law School. Retrieved March 18, 2007, from http://www2.law.columbia.edu/brokensystem2/index2.html.

Lockhart v. McCree, 476 U.S. 162 (1986).

Lord, Charles G., Lee Ross, and Mark R. Lepper. 1979. Biased Assimilation and Attitude Polarization: The Effects of Prior Theories on Subsequently Considered Evidence. *Journal of Personality and Social Psychology* 37 (11): 2098–2109.

McGautha v. California, 402 U.S. 183 (1971).

McPherson, Marlys. 1978. Realities and Perceptions of Crime at the Neighborhood Level. *Victimology* 3 (3–4): 319–328.

Mueller, Robert S., III. 2006. Preliminary Semiannual Uniform Crime Report 2006. Washington, D.C.: U.S. Department of Justice, Federal Bureau of Investigation.

National Prisoner Statistics. 1974. Capital Punishment, 1971–1972 (SD-NPS-CP-1). Washington, D.C.: U.S. Department of Justice, Law Enforcement Assistance Administration.

Nelson, Thomas E., Rosalee A. Clawson, and Zoe M. Oxley. 1997. Media Framing of a Civil Liberties Conflict and Its Effect on Tolerance. *American Political Science Review* 91 (3): 567–583.

Nice, David C. 1992. The States and the Death Penalty. *The Western Political Quarterly* 45 (4): 1037–1048.

Oregon v. Guzek, 546 U.S. 517 (2006).

Page, Benjamin I., and Robert Y. Shapiro. 1983. Effects of Public Opinion on Public Policy. *The American Political Science Review* 77 (1): 175–190.

Page, Benjamin I., and Robert Y. Shapiro. 1992. *The Rational Public: Fifty Years of Trends in Americans' Policy Preferences*. Chicago, Ill.: University of Chicago Press.

Penry v. Lynaugh, 492 U.S. 302 (1989).

Pierce, Glenn L., and Michael L. Radelet. 2005. The Impact of Legally Inappropriate Factors on Death Sentencing for California Homicides, 1990–1999. *Santa Clara Law Review* 46: 1–47.

Pollock, Philip H., III. 1994. Issues, Values, and Critical Moments: Did "Magic" Johnson Transform Public Opinion on AIDS? *American Journal of Political Science* 38 (2): 426–446.

Poole, Keith T., and Howard Rosenthal. 1984. The Polarization of American Politics. *The Journal of Politics* 46 (4): 1061–1079.

Proffitt v. Florida, 428 U.S. 153 (1976).

Quattrone, George A., and Amos Tversky. 1988. Contrasting Rational and Psychological Analyses of Political Choice. *American Political Science Review* 82 (3): 719–736.

Radelet, Michael L., Hugo Adam Bedau, and Constance E. Putnam. 1992. *In Spite of Innocence*. Boston, Mass.: Northeastern University Press.

Radelet, Michael L., and Marian J. Borg. 2000. The Changing Nature of the Death Penalty Debates. *Annual Review of Sociology* 26: 43–61.

Rankin, Joseph H. 1979. Changing Attitudes toward Capital Punishment. *Social Forces* 58 (1): 194–211.

Riker, William H. 1980. Implications from the Disequilibrium of Majority Rule for the Study of Institutions. *American Political Science Review* 74 (2): 432–446.

Riker, William H. 1982. *Liberalism against Populism: A Confrontation between the Theory of Democracy and the Theory of Social Choice*. Prospect Heights, Ill.: Waveland Press.

Riker, William H. 1983. Political Theory and the Art of Heresthetics. In Ada Finifter, ed., *Political Science: The State of the Discipline*. Washington, D.C.: American Political Science Association.

Riker, William H. 1984. The Heresthetics of Constitution-Making: The Presidency in 1787, with Comments on Determinism and Rational Choice. *American Political Science Review* 78 (1): 1–16.

Riker, William H. 1986. *The Art of Political Manipulation*. New Haven, Conn.: Yale University Press.

Riker, William H. 1988. *Liberalism against Populism*. Prospect Heights, Ill.: Waveland Press.

Riker, William H. 1990. Heresthetic and Rhetoric in the Spatial Model. In James M. Enelow and Melvin J. Hinich, eds., *Advances in the Spatial Theory of Voting*. New York, N.Y.: Cambridge University Press.

Riker, William H. 1996. *The Strategy of Rhetoric*. New Haven, Conn.: Yale University Press.

Roberts v. Louisiana, 428 U.S. 153 (1976).

Roper v. Simmons, 534 U.S. 551 (2005).

Sarat, Austin, and Neil Vidmar. 1976. Public Opinion, the Death Penalty, and the Eighth Amendment: Testing the Marshall Hypothesis. *Wisconsin Law Review* 1: 171.

Scheck, Barry, Peter Neufeld, and Jim Dwyer. 2000. *Actual Innocence: Five Days to Execution, and Other Dispatches from the Wrongly Convicted*. New York, N.Y.: Doubleday.

Schelling, Thomas C. 1971. Dynamic Models of Segregation. *Journal of Mathematical Sociology* 1 (2): 143–186.

Schelling, Thomas C. 1978. *Micromotives and Macrobehavior*. New York, N.Y.: W. W. Norton & Company.

Schlup v. Delo, 513 U.S. 298 (1995).

Schneider, Anne, and Helen Ingram. 1993. Social Construction of Target Populations: Implications for Politics and Policy. *The American Political Science Review* 87 (2): 334–347.

Shepsle, Kenneth A. 1979. Institutional Arrangements and Equilibrium in Multidimensional Voting. *American Journal of Political Science* 23 (1): 27–59.

Shepsle, Kenneth A., and Barry R. Weingast. 1981. Structure-Induced Equilibrium and Legislative Choice. *Public Choice* 37 (3): 503–519.

Shepsle, Kenneth A., and Barry R. Weingast. 1987. The Institutional Foundations of Committee Power. *American Political Science Review* 81 (1): 85–104.

Snell, Tracy L. 2005. Capital Punishment, 2005 (NCJ-215083). Washington, D.C.: U.S. Department of Justice, Bureau of Justice Statistics. Retrieved March 13, 2007, from http://www.ojp.usdoj.gov/bjs/pub/pdf/cp05.pdf.

Soroka, Stuart Neil. 2002. *Agenda-Setting Dynamics in Canada*. Vancouver, B.C.: UBC Press.

Soss, Joe, Laura Langbein, and Alan R. Metelko. 2003. Why Do White Americans Support the Death Penalty? *The Journal of Politics* 65 (2): 397–421.

Sparks, Holloway. 2003. Queens, Teens, and Model Mothers: Race, Gender, and the Discourse of Welfare Reform. In Sanford Schram, Joe Soss, and Richard C.

Fording, eds., *Race and the Politics of Welfare Reform*. Ann Arbor: University of Michigan Press.

Stack, Steven. 2000. Support for the Death Penalty: A Gender-Specific Model. *Sex Roles* 43 (3–4): 163–179.

Stafford, Mark C., and Omer R. Galle. 1984. Victimization Rates, Exposure to Risk, and Fear of Crime. *Criminology* 22 (2): 173–185.

Stimson, James A. 1991. *Public Opinion in America: Moods, Cycles, and Swings.* Boulder, Colo.: Westview Press.

Taylor, D. Garth, Kim Lane Scheppele, and Arthur L. Stinchcombe. 1979. Salience of Crime and Support for Harsher Criminal Sanctions. *Social Problems* 26 (4): 413–424.

Terkildsen, Nayda, and David F. Damore. 1999. The Dynamics of Racialized Media Coverage in Congressional Elections. *The Journal of Politics* 61 (3): 680–699.

Terkildsen, Nayda, and Frauke Schnell. 1997. How Media Frames Move Public Opinion: An Analysis of the Women's Movement. *Political Research Quarterly* 50 (4): 879–900.

Tyler, Tom R., and Renee Weber. 1982. Support for the Death Penalty; Instrumental Response to Crime, or Symbolic Attitude? *Law & Society Review* 17 (1): 21–46.

Uniform Crime Reporting Program. 2006. Crime in the United States 2005. Washington, D.C.: U.S. Department of Justice, Federal Bureau of Investigation. Retrieved March 16, 2007, from http://www.fbi.gov/ucr/05cius/data/table_01.html.

United States v. Jackson, 390 U.S. 570 (1968).

Vidmar, Neil, and Phoebe Ellsworth. 1974. Public Opinion and the Death Penalty. *Stanford Law Review* 26 (6): 1245–1270.

Warden, Rob, and Michael L. Radelet. 2008. *Encyclopedia of Wrongful Convictions*. Evanston, Ill.: Northwestern University Press.

Warr, Mark. 1980. The Accuracy of Public Beliefs about Crime. *Social Forces* 59 (2): 456–470.

Warr, Mark. 1982. The Accuracy of Public Beliefs about Crime: Further Evidence. *Criminology* 20 (2): 185–204.

Warr, Mark. 1995. Poll Trends: Public Opinion on Crime and Punishment. *The Public Opinion Quarterly* 59 (2): 296–310.

Watts, Duncan J. 1999. Networks, Dynamics, and the Small-World Phenomenon. *American Journal of Sociology* 105 (2): 493–527.

Watts, Duncan J. 2003. *Six Degrees: The Science of a Connected Age*. New York, N.Y.: Norton.

Weems v. United States, 217 U.S. 349 (1910).

Witherspoon v. Illinois, 391 U.S. 510 (1968).

Wood, B. Dan, and Alesha Doan. 2003. The Politics of Problem Definition: Applying and Testing Threshold Models. *American Journal of Political Science* 47 (4): 640–653.

Woodson v. North Carolina, 428 U.S. 153 (1976).

Woolley, John T. 2000. Using Media-Based Data in Studies of Politics. *American Journal of Political Science* 44 (1): 156–173.

Young, Robert L. 1991. Race, Conceptions of Crime and Justice, and Support for the Death Penalty. *Social Psychology Quarterly* 54 (1): 67–75.

Young, Robert L. 1992. Religious Orientation, Race and Support for the Death Penalty. *Journal for the Scientific Study of Religion* 31 (1): 76–87.

Zaller, John R. 1992. *The Nature and Origins of Mass Opinion*. New York, N.Y.: Cambridge University Press.

INDEX